MW00963425

MIDFIELD LIAISON

The Frank Bunce, Walter Little Story

MIDFIELD LIAISON

The Frank Bunce, Walter Little Story

By Bob Howitt

rugby publishing limited
Auckland, New Zealand

Acknowledgements

The author wishes to acknowledge the following
people for their support and assistance: Joe
Anderson, Bryan Craies, Frankie Deges, Lindsay
Ellery, Peter Fatialofa, John Hart, Dick Garratt,
Lindsay Knight, Merv and Margaret Jamieson, Brian
Lochore, Laurie Mains, Brad Meurant, Geoff Miller,
Alby Pryor, Eric Rush, Peter Thorburn, Mike Scott
and his 1967 Mustang and Northern Zone,
Shore City Galleria.

Special thanks to Margaret Jamieson and Tracy Little
for the use of your comprehensive scrapbooks.

© Bob Howitt, Walter Little, Frank Bunce
First published in 1996 by Rugby Publishing Ltd
67-73 View Road, Glenfield, Auckland, New Zealand.

Typesetting/design by Sportz Graphics Ltd, Glenfield,
Auckland. Printed through Colorcraft Ltd, Hong Kong.

Rugby Publishing Ltd is a member of the Medialine Group
of Companies. P.O. Box 100-243, North Shore Mail
Centre, Auckland 10, New Zealand.

ISBN 0-908630-59-X

Contents

Dedicated

to
Frank Bunce senior,
who died in 1991, a year before
his son became an All Black
and
Maurice Dick,
Walter's good friend whose dream
was to write his autobiography

Introduction

That this joint biography linking the diverse careers of Frank Bunce and Walter Little is being published has much to do with Laurie Mains' appointment as All Black coach in 1992.

Until Mains entered the national scene, in the wake of New Zealand's unhappy World Cup campaign in the UK, Bunce, then 30, had been a bit player for Auckland for many years before transferring to North Harbour in search of regular first-class play.

And Little, after a dazzling schoolboy career and promotion to the All Blacks as a teenager, had dropped out of his country's test line-up and sat rather forlornly on the reserves bench for most of the World Cup watching his team come horribly unstuck.

The midfield liaison that would become the most formidable in the world had not yet been formed.

Jason Little and Tim Horan, acknowledged as rugby's best midfield pairing, were being hailed for their contribution to Australia's World Cup triumph.

Will Carling and Jeremy Guscott of England were undoubtedly the most potent pairing in the UK.

And Philippe Sella and Franck Mesnel were, like the entire French team, always dangerous, if prone to inconsistency.

But Bunce and Little? Destined to become the premier midfield combination in the world? And in four years rise to such international prominence that their careers and achievements would be recorded in a book?

Not likely, mate. Not when the 30-year-old has a diabolical reputation for being unreliable, has played more games for the Auckland B team than the As and is seriously contemplating a career in league.

And his cigarette smoking, beer-loving partner can't make up his mind whether he's a first-five or a second-five.

Who could possibly put this seemingly incongruous pair together and strike the jackpot?

Laurie Mains, that's who, although not without a pinch of experimentation, that would see Bunce tried at second-five and Little at centre and first-five before they finally settled into their Nos 12 and 13 All Black jerseys.

Mains, who had been enormously impressed with Bunce's play for Western Samoa at the World Cup, recognised in him the mongrel that would make him a feared centre at international level.

Bunce's devastating tackling ability and thrustful running would combine perfectly with Little's remarkable tackle-breaking skills, startling acceleration and magic hands.

Not only would they put steel into the All Black backline, they would become the closest of mates, with Frank featuring as best man when Walter married Tracy Wishnowski prior to the World Cup in 1995.

There have been other joint biographies of rugby personalities published in the past dozen years, of Wellington threequarters Stu Wilson and Bernie Fraser, of twins Gary and Alan Whetton, of the Wallaby wonders Horan and Little and of The Geriatrics, Andy Dalton, John Ashworth and Gary Knight.

In each instance, the pairings' careers parallelled each other.

Which makes *Midfield Liaison* the more remarkable because Bunce and Little etched completely independent lives and careers before circumstances brought them together as North Harbour representatives in 1991.

Bunce, the third of eight children (with more Niuean blood than Western Samoan) grew up in the Auckland working class suburb of Mangere, where he flirted with a gang element, his entry into senior rugby being delayed a year while he served a nine month periodic detention sentence.

Frank is the first to admit that rugby was his salvation. When in his impressionable youth several paths appeared before him, he is eternally grateful that the one he chose was the Avenue de Rugby.

If rugby has been a lifesaver for Frank, it would be easy to convene a hall full of people who would verify that Frank has been incredibly good for rugby.

It was his loyalty to the Manukau club which made him decline invitations to switch unions and his intense passion for rugby which resulted in his rejecting lucrative league offers.

His unassuming and easygoing nature meant that he continued to nurture the ambition to represent the All Blacks when all logic declared that he had missed the bus. Before Frank, had there ever been a back debut for the All Blacks at 30?

Little's story is completely different. The youngest of six brothers born to Fijian parents in Tokoroa, Walter was a natural and gifted sportsman who made an impact the moment he first took the field.

Not only did he represent virtually every age grade team for which he was eligible, in Tokoroa, south Waikato, Auckland, North Harbour and eventually New Zealand, but he became synonymous with success.

Such obvious talent did he possess that Peter Thorburn – who was to become a huge influence on his career – plucked him from the first fifteen at Hato Petera College and introduced him to his North Harbour representative squad to train alongside such giants of the game as Buck Shelford and Frano Botica.

If Little's rugby career was a breeze through until 1989 when he bolted into the All Blacks for the tour of Wales and Ireland, he was to discover frustration and agony in the years ahead.

His first major trauma was working out how to operate alongside Grant Fox, then followed disillusionment as the All Blacks came crashing down under Gary Whetton's captaincy and frustration as various selectors and coaches moved him about the backline at their whim.

Even under Mains there were disappointments and in 1993, after walking out on the All Blacks – but fortunately being persuaded to return – he, like Bunce the year before, teetered on a career in league.

Eventually, he was restored to the All Black backline alongside Bunce (and given an apology for being left out), becoming an integral member of the team which dazzled the rugby world throughout 1995.

Like Frank, Walter is one of sport's nice guys, humble, loyal and dedicated.

When Frank, Walter and I first came together to plot the contents of this book, we were unanimous that it should be, first and foremost, entertaining.

That rather depended on how vivid was their recall of events and how many interesting anecdotes they could toss up.

"You might struggle with this book," a colleague warned, "Frank and Walter being the quiet types that they are. What if they haven't got any good stories to tell?"

What indeed. I was sure they had loads of stories to tell. It was a case of whether they could remember them. A lot of players can't.

Well, by the time you've read *Midfield Liaison* I'm sure you'll acknowledge that not only do Frank and Walter possess exceptional recall, but between them (and with a bit of help from their mates, particularly Eric Rush) we've come up with enough entertaining and amusing stories to have this book almost categorised in the humour section.

A more outrageous assortment of rugby stories would be hard to find than those contained in the Los Mongreles chapter.

Then there's an irreverent shakedown on the All Black World Cup squad in the chapter entitled The Class of '95. You'll be surprised at some of the revelations made about your international rugby heroes – the player who likes to go nude while on tour, the player who ran up toll bills of $3500 while in France, the player who startled Sean Fitzpatrick while wearing camouflage gear, and how Jonah Lomu ran bubble baths for Frank.

Frank and Walter have been candid, alarmingly so at times, in their assessment of the managers, coaches and captains they have played under throughout their first-class career.

But, most importantly, throughout they have been totally honest.

Compiling this work has been an all-consuming task, requiring total commitment and dedication on many fronts.

And in that regard, I have been enormously fortunate. Frank and Walter could not have been more co-operative or open, without ever forfeiting their senses of humour.

Equally as important, the dozens of people I approached for background, advice and stories were all enthusiastic about assisting, which reflects the esteem in which the pair are held.

Laurie Mains, who played such a major role in their careers, described them as a delight to work with. "I couldn't have wished for a more dedicated pair," he said, adding that he was available to assist in any manner with the promotion of the book.

As an author I consider myself fortunate to have been assigned the task of writing this book and of chronicling the lives of two exceptional footballers whom I hold in such high regard.

Bob Howitt
Auckland, April, 1996

The Team From Hell

Hundreds of thousands of New Zealanders have passed close by the Manukau Rugby Football Club's headquarters on Williams Park. But only a small number would know it.

The clubrooms are in Viscount Street, an undistinguished thoroughfare in Mangere running off Kirkbride Rd, part of the main route into Auckland city for passengers arriving at Auckland's domestic and international airports, the road upon which seemingly dozens of hotels and motels have sprouted over the past couple of decades.

The decision to relocate Manukau "over the bridge (Mangere Bridge)" in Viscount Street in 1972, wasn't taken lightly as the club had previously existed in Onehunga, one of Auckland's oldest suburbs, for 47 years. It was a move resisted by many of the club's stalwarts; indeed, most of Manukau's veteran members stubbornly refused to venture out of their traditional territory and, to this day, the old boys' association remains in Onehunga.

However, the club's younger, more progressive administrators saw a limited future in Onehunga where matches were being played on Waikaraka Park which was becoming the headquarters for stock car racing in Auckland.

By moving across the bridge to Williams Park, it would mean autonomy for the club. There was room for three playing fields and spacious, new premises. It also meant Manukau would be able to tap into Mangere's vast working class population, which was predominantly Maori and Polynesian.

The Manukau City Council offered sporting clubs in those days an attractive proposition. If the club put up one-quarter of the finance required, Manukau would match it dollar for dollar and lend the remaining 50 per cent at a basic interest rate of 3 per cent. Manukau went for it, engaging JBL, which was to crash spectacularly a decade later, to design and build the new premises.

By 1970s standards, the clubrooms were among the most palatial of their kind in New Zealand. They gave Manukau a status and when, the next year, with Wally Rawiri and former All Black Mac Herewini as co-coaches, the senior team won, for only the second time in the club's history, Auckland club rugby's premier trophy, the Gallaher Shield, it was boom time for Manukau rugby.

A club commitee member at the time was Alby Pryor, a powerful personality who had made his mark representing Auckland and New Zealand Maori and who had coached Manukau to its first Gallaher Shield success in 1968.

"There's nothing like success to boost a club," recalls Pryor. "When we were advancing towards the championship in 1973 and after winning it, you couldn't move in the new clubrooms."

That team of '73 was a formidable one featuring one All Black, Herewini (who doubled as a player-coach), New Zealand Maori rep Alby Hansen and several distinguished Auckland representatives including the fleet-footed midfielder Teroi Tataurangi (father of golf professional Philip Tataurangi), fullback Roger Whatman and former New Zealand Colt prop Ron Webb who, as the captain, was chaired from Eden Park after his team's thrilling victory over the more fancied Grammar Old Boys in a midweek play-off for the title.

However, fame can be despairingly fleeting as Manukau followers were to discover. Because many of the key personnel in that team of '73 stepped down after the Gallaher Shield triumph, the side struggled to stay with the Ponsonbys, Grammars and Waitematas the next season.

Worse was to follow. Within five years, Manukau had plummeted to third division status, the senior team but a shadow of that which in 1973 had regularly featured in the main fixture on Eden Park No 1.

Support for the team dwindled and the clubrooms, which had been bursting at the seams four and five years earlier, were now sparsely attended. This was not entirely the ailing senior team's fault. A gang element had involved itself in the club and had frightened off many of the regular clubroom patrons.

The revival started when Barry Thomas, the former All Black who had captained Manukau to its first senior club title in 1968 and who was affectionately known as Bear, approached Alby Pryor, who had given away the time-consuming role of rugby coach to concentrate upon his butcher's shop.

"Barry suggested that I become president, that he would take over as secretary-manager," said Pryor, "and that together we would address the many issues that were troubling the club. There had been a lot of infighting within the management committee and the gang factor had been terribly disruptive.

"It was important to re-introduce discipline, to set rules and dress codes, to get some pride back into the club. And on the playing front we had to start building for the future."

Thomas and Pryor, with some enthusiastic support, soon had Manukau functioning efficiently again. The gang element disappeared, encouraging former members to return to the clubrooms. The club was back on the rails.

The next important assignment was to develop the club's young players, to ensure that in the coming years Manukau wouldn't continue to languish in the lower reaches of the Auckland Rugby Union's senior competition.

It was on the third grade, the under 21s, that Thomas (who had two of his sons, Greg and Mike, involved), Pryor and the new, energetic committee focused their attentions in 1980. Although it's probably an exaggeration to say no expense was spared in nurturing this highly promising team – which was to reward the club by winning the championship – vast resources were invested.

Pryor recalls that $4000, a substantial sum at the time, was approved to send the team away to a pre-season training camp at the Onemana Beach Resort on the Coromandel peninsula. Graham Henry, later to become a highly successful coach of Auckland, John Graham, who would be Henry's forward coach, and Pat Walsh, the former All Black selector, were all brought in to assist.

"We made a substantial investment in our colts," said Pryor. "We saw these players as our seniors of the future, the players who would haul Manukau back to first division. It was all professionally done."

Such was the level of concentration upon the third grade team, which had become the club's showpiece, that almost no one noticed what was going on two grades down. In the fifth grade (under 19) Manukau was harbouring The Team From Hell.

It was club stalwart Dick Garratt who first drew the Manukau committee's attention to "certain problems" associated with the team. They were, he reported, a lawless group, totally anti-establishment – scarcely any of them had stepped foot inside the clubrooms – with a reputation for drinking vast amounts of beer and getting into fights. The team's basic discipline had broken down.

"They sounded exactly what the Manukau club didn't need," said Pryor. "We had been working hard to improve our image and set certain standards within the club. We'd eradicated the rough element. We certainly didn't need this."

So Pryor and Garratt were delegated to attend the fifth grade team's next match with the power, if needed, to rid the club of these troublemakers.

"Dick and I genuinely expected we were going along to terminate their association with the club," said Pryor, "so bad were the reports we'd been getting."

What Pryor and Garratt were to encounter, that fateful Saturday at the Auckland Domain, and for the balance of the season, was the stuff of which legends are made.

"They certainly were the team from hell when we first sighted them," said Pryor. "They were a motley assortment of bikies and drop-outs. Some were swigging from beer bottles, others carried love bites. They looked anything but a rugby team. And their initial reaction, upon being told we represented the club's management committee, was to advise us to 'get stuffed...!'"

The manager was a colourful personality, Harry Korewha, known as The Keg. His drinking habits were legendary. He stood 4ft 8in and was approximately as wide as he was tall.

Almost the entire team were fed by The Keg and his wife on Friday nights and slept over at their house, it being the only way The Keg and the coach could be certain they would have a starting fifteen the next afternoon!

The coach, who admitted to Pryor and Garratt that he'd lost control of his charges, was Buck Hohaia. There was no point in his issuing playing instructions, he lamented. They usually told him to shut up. And on the odd occasions they did appear to be listening, which were usually because they were excessively hungover, they went out and did their own thing anyway!

In their midst, one of the bikies, was Frank Bunce who played on the side of the scrum. His attire appeared to be a cut above most of the others.

Pryor and Garratt had no idea what to expect from the team on the field but retained an open mind upon learning that they were undefeated.

"We suddenly realised that they were a team possessed of some uncommonly good footballers," said Pryor. "Their scrum was powerful, mainly because of the presence in the front row of a huge, ferocious-looking individual called Tony Roberts. He reminded us of Keith Murdoch.

"In the backline they possessed a clever runner, a boy named Jonathan Tukerangi. And then there was Frank. He had an aura about him. He was above average as a flanker but the manner in which he beat opponents with minimum effort and created opportunities from nothing suggested straightaway that he could be more strategically placed than on the side of the scrum. You could see that he did a lot of other people's work.

"The players didn't do a lot of passing. They were such natural footballers that when it was their turn, they just ran."

Pryor and Garratt went away from the Domain far from despondent, as they suspected they would be after firing their bullets. They were, instead, stimulated by what they'd seen. This was a team to nurture. This team complemented the third grade side beautifully. All it would take was strong management, discipline and some tender, loving care.

Few of the Manukau fifth graders looked as though they'd experienced much TLC in their lives. "We obviously had to get them club orientated," said Pryor.

The club orientation bit didn't start immediately. But there were some instant changes. It was agreed that while Harry Korewha, The Keg, would remain as the manager, Alby Pryor would take over as coach, with assistance from Dick Garratt and Buck Hohaia.

The team's first outing under the new regime would be against East Coast Bays, the champion side from 1979, at the Domain. Start time was 1pm.

When Pryor and Garratt arrived at the Domain at about twenty minutes to one, it was to find the East Coast Bays players, coached by Peter Thorburn (later to become North Harbour's first representative coach), resplendent in matching track suits, warming up and going through their stretching exercises.

By five minutes to one, not a solitary Manukau player had arrived. A worried Alby looked at Dick. "I hope they're not staying away in protest," he said.

In the next couple of minutes the Manukau fifth grade team began to materialise, aboard a collection of suped-up cars, mostly Mark II Zephyrs, and motor bikes.

One of those on a motor bike was Frank Bunce. It was three minutes to one as he ambled across towards the changing room, a pie in his hand.

"Come on, hurry up," said Alby. "Get your jersey on."

"I can't," said Frank, "till I finish eating my pie."

"You're not eating *that*," said Alby.

"Says who?" barked back Frank, not accustomed to having his statements challenged on match days.

"Me!" Whereupon Alby reached forward and crushed the pie in Bunce's hand, causing him to shout in pain because it was hot.

"What the hell!" shouted Frank, shaping aggressively at Alby.

"Come on," said Alby, "do you want to take me on?"

Frank was all menace as he glowered at his new coach, but his natural instincts told him to save his aggression for the enemy on the field. Somewhere in the back of his mind he remembered someone telling him about how Alby Pryor had had a reputation as one of the roughest, toughest players to represent Auckland and how he'd achieved notoriety by flattening a British Lion while playing for New Zealand Maoris at Eden Park once.

Frank walked calmly to the rubbish bin and scraped the glutinous remains of the pie into it, returning to pull on his playing jersey.

When the referee blew his whistle to start proceedings, East Coast Bays boasted 15 players, all immaculately attired, Manukau nine. The nine, which included five members of the Tukerangi household and

Frank, had a commonality through their jerseys, but their shorts and socks were all distinctly original.

Within seconds of kick-off East Coast Bays was awarded a penalty goal which it converted into points. Three-nil. From the re-start, by which time Manukau's numbers had swelled to eleven, East Coast Bays swept back on to attack, to be awarded another penalty.

"This is embarrassing," Dick Garratt said to Alby Pryor. "If things don't improve, I think we should go to Eden Park to watch our seniors."

East Coast Bays' second penalty attempt dropped under the bar where it was fielded by Jonathan Tukerangi. He didn't kick for touch. That wasn't how the Manukau fifth grade team played its rugby. He took off upfield, linking with Frank Bunce. They so bewildered the defence with their interpassing that Tukerangi scored between the posts 100 metres away.

The eleven of Manukau would probably have been a fair match for East Coast Bays. But within five minutes, with a full complement of players on the field, Manukau took charge, going on to win the game 47-3.

"It was an astonishing performance," recalls Pryor. "East Coast Bays didn't get a look in. They couldn't handle Tony Roberts (who'd acquired the nickname of The Animal) in the scrums, and players like Tukerangi and Bunce just kept running through them."

The Animal was only eighteen but he had quite a bit of grey hair, which was to bring protests from every opponent that year. They were always claiming he was over age, but he carried his birth certificate with him to silence his critics.

From being outsiders, the Manukau fifth graders were gradually coaxed into participation in the club. To encourage this, the clubrooms became the assembly point each Saturday, with the club van being used to transport the players to and from their matches.

Under Pryor's expert tutelage – "all they needed," he claimed, "was some discipline" – the players went on to win every match, most by wide margins. But sadly they didn't win the championship, losing the title on a protest for fielding an unregistered player.

"It's something we'd been cautious about all season," said Pryor. "With our assortment of offbeat individuals, it was natural for opponents to treat us suspiciously and after every match they'd check the team lists against the names of players registered with the Auckland Rugby Union.

"Right towards the end of the season a player called Lucky Cecil, who'd been holidaying on Her Majesty's Service, turned up one Saturday and said to Buck Hohaia, 'Hey, Buck, how about givin' us a game.' The Keg was happy enough to field him because he wasn't a bad player, but they unwittingly listed him as Lucky Cecil on the team sheet, and of course he wasn't registered.

"Our opponents protested and we had the game taken off us. It cost us the championship."

Pryor says that although it upset the club, the players didn't react to their being penalised. "It worried the club a lot more than the players. Those guys were used to taking knocks. They weren't visibly upset with the news."

Probably because it felt guilty about denying the title to what was patently the best team in the competition, the Auckland Rugby Union agreed to a special fixture between the Auckland fifth grade representative side and Manukau at Williams Park.

Manukau, allowed to retain its representative members, of which Bunce was one, dealt a 36-nil towelling to the Auckland side, to complete a most impressive season.

Pryor looks back on his involvement with the fifth graders of '80 as one of the most satisfying experiences of his career.

"It's incredible to think that the first time I sighted them, Dick and I were going along to boot them out of the club. But thirty per cent of those players went through to play senior club football. Out of nothing came an All Black and the basis of a team that put Manukau in good stead for years to come. It was a classic example of a club picking up players and nurturing them. If we hadn't taken them in and got them involved in the club, chances are they would have been lost to rugby. Before we began working with them, a lot had a dreadful history of getting involved in bar room brawls."

Pryor and Garratt found that the players' own "blunt Maori humour" worked more effectively than any criticism they might direct at them. A dropped pass would incur derision from their peers. Comments like "You dropped the ball, you stupid Maori" would make them grimly determined not to be the culprit again.

Towards the end of the season, Pryor switched Bunce from the side of the scrum to centre. Bunce hated it but Pryor was convinced that that was where his future lay.

"He was too classy to be a flanker. When you got the ball to Frank, things happened. With a minimum of effort, he could beat an opponent and set things up. He wasn't just a finisher, he was a creator."

Bunce, who'd played all his rugby from the age of eight, when he first weighed in with Manukau, as a flanker, was thoroughly bemused by life in midfield.

"I'd never wanted to play anywhere except flanker. My heroes were Ian Kirkpatrick, Ken Stewart, Kevin Eveleigh and Barry Ashworth, with Kirkpatrick definitely number one. I was completely won over by that try he scored at Lancaster Park against the Lions.

"I remember reading an extract from a book in which Kevin Eveleigh described his training programme. He basically used to run till he dropped. I recall how he said he used to sprint from lamp post to lamp post. I tried that once and I was hopeless. 'This is not for you, Frank,' I said to myself. I could manage the same challenge the next day with a group, talking all the way, but on my own I was a hopeless trainer."

Anyway, coach Pryor ordered Bunce to move to centre. His first game in the No 13 jersey was back at the Domain on a cold, windy day. "I thought it was a stupid bloody position," recalls Frank. "I remember standing around waiting for something to happen, advancing one step at a time while the forwards agonisingly improved their position. There was nothing to do. At least the wingers could go looking for extra work. The centre was transfixed. I couldn't get involved in the rucks and mauls; in fact, the first couple of matches I played at centre produced almost no physical involvement whatsoever. That wasn't me."

When Mac Herewini (among whose claims to fame as an All Black was that he once took over the goalkicking duties from Don "The Boot" Clarke in a test, because Clarke kept missing) stepped down as coach of the struggling Manukau senior team at the conclusion of the 1980 season, Alby Pryor was pressed into taking up the coaching reigns again.

He agreed to, because he saw so much exciting talent coming through from the third and fifth grade teams. One player he had in mind as his centre was Frank Bunce. But fate was to intervene. The gifted footballer from The Team From Hell wouldn't be playing any rugby in 1981.

Bunce fell foul of the traffic department. Not once, but twice. He was to pay a heavy penalty. It was, he reflects now, an inevitable situation given his circumstances.

He wasn't short on intelligence, or encouragement from his family. A mischievous child, he certainly didn't lack for love from his parents or from his brothers and sisters of which there were seven – Margaret, Sifa, Jennifer, Tony, Stephen, Joanna and Chris (Chris's claim to fame being that he was the heaviest baby, at 20lb, ever born at Middlemore Hospital).

Frank's father dealt severely, but reasonably, with his children when the occasion called for it.

Such as when young Frank stayed home from primary school once because he was ill. Feeling better in the afternoon he decided to experiment with a cigarette. He ignited not only the cigarette but the kitchen curtains, watching in horror as the flames raced up them and threatened to engulf the entire house. Fortunately, his screams were heard immediately by the neighbour who rushed in and helped a panic-stricken Frank douse the fire.

Frank's mother was surprised to see him hurrying down the road as she returned home with the groceries. "I'm feeling a lot better," wee Frank blurted out. "I think I'll go to school!"

He can only imagine his mother's reaction when she discovered her charred kitchen. "I returned home in great trepidation that day," says Bunce, "and was told to wait in my room till my father arrived. He could have done a lot of things but he just lectured me and ordered me to bed without dinner.

"One good thing came out of that experience - I have never smoked another cigarette to this day."

Laziness, Bunce admits, is one of his worst traits. He confesses to having always been lazy. When a student at Mangere College, two streets from where he lived, he used to remain in bed in the mornings until the first bell rang at 8.40am. Then he'd make a mad dash for it, and stroll into school just before the second, and final, bell tolled at 9am!

An academic he wasn't. He lived for the sport; rugby (which was not of any great consequence at Mangere College, at the bottom of the ladder among Auckland's rugby schools), volleyball, basketball and gymnastics. He wagged school often, to do nothing in particular, except mix all too often with the wrong types.

"One of the guys I used to hang out with was later jailed for life for murder. He killed a milkman. There was a strong criminal element and, of course, there were always drugs which fortunately didn't appeal to me any more than cigarettes.

"I heard Jonah Lomu say in a documentary in 1995, after he'd become an international superstar, that he was desperately close to going off the rails as a teenager, that rugby was eventually his salvation. I guess you could say the same about me. The temptation to turn to crime was always confronting me, but fortunately my conscience always held me back."

Naturally bright, young Frank was always in the top classes at college and, notwithstanding an absolute minimum of study, he passed School Certificate at his first attempt, unlike most of his class mates and friends.

But then, contrary to everyone's advice, he left school. "It seemed like a good idea at the time," says Bunce. "It was probably the stupidest thing I ever did. I went against everyone's advice. I thought I knew best, which I didn't. It's still a huge regret. I was intelligent enough to have prospered at school and Mangere College gave me every opportunity, but I just quit.

"I remember when I was finishing my primary education, a teacher calling on my parents and recommending they send me to a boarding school. The teacher had identified my basic laziness and was concerned I would become a drifter without strong supervision.

"Application was never a word to feature in my school reports. Otherwise, I might have utilised my sports sessions to practise kicking with my left foot. Or even with my right foot would have been a help! I was easily led in those days and spent too much time mixing with the wrong types, guys who would inevitably finish up on the scrapheap.

"I was in on a couple of car conversions, the worst thing I ever stooped to. Thank goodness rugby hoisted me out of that mire."

Bunce recalls how his family took in a boarder at one stage. He offered him a ride in his car. "For a joke, I said the car had been stolen.

The boarder refused to get in it! They were my worst years, when I was nineteen and twenty."

Late in 1980, mildly intoxicated, he was stopped by the police while driving home from a party one night. It cost him a hefty fine and led to his driving licence being cancelled for six months.

A couple of months later he drove out of the Otahuhu Rugby Club one night in his showy 1958 Plymouth... "a great big thing with wings"...having consumed an excess of beer. He hadn't gone far when flashing lights let him know the law was upon him again. "The cop claimed I hadn't given way at a stop sign. When I turned the crystals green again, I knew I was in deep trouble."

Bunce was remanded in a cell overnight when it was established that he was a disqualified driver.

"While I was sitting there, with drug addicts and all sorts of weird people around me, a policeman, who must have recognised me, came up and said, 'Why don't you stop fucking around with your life and concentrate on rugby.' He was talking a lot of sense but somehow I felt I was caught in a web from which it was almost impossible to disentangle myself."

Bunce was trembling when he appeared before the judge in December for sentencing. The judge did not take kindly to citizens driving while disqualified and certainly not intoxicated citizens. "I am warning you," he told Bunce, "that you could go to prison for this offence. Fortunately, you did not cause harm to any other person, so I am sentencing you to nine months periodic detention and disqualifying your driver's licence for a *further* six months. You will not drive again until that period of suspension is completed."

It was a sober, contrite Frank Bunce who exited the court. The thought that his misdemeanour could have landed him in prison brought him out in a cold sweat. "I wasn't seriously over the limit when I was picked up, but being a suspended driver meant I was in deep trouble."

The significance of nine months periodic detention didn't hit home to Bunce immediately, until he discovered that his PD was to be served from 8am to 5pm every Saturday. And nine months from December meant he wouldn't have a Saturday spare until September 1981. That was his debut year in senior club rugby gone.

The positive aspects of his nine months of PD were that it curtailed his wild Friday night social activities, got him out of bed early on Saturday mornings, meant plenty of fresh air each weekend and caused him to take a long, hard look at himself.

Every Saturday he and the other mostly petty criminals would assemble early and be driven to Ambury Farm near Mangere Cemetery where they would either build stone walls or cut scrub.

The routine never varied. There would be a ten minute smoko in mid-morning when tea, so potent it almost held the spoon upright, was served in tin cups. During their thirty minute lunch break they would be given three sandwiches, one cheese and onion and two luncheon sausage. "The menu never varied," says Bunce. "The chef obviously didn't have a lot of imagination."

Punctuality has never been, and still isn't, Bunce's greatest quality, but after a first weekend mix-up, he made certain that throughout his nine month 'sentence' he never turned up late.

He had been instructed to register at the PD centre on the Friday before his first day's detention. Through a misunderstanding, he failed to report, but was on hand for the roll call the next morning. He became perplexed when his name was not called out, the supervisor having no record of him. After a brief inquiry it was established that Bunce was at fault. His punishment was an extra day's detention. He would report at 8am on the Sunday morning as well.

"I made certain, from that moment, that I was a model citizen. Nine months of Saturdays was more than enough. I didn't fancy building rock walls on Sundays as well as Saturdays!"

Usually there were about 30 in the PD gang that Bunce was involved with each Saturday. They were, Bunce recalls, "a bunch of losers" serving their penance for such offences as breaking and entering and assaults.

Having to sacrifice a season of rugby hurt. He was missing the camaraderie of his Manukau team mates. On many occasions during the year he permitted himself moments of introspection as he munched unenthusiastically on his cheese and onion and luncheon sausage sandwiches. "What the hell am I doing here?" he would ask himself as he scanned the losers around him. "I don't belong with these people. They don't want to play rugby or get out of this environment. Most of them just don't care."

Bunce resolved to be a model PD worker and to never get himself into this situation again. He sensed deep down that he had something to offer this world. He wasn't quite sure what, but building rock gardens and scrub cutting for the Justice Department every Saturday sure as hell wasn't going to help him achieve it.

How different 1982 would be. No Team From Hell, no PD, no confrontations with rugby coaches, no huge regrets about the direction his career was taking.

Although he had regular employment, serving his apprenticeship as a French polisher with the firm of J and B Sands, more significant in the context of his attitude to life was the fact that he was included in the Manukau senior club squad, coming under Alby Pryor's fatherly guidance again. It was a super year to be involved with Manukau because the club had approved an overseas trip, to the Michelob tournament in Tucson, Arizona. Frank would participate in the fundraising and the travel, which he would see as a turning point in his life.

Although he had been sidelined effectively for a season Bunce hadn't missed out on rugby altogether. The Manukau club had a strong association with Bay of Plenty and in particular the Te Tirahau people of Tuhoe (which translated means the children of the mist) and there was a regular interchange of visits, usually on Sundays. Frank was always encouraged to travel with Manukau when it visited Tuhoe (about 20 kilometres from Taneatua).

Another Sunday tradition that developed in those days, largely thanks to Dick Garratt, was the one hour runs from the local tennis club.

"Prising Frank away from his bed on a Sunday morning was an agony," remembers Garratt. "Frank was basically lazy and not a great trainer. But we worked on him, and he became part of our Sunday morning runs. We'd circle the airport and come back down past the Travelodge to the tennis club."

When Frank resumed his rugby career in 1982 he presumed he would pack down on the side of the scrum again, but coach Pryor had other ideas.

In the early season trials, Bunce found himself wearing the No 13 jersey and marking George Stirling, the established centre who was distinctive with dreadlocks.

Whether it was because Bunce had the better of him or for personal reasons, Stirling soon opted out of rugby for the year, leaving the graduate from the 1980 fifth grade team to link up in midfield with the Thomas brothers, Greg and Mike.

In his first senior game, against Marist, Bunce came up against James Buutveldt, a player who had worn the Auckland jersey the previous season. As Bunce went to follow a kick through, he was held back by Buutveldt. Bunce did no more than protest.

"Don't stand for any of that nonsense," Mike Thomas said, "next time he does it, smack him!"

"I can't do that," pleaded Bunce, "He's an Auckland A rep and I'm playing my first senior game."

"Listen, if you don't sort it out now, he'll just keep doing it."

"Okay."

Not long after, Buutveldt, obviously believing he'd located someone of genial nature among the opposition, grabbed hold of Bunce's jersey and obstructed him again.

But this time Bunce rounded on him and with a telling punch knocked the would-be Auckland representative to the ground.

"I was worried about the consequences," says Bunce, "but no one saw the punch, not even James Buutveldt, I suspect. The retaliation worked - he didn't hold me back again! It was a valuable lesson in my first senior game."

Eleven years on Bunce would proffer the same advice to a youthful Liam Barry during North Harbour's NPC semi-final against Otago at Carisbrook - the classic encounter that went to extra time – when Jamie

Joseph was doing the jersey-pulling. The circumstances were almost identical, with Barry loath to retaliate.

"Whack him," ordered Bunce, "or he'll just keep doing it."

Some time later Barry, heeding the advice of someone a full 10 years older than himself, struck out at Joseph when the Otago flanker tried to impede his progress.

However, on this occasion the referee saw Barry throw the punch, penalised him, and Otago kicked the goal.

"Thanks a lot for that advice," said Barry the next time he passed Bunce!

Although he would have jumped at the opportunity to revert to a loose forward role, Bunce accepted his appointment at centre and worked diligently at developing the skills required. Because Manukau was a survivor in the first division of the Auckland competition rather than one of the glamorous teams, Bunce was consistently thrust into a defensive role. If he'd had limitations they would have been exposed but, like most Polynesians, tackling came naturally to him.

"My brothers were all strong tacklers," says Bunce. "It's something we seemed able to do from the start. I'd have to say that playing for Manukau, I certainly got plenty of practice at it!"

Having survived comfortably in division one and after a year of furious fundraising, Alby Pryor's men of Manukau headed for the United States. For most of them it was a mind-boggling experience. "The furthest any of us had been was Australia," says Bunce. "Here we were with an itinerary that had us doing Arizona, Las Vegas, San Francisco, San Diego, Disneyland, Tijuana and Hawaii. It was all a bit overwhelming."

There was rugby to be played, which didn't interfere too seriously with the socialising. Not once the players discovered they could purchase two dozen cans of beer at the local supermarket for $6. "I knew then," says Bunce, "this was going to be a great trip!"

Manukau actually made it to the final of the Michelob tournament where it was defeated by Kiwi compatriots Otahuhu. Along the way it played a couple of warm-up fixtures against American sides. At San Diego, Bunce recalls watching in astonishment as gophers kept appearing out of holes in the ground. "How can you prepare yourself seriously for a tackle when there's a gopher between you and the guy with the ball!"

Another time, fired up by coach Pryor after a couple of disappointing performances, the Manukau players decided to give their American opposition a taste of genuine New Zealand rucking. They exploded into one ruck, delivering an opponent along with the ball to their halfback. "Jesus, you guys are crazy," declared the fellow marking Bunce. "We're just here to play rugby."

Bunce fell head over heels in love with the whole American

experience. For a young guy from Auckland it was unbelievable. "What it brought home to me was that rugby could open the world to you. Until then, my world had revolved around Mangere. My work, my rugby, my entire social life happened in Mangere. Now here I was in places like Phoenix, Arizona, the city Elvis Presley had written one of his classic songs about."

Just being in Phoenix was special enough but when, at the conclusion of the tournament, a Michelob beer tanker was driven on to the field and each player presented with a beer mug...well, that was the ultimate.

Unwinding in Honolulu on the way home, Bunce and Jonathan Tukerangi, two of Manukau's most promising young backs, were called aside one day by Alby Pryor. "You've obviously enjoyed yourselves immensely," he told them. "You see what you can get out of the game. So my advice to you both is to stop mucking around when you get home. Give rugby one hundred per cent and it will reward you ten times over. Do you understand what I'm saying?"

Fourteen years on, Pryor says he felt Bunce knew exactly what he was talking about. "You could tell he was a boy who wanted to achieve, someone who was only just beginning to appreciate what life had to offer. I didn't get the feeling that other fellow understood me at all."

1986 And All That

Rugby seasons don't come much more screwball than 1986. That was the year the All Blacks – with two notable exceptions, David Kirk and John Kirwan – dubbed themselves the Cavaliers and undertook their illicit tour of South Africa, playing a full series against the Springboks.

Their daring mission, a masterpiece of clandestine planning, was greeted with mixed sentiments back in New Zealand.

The (Labour) Government, which in cahoots with prominent members of the legal profession had forced the cancellation of the scheduled tour of the republic the previous year, was livid; the New Zealand Rugby Union was angry, and duly slapped a two-test ban on the 31 players; those clubs and unions which unexpectedly found themselves without their most celebrated players were frustrated; and the man in the street wasn't quite sure how to feel.

There was no question, however, about how Brian Lochore felt. As New Zealand rugby's chairman of selectors in 1986, he was charged with producing quality results in a one-off test against Jacques Fouroux's Frenchmen, in a three-test series against Alan Jones' Wallabies – who were riding high after their Grand Slam triumph in the UK in 1984 – and, at season's end, on a full-scale tour of France.

Lochore had stoically accepted the disruptions of the previous season, one which had seen the pin pulled on the tour of South Africa – the ultimate challenge for any New Zealand rugby player – just days before assembly.

One could not measure the level of disappointment that Lochore must have felt but, like the great statesman he is, he kept almost all his feelings private, and was partly consoled with a substitute tour of Argentina.

The traumas of '85 behind him, Lochore was readying for the challenges of the new rugby season – an important one with the inaugural

Rugby World Cup approaching – when news broke of the Cavaliers' audacious, and unauthorised, journey to South Africa.

Lochore was stunned. "I thought the South African saga was behind us," he said. Far from it. Lochore gloomily contemplated entering the new season without 30 of the country's leading players and one of his fellow selectors, Colin "Pinetree" Meads, who had gone to South Africa as the Cavaliers' coach.

Technically, the Cavaliers, whose matches in the republic stretched from 23 April to 31 May, would be back in New Zealand in time for the year's first international, against France at Lancaster Park. But you didn't have to be a Rhodes Scholar, like David Kirk who'd subtlely sidestepped involvement with the Cavaliers, to know that all those involved would be penalised upon their return. After all, by flaunting existing procedures in organising their overseas venture their actions were tantamount to mutiny.

When the New Zealand Rugby Football Union announced a two test ban for the rebels, Lochore and his fellow selectors, Tiny Hill and Colin Meads (who had coached the Cavaliers) realised that a monumental assignment confronted them: They were going to have to take on the might of France and Australia, in tests at Christchurch and Wellington, with a brand new team. Only Kirwan and Kirk remained of the 30 players originally selected to tour South Africa the previous year.

Although he was unaware of the player's existence at the beginning of the year, one individual who would challenge strongly for selection in the Baby Blacks was a 24-year-old Aucklander Frank Bunce.

Bunce had been playing senior club rugby for Manukau since 1982 without winning any startling recognition. He'd tripped north in 1983 with Auckland C, a team that also included Terry Wright on the wing and Lindsay Harris at fullback. Billeted throughout, the team, according to Bunce, quickly appreciated that in Wright it possessed a player of Olympic pace, so they concentrated on working the ball to him at maximum velocity and stood back and applauded as he regularly scorched a path to the goalline at such delightful rugby outposts as Warkworth and Dargaville.

The next year Bunce stepped up to the Auckland B team, or second XV as it has always been rather unromantically labelled by the Auckland Rugby Union, to make his first-class debut against the the full strength King Country team in the rain at Eden Park.

Auckland B, then coached by Maurice Trapp and Bryan Williams, trailed by 12 points to nil at halftime against a team that had won six representative matches already that season when Bunce, according to the *8 O'Clock*, "surged through five or six tackles to score a spectacular try." He also "cut back" for another excellent try late in the game to help secure a 24-12 victory for his team.

Marking him that afternoon was former All Black trialist Murray Kidd, who at the beginning of 1996 was appointed coach of Ireland. Kidd, who came desperately close to All Black selection on more than one occasion, remembers vividly the impact Bunce made that afternoon back in 1984.

"My reason for retiring (after 109 games for King Country) was because of what Frank did to me that day. He ran clean over me to score his try. He may not have been the most skilful player I ever marked but he was undoubtedly the most physical. It surprised me, after what he showed on that occasion, that he took so long to become an established player at top level.

"Frank convinced me that I was too old for the modern game. I was always honest about what (or who) prompted me to retire. It was a long time before people appreciated what I was trying to tell them."

Although Bunce's play was of a consistently high standard for Manukau and Auckland B through those seasons in the mid-1980s, he failed to convince the then Auckland coach John Hart of his true potential, Hart being more than satisfied with the man he had wearing the No 13 jersey, Joe Stanley.

Hart did acknowledge Bunce's promise fleetingly in 1985 when he introduced him to the A squad for an early-season game against the Wasps at Rotorua. Bunce didn't get on the field but got a great buzz out of rubbing shoulders with such celebrated players as Grant Fox, Joe Stanley and the Whetton brothers.

If he was somewhat overawed in a rugby context at finding himself in such illustrious company, Bunce, after downing a considerable quantity of beer that evening, certainly wasn't shy when it came to socialising alongside his team mates.

He was feeling no pain when he took himself off to the toilet at one stage. Suddenly, alongside, was Lindsay Harris, his old buddy from the Auckland B and C days.

"Hey, Frank, can I offer a word of advice," said Harris.

"Sure, mate."

"Quieten down on the partying with people like Joe (Stanley) and AJ (Whetton). They've been there, done that. You're a new kid. You haven't even worn the Auckland jersey yet. Just don't overplay your hand. People like John Hart take notice of these things."

It was a subdued Frank Bunce who returned to the party. He was to remember Harris' words and sometimes wondered, when Hart consistently ignored his claims throughout 1985 and most of 1986, whether it was because he had "overplayed his hand" that night in Rotorua.

Not that it entirely quelled the impish spirit that has always existed within him.

During an Auckland B team visit to the King Country in 1986, Bunce was dining with team mate Mike Dowd at Taumarunui's Cobb and Co on the eve of the game.

"A wine would be a pleasant accompaniment to our meal," observed Bunce, who wasn't playing the next day because of an ankle injury. Dowd concurred.

"Waiter," commanded Bunce, "a bottle of Moet and Chandon, please."

"Certainly, sir," responded the waiter, not accustomed to serving finest French champagne to Cobb and Co clientele.

"Oh yes, and would you also deliver a bottle to the gentlemen sitting over there, with my compliments," added Bunce, pointing to the Auckland B team manager Kevin Gimblett and coach Tank Herring.

Bunce was savouring the bubbles, which cost about $70 a bottle, and which was charged to the team's expense account, when the wine was delivered to Gimblett.

"With the compliments of the gentleman at the table over there," said the waiter.

"Fantastic," said Gimblett, not noticing who the 'gentleman' was. "Pour away."

Just as Gimblett was about to put the nectar to his lips, he caught a glimpse, through the rows of tables, of Bunce raising his glass in a toast. "Oh shit," he said to Herring, "excuse me a moment, I think someone's having us on."

It's not known if the Auckland Rugby Union expressed surprise at such a large wine bill the night before the team played its game. Perhaps it was placated by the fact the mighty Bs defeated King Country 9-7 the next day.

Bunce may have languished in the Bs forevermore had it not been for Bryan Craies, the effervescent former Auckland coach who had become the Auckland Rugby Union's chairman of coaching and, more significantly in 1986, Leo Walsh's assistant as coach of the North Island team.

With 30 of the nation's best players away in South Africa, and in big trouble with the NZRFU, suddenly the inter-island fixture, scheduled for Oamaru in June, took on major significance.

Craies had been aware of Bunce's talent for several seasons.

"I was one of the few people around consistently watching the Auckland club scene and I had seen Frank performing regularly for Manukau.

"It was against Frank that Manukau was a rather unfashionable club. If he'd been doing his thing for Ponsonby or Marist, probably he would have had a higher profile.

"What impressed me instantly about Frank was that he could make a clean break, one of the few who could. He didn't have to bullock through, something that he's tended to do in recent years. In those early days, he was incisive, and he set up his wingers outside him brilliantly. "By the time 1986 came around, I regarded Frank as a complete footballer as a centre. He had pace and all the skills. What he couldn't do was kick. He still can't, but that's not necessarily a bad thing. You tell me a top-class centre who can kick well. If you can't kick, you've got to do something when you get the ball, and Frank always did."

Craies suspects that Bunce's image counted against him. "He was regarded as something of a rebel. He certainly had a devil-may-care attitude and his personal life was something of a mystery.

"Possibly that counted against him with Harty (John Hart, the Auckland coach) which is a shame because Buncey was deceptive. He looked like a rebel but underneath he had a huge heart for rugby. And he was totally loyal to his club Manukau."

When Bryan Craies and Leo Walsh had their first meeting as selectors, early in '86, it was to acknowledge that halfback David Kirk, winger Terry Wright, who'd scored a hat-trick of tries for North Island the previous year, and hooker Bruce Hemara, another survivor from North's decisive victory in '86, were probably about the only certainties.

Kirwan was in doubt because he was late returning from club commitments in Italy. Overall, Craies and Walsh had a lot of yawning gaps to fill. Walsh said he would largely concern himself with the forwards, leaving Craies to sort out a likely backline combination.

Midfielders missing on Cavaliers duty in South Africa were Steven Pokere and Bill Osborne of the North Island and Vic Simpson and Warwick Taylor from the South. Who would their substitutes be?

When Walsh and Craies reconvened in May, Craies had his midfielders sorted out. "One guy from Wellington and one from Auckland are going in, and they'll be sensational – John Schuster and Frank Bunce," he informed his colleague.

"Who the hell are they?" responded Walsh.

"You'll just have to rely on my judgment," said Craies.

"Hmmmm!" was all Walsh could offer.

Craies explained that Bunce had been doing great things for Auckland B (but had yet to wear the Auckland A jersey) while Schuster was making his mark with Wellington having previously represented Auckland Colts.

In any other year, Walsh would probably have insisted on a more orthodox selection policy. But this was a screwball year anyway. If his selecting partner was convinced Bunce and Schuster were players of the future, why not run with them!

Bunce had an inkling something special was in the wind when he was selected to play in Palmerston North at the beginning of June for a Manawatu Centennial Invitation XV coached by Brian Lochore and again when the national selectors looked in on a Manukau v Ponsonby senior club contest at Eden Park, a game in which he marked Joe Stanley.

"People said the selectors were interested in me. I was sort of flattered, but in my heart I thought, 'Nah, they wouldn't be looking at me. It's Joe (Stanley) they'd be more interested in.'"

It was Joe's wife Evelyn who broke the news. She telephoned Frank and told him she'd heard he'd been selected for the North Island team.

Frank wasn't convinced. "I'd heard nothing on the radio, I thought she must have got it wrong."

The *New Zealand Herald* photographer waiting for him outside the Manukau clubrooms ended any doubts. Suddenly, Frank was a personality. "I was in the North Island team, all right, and the media descended upon me. I had to do about a dozen runs towards the camera, with the Thomas brothers Greg and Mike, who were giving me a fearful ribbing, on either side of me. Then I had to answer a barrage of questions. It was my first experience of dealing with the media and, frankly, I didn't know what the hell to say."

What Bunce *did* say, according to his scrapbook clippings, was that it was "a real shock" to be selected. "I had read in the newspapers that my name was being mentioned, but I've only played club rugby."

Bunce's elevation to stardom created quite a stir among club members. It was a long time since Manukau had had a player recognised nationally – present club manager Barry "Bear" Thomas, an All Black in 1962 and 1964 was the last – and this was cause for celebration. The bar at Viscount Street stayed open late that night.

If Bunce had remained in the sanctuary of the Manukau clubrooms until the interisland fixture on 18 June he may well have become an All Black six years earlier than he did. Bryan Craies has not the slightest doubt that a fully fit Frank Bunce would have made such an impact against South Island the national selectors could not have resisted selecting him.

But it wasn't a fully fit Frank Bunce who took the field at Centennial Park in Oamaru (to a smaller crowd, ironically, than had watched the curtainraiser between traditional college rivals Waitaki Boys High and St Kevins College), it was a Frank Bunce carrying a painful ankle injury, one which forced him out of the game after 30 minutes.

He'd damaged the ligaments in his right ankle playing for Manukau against Waitemata. It was to be the start of a frustrating run of injuries leading into important games that were to impair Bunce's career opportunities.

Bunce flew into Oamaru nursing the ankle injury, praying it would respond rapidly to physiotherapy treatment. When it did not, he mentioned to Peter Fatialofa, who was propping the North Island scrum with Kevin Boroevich, his concern, suggesting he might pull out.

Fatialofa convinced him otherwise. "Hey, man," he said, "you didn't come all this way for nothing. Go for it!"

Bunce found himself rooming with fellow rookie midfielder John Schuster who, unfortunately for Bunce, turned out to be a soccer enthusiast. Normally, that wouldn't have mattered but while the players were quartered in Oamaru, the soccer World Cup was happening in Italy with live telecasts running late into the night.

"John insisted on watching every minute of every game," recalls Bunce. "I can't say I got a lot of sleep the night before our game!"

Bunce, although conscious of his ankle injury, felt he combined well in training with Frano Botica and Schuster and was excited about the attacking possibilities the North backline possessed. He would be marking Mid-Canterbury's Murray McLeod, a late replacement for Mike Gibson of Otago.

Although the black jersey he pulled on in the dressing room did not possess a silver fern, it was near enough to the sacred All Black jersey for Bunce to feel a surge of pride. "There's something special about a black rugby jersey. I think I knew that day in Oamaru that I wouldn't be satisfied until I had worn the real thing...!"

Bunce was hopeful that his adrenalin rush would disguise the discomfort the damaged ankle ligaments were causing. But it didn't happen that way. The jarring sensation was there from the start. He couldn't focus on the role for which he'd been selected because the injury was such a distraction.

"I was weighing up the options. If I stayed on, I could make a fool of myself and ruin my chances for the future. If I went straight off, it wouldn't look good, and it would certainly spell an end to my prospects for 1986.

"Reluctantly, after about thirty minutes play, I advised my captain (David Kirk) that I couldn't carry on. I moved despondently to the sideline and shortly thereafter joined our lock Mata'afa Keenan in the first aid room. He'd been considered a certainty for All Black selection but his season came to an abrupt finish when he tore his knee ligaments soon after the start.

"It didn't seem possible at the time, but Mata'afa and I were to play test rugby together for Western Samoa five years on."

Bunce drowned his disappointment in Speights that evening. The final frustration in the small north Otago town came after midnight when he couldn't find a piecart or a takeaway bar open!

Unable to play in the national trial in Blenheim three days later, Bunce saw his chances of All Black selection evaporate. The selectors eventually disregarded all the centres who were on display at Oamaru and Blenheim (Iain Wood and Scott Pierce wore the No 13 jerseys in the trial) and introduced Joe Stanley for the international against France.

Brian Lochore admits that Bunce was "clearly in the frame" for selection. "It was against Frank that he wasn't being used by Auckland, so he had to prove himself in the trial games. Having had him brought to my attention by Bryan Craies, I watched him play a couple of times and I must say I regarded him as a player with a lot of talent, a lot of skill. I wouldn't discount the fact that Frank could have been an All Black in 1986 if he'd taken the opportunity with which he'd been presented."

Lochore said his selection panel eventually settled for Joe Stanley because he'd proved himself playing inside John Kirwan and Terry Wright for Auckland. "Even though we didn't use him in the trials, we'd seen him operating for Auckland and knew his capabilities."

Bryan Craies accepts that Lochore made the correct choice in the circumstances, pairing Stanley up in midfield with Arthur Stone.

"However, I had no doubt that, once given the break, Frank would never look back. He had been injured. If fit, he would have turned on a blinder and Lochore would have had to select him. He and Schuster would have been brilliant together in midfield. They were my dream pairing. I could see them operating together in the All Black backline. Sadly, they were never to play together again."

John Hart, the Auckland selector-coach, didn't approve of the North Island selectors' approach at all. "I thought at the time their disregard for Joe Stanley was grossly unfair. He was one of the mainstays of the Auckland team and over the next four or five years he was to prove his class for Auckland and New Zealand.

"I have to say I hadn't seen a lot of Bunce, although I know I questioned his discipline and commitment to the game at the time, and in those days I wondered whether he could take the outside break, which he subsequently developed. I am prepared to concede that I possibly underestimated him. I suspect Frank is one of those rare individuals who got better with every step he took up the rugby ladder. Many players get found out as they advance – Frank seemed to blossom as he advanced."

Bunce tried to put the disappointment of Oamaru behind him. There were important Gallaher Shield matches coming up with Manukau, and now that he had been recognised nationally, he hoped Hart might look more favourably in his direction.

But the damaged ankle ligaments took an age to mend. "I spent weeks – it began to feel like months – at the physiotherapist's," said Bunce. "It was depressing. I began to feel the damned thing would never come right."

Bunce can claim that in the 15 years since he first became a senior club player he has been mercifully free of serious injuries. "That ankle back in 1986…that was one of the worst." X-rays had revealed no broken bones but still the ligaments refused to mend.

Bunce spent hours on the balancing board in an endeavour to strengthen the ankle but signs of improvement were painstakingly slow. He could walk and he could work out at the gym but the moment he attempted any sidewards movement, the pain bit in.

Standing gloomily at Eden Park one Saturday afternoon, watching his Manukau team in action, he got into conversation with Andy Haden whose celebrated international career had finally come to a halt the previous year.

Haden listened to Bunce's tale of woe and proffered a piece of homespun philosophy. "Sometimes, Frank," he said, "you reach a point where you've just got to go out and play."

The following week, his ankle still a source of concern, Bunce was mooching around at Eden Park again when Auckland selector Hart wandered up. "I see your name's still not in the programme, Frank. When do you hope to play again?"

Frank explained his dilemma and mentioned Haden's comment. "Maybe he's got something – who knows?" said Hart, wandering off to focus on potential Auckland squad members who didn't have crocked ankles.

Bunce felt disconsolate. He also felt an urge to make things start happening. He hastened to the Manukau dressing room where he found coach Pat Walsh and asked him how his line-up was looking for that day.

"Well, to be honest, I'm a back short – do you want to play?" said Walsh.

"Yeah – give me a jersey."

When Manukau ran on to Eden Park, John Hart did a double take. There in the No 13 jersey was Bunce. "Funny," he commented to a friend, "I thought Frank said he wasn't ready to start playing yet."

Bunce admits to a moment of panic as the referee signalled the start of the game. "What am I doing here?" I thought. "I'm supposed to be injured. I've got an ankle that won't come right – what if…what… what…what the hell, let's get on with it."

To his surprise, and sheer delight, he completed eighty minutes of action with no discomfort in the ankle whatsoever. He'd done it without any injections. "I wanted to shout 'Eureka' when I returned to the changing room, but I was rather perplexed. I had a terrible feeling I could have been back playing rugby a month earlier!"

It was a timely return to action, for Hart was canvassing talent to supplement his squad for the upcoming Ranfurly Shield defence against lowly Horowhenua. The game would be played on a Sunday, 24 hours after the All Blacks tackled Australia in Dunedin. And in the All Black starting line-up were seven Aucklanders.

Among the reinforcements Hart required were a centre to replace Joe Stanley (come in Frank Bunce), a first-five to take over from Grant Fox (Brett Craies, North Island selector Bryan's son, got the job) and a blindside flanker for Alan Whetton (Eric Rush was preferred).

Auckland cantered to victory, winning 82-6. Bunce scored a try while Craies kicked 30 points, only two short of Robbie Deans' Ranfurly Shield record. Bunce, Craies and Rush were credited with turning in "distinguished performances." They were all making their Auckland debuts.

It was Brett Craies who, in high spirits that evening, provided what was to be a classic throwaway line. "Only thirteen more appearances for a blazer, guys," he quipped. Bunce and Rush laughed with him at the time. If only they were to know...

Craies was to get just three appearances in three seasons for Auckland before moving to Waikato where he was to fashion an impressive record for the Mooloo men and Rush would manage just 13 outings in five years before switching to North Harbour, from where he would go on to become an All Black winger. Bunce would be the only one to qualify for an Auckland blazer...four years on (with five of his twenty appearances being as a replacement). He too would head across the bridge to North Harbour before achieving international stardom.

Bunce, operating outside Kurt Sherlock and with Bernie McCahill on the wing and Terry Wright at fullback, enjoyed his first outing for Auckland but even though the game was against third division minnow Horowhenua he was surprised at the greater tempo at which it was played. "It was a huge step-up from club play and a lot different from what I'd experienced with the Auckland second fifteen."

This was Bunce's second big opportunity in a little over two months, but as in Oamaru he was to depart the field early with an injury. This time the damage was obvious for all to see. He'd had his hand on the ball when an over exuberant Horowhenua forward took a hefty kick at it. A sprig ripped between the third and fourth fingers of Bunce's left hand, slicing the hand open.

"It was horrible," recalls Bunce. "It was a huge gash that exposed all the sinew. There was a lot of blood. I just presumed I would go off."

Andy Haden, Auckland's captain, didn't see it that way. "You can't go off on your debut," he said in a deadly serious tone.

Bunce reluctantly accepted the great man's pronouncement. He was privileged to be playing for the best provincial rugby team in the world. Lacerated hand or not, he would battle on to the finish.

Just as he was about to instruct the St Johns ambulanceman to apply a bandage, to close the gaping wound and soak up the blood, Auckland's No 8 John McDermott intervened. "You can't play on with an injury like that," he said. "It's awful – go and get it treated."

Bunce looked towards the scoreboard. His team was seventy points ahead with fewer than ten minutes to play. He didn't feel he was letting them down by retiring at that stage. He heeded McDermott's, rather than Haden's, advice and went off, to be replaced by John Kirwan who had featured in New Zealand's one-point test victory over the Wallabies at Carisbrook the previous afternoon.

"Not a bad replacement," Bunce remembers thinking as he wandered down the tunnel towards the Auckland dressing room, the loose bandage around his hand bright scarlet.

Bunce felt rather sheepish when Haden approached him at the after-match function. He anticipated a scolding for ignoring his advice. "Probably the smartest thing you could have done, coming off," declared Haden. "When I played on with the same injury a couple of seasons back, the hand was such a mess I couldn't play for another two months!"

Kirwan would play for Auckland for the remainder of the season. So, too, as Auckland impressively defended the Ranfurly Shield it had prised from Canterbury the previous September, would Joe Stanley. Bunce would not be required again. His moments in the limelight for 1986 had passed.

John Hart was about to step aside as Auckland coach. Maurice Trapp and Bryan Williams, who'd shaped an impressive record with the Auckland second XV, where they'd regularly used Bunce at centre, would take over. Perhaps better things lay ahead for the aspiring Manukau centre in 1987.

3

Rubbish Carts And Rugby League

Frank Bunce could have happily become a professional rugby player in the mid to late 1980s when he was starting to make his name as a strong running centre threequarter.

Sport, and particularly rugby, was his great passion. Work was a necessary nuisance to provide him with enough money to exist. From the time he'd walked out of Mangere College after his fifth form year, he had worked as a French polisher. It wasn't a bad job but it occupied Frank for more hours in the day than he really wanted to spend on his vocation. He'd rather be out throwing a ball around, having a game of touch or indulging himself in a game of sevens. And then there was the social scene and his propensity for guzzling beer. That wasn't exactly compatible with 8am starts and the potent fumes emitted by the various polishes when he hit the workplace each morning.

There had to be a happy compromise somewhere but Frank couldn't fathom it at that stage of his life. Rugby being amateur, he obviously wasn't able to sustain himself in that direction. It would be almost another decade before newspaper magnate Rupert Murdoch would lavish his millions upon the game and allow players like Bunce to become truly professional. Without that option back in the 1980s, Bunce eventually quit the French polishing profession and took a job with Telecom, becoming part of a work gang responsible for installing, among other things, lamp posts.

He appreciated the outdoor work but what he didn't appreciate was having to dig the deep holes to accommodate the posts. "It was," he admits, "too much like hard work. You can only dig so many holes before you start having nightmares about them."

So when Bryce Edwards, the coach of the Otahuhu senior club team, who Bunce had befriended socially, invited him to help out on his rubbish truck over the Christmas holidays, Frank jumped at the chance.

When Frank began asking questions after reporting for duty on his first morning, he was given the classic dustmen's throwaway line... "you'll pick it up as you go."

Garbologist is a term by which some rubbish workers have wished to be known. Frank never went for those highfalutin terms. He regarded himself purely and simply as a dustman and he enjoyed himself in the role so totally during that first summer that he was to retain the job for almost five years.

It was, says Bunce, the ideal occupation for him at that time. The daily routine involved a 6am start with three and a half to four hours rubbish collecting. By mid-morning he was finished, free to shower and dedicate the remainder of his day to his own pursuits.

Initially, he was so exhausted he went straight home, showered and crashed into bed, but as he adjusted he realised that the free afternoons afforded him time to work out at the gym. Which eventually became the norm. The mix of physical work and exercising at the gym dramatically reduced his body fat while increasing his aerobic conditioning, making him the fittest he had ever been. He would not achieve a comparable level of fitness again until the All Blacks were put through a virtual commando course as they prepared for the 1995 World Cup in South Africa. At one point his doctor told him his body fat count was so low it was dangerous.

The rubbish truck had one driver and two or three 'runners.' Frank was always a runner and there can be few more physically demanding jobs. "We literally ran from 6am till 9.30 or 10 every day, lifting and throwing rubbish bags the whole way. Some bags were light, some unbelievably heavy. If you fell behind, because a bag broke or there was some complication, you'd have to sprint to catch up."

Their 'territory' was Otahuhu, Panmure, Mt Wellington and a corner of Ellerslie. The only days off were statutory holidays such as Christmas Day, Good Friday and Anzac Day when they'd have to work Saturdays, or do an afternoon shift, to compensate.

The Auckland climate being such a weird sub-tropical mix, Frank and his fellow dusties experienced the extremes in work conditions. "Summer generally was brilliant," he recalls. "Usually we'd be finishing just as the temperature was building up and becoming uncomfortable.

"But winter was a bitch. It always seemed to be raining and often at 6 o'clock in the morning it would be freezing cold. In summer we scarcely wore anything at all but on those cruel winter mornings we'd be togged up in sweatshirts, jerseys, tracksuit pants and often heavy jackets as well."

Bunce never ceased to be astonished at what some people expected of dustmen. "You'd get people asking us to stop and clean out their garden for them. We always politely declined!

"You'd wonder what some people put in their rubbish bags because they'd stink to high heaven. That was the downside of being a dustman, that and when overnight rain brought all the maggots out of the bags."

Bunce's worst moment, though, came when broken glass, which hadn't been wrapped, cut through the side of the bag and jagged into his leg as he hoisted it up. "That was a major concern," he says. "I was rushed to hospital and needed thirty stitches to repair the damage."

It was Bryce Edwards' responsibility to bring enough cash each day to fund a round of meat pies during the dusties' ten-minute breakfast stop. On the odd occasion he forgot the money, he'd inform his workmates that "today it's a dingo's breakfast, boys – a drink of water and a look around!"

"Bryce was a real character. We accepted the occasional dingo's breakfast because often he'd go fishing and bring us fresh, smoked fish, which was a real delicacy."

Eric Rush, who'd made his Auckland debut the same day as Bunce in 1986, occasionally helped out on the truck during his university holidays.

Dustmen's greatest hazard are dogs and the Edwards team certainly had their moments, although Frank proudly announces that in five years, often with the odds seriously stacked against him, he was never once bitten. "That's where my sprint work came in valuable," he says. "A swift kick would always take the stuffing out of the little dogs and a punch in the nose worked wonders at other times. Usually the little fellows just yapped at you. You had to watch out for the bigger dogs especially if they were in packs. You'd stir them up running past.

"My biggest concern were rottweilers. I remember this one that as a pup was a cuddly little thing. We used to play with it. But as it grew it developed decidedly unfriendly tendencies. I used to hate collecting the bag outside its property and in the finish I used to take an extra bag with me in case it jumped the fence. I'd whack it with the spare bag and while it was recovering sprint to the truck!"

Bunce cherished his days as a dustman, for they complemented his rugby (and touch and sevens) commitments perfectly. Things *could* have been better. The new Auckland selectors, Maurice Trapp and Bryan Williams, could have acknowledged his talents more enthusiastically instead of, like Hart before them, refusing to look beyond Smokin' Joe Stanley for the centre berth in their representative team. And Frank, like many aspiring footballers of the time, would have appreciated some financial reimbursement for the hours put into travelling, training and playing in the cause of rugby.

There was one recourse open to rugby players wanting to embrace professionalism – a switch to league. It was something Bunce was to contemplate seriously on at least two occasions before cementing a place in the All Blacks.

The first time he thought about league was after fielding a call from a representative of the North Sydney Bears. It was 1988. Bunce had been recommended to the club by the New Zealand league representative Clayton Friend. "Are you fast?" the caller asked Bunce. "Fast enough," he replied, not certain where the conversation was leading. "Well, are you interested in playing league for the Bears?" "I could be." "Right, we'll get back to you."

Chuffed that a prominent Winfield Cup club had seen fit to approach him, Bunce waited for the call back. It never came. "It didn't bother me," he says, "I was intrigued to think they were even considering me." The next time Bunce and an Australian league club rubbed shoulders, in 1989, he would cross the Tasman and be offered a contract.

Before then, however, Bunce was to cause a few more ripples in the rugby pond, without ever threatening to displace Stanley from the Auckland team. In fact, the worst possible scenario eventuated with the emergence of another classy centre, teenage star Craig Innes. It was Innes, not Bunce, who would become Stanley's successor in the No 13 Auckland jersey.

If Bunce expected that his Auckland prospects would improve once Trapp and Williams were running the show, he was seriously misguided. They gave him just one outing in 1987, an early season game against North Harbour at Takapuna when the team's international stars were unavailable, preparing as they were for the World Cup.

The next year he played eight times for Trapp's team. If that sounds impressive, note that only one appearance was at centre – against Manawatu when he scored three tries and took the player of the day award – three were on the wing and the other four were as a replacement.

Bunce did remain in the national selectors' minds, however, and they named him at centre, opposite 18-year-old Innes, in the specially arranged New Zealand trial at Palmerston North, for players not involved in the South Pacific championship series.

Three days before the trial Bunce was on the reserves bench for Auckland's Southpac contest against Wellington at Eden Park, a game Auckland was to win by an embarrassing 58 points to nil.

Late in the game Bunce went on as a replacement for Lindsay Harris. Scarcely had he arrived on the field than Auckland called a well-rehearsed move which created the overlap for Terry Wright motoring in from fullback. "He sprinted probably eighty metres," recalls Bunce, "and having come on cold – I hadn't even stretched my muscles since before the game started – I was struggling to stay with him. However, as he drew the fullback I made the supreme effort. After all, he was presenting me with a try on a plate. But as I went for his pass I felt my hamstring tear, and I dropped the ball! It hardly mattered with Auckland so far ahead but I felt totally embarrassed in front of about twenty thousand spectators. And to compound the error I fumbled the next pass as well.

"The only good to come out my misfortune, which didn't do anything for my reputation at the time, was that the Auckland management ruled that in future the reserves would go through a warm-up routine and stretch muscles at halftime."

The day following Bunce's unfortunate experience against Wellington, an 18-year-old was to make an impressive debut for North Harbour at Pukekohe. That player was Walter Little.

Having bombed his golden opportunity with North Island in 1986 because of an ankle injury, Bunce now found himself heading for the Palmerston North trial with a damaged hamstring.

"It seemed I was fated to be always injured on major occasions. There was no opportunity of getting myself right in three days, even though a physiotherapist worked on the hamstring until a few hours before I took the field."

Although Bunce's team, captained by Buck Shelford, won handsomely, the Manukau centre experienced a forlorn afternoon. "It's impossible to produce quality rugby when you're conscious of an injury and I did just about everything wrong. Richard Becht, writing in the *Auckland Sun* newspaper (now defunct), gave me a three out of ten."

Bunce's performance was epitomised by an incident late in the game. Desperately striving to make some impact, he raced into the clear, only Counties fullback Lindsay Raki between him and the goalline.

"All I had to do was draw Lindsay, like a good centre should," said Bunce, "and pass the ball to either of my two team mates outside."

However, Bunce allowed himself to be conned by a piece of Maori trickery. "Lindsay's eyes turned away to the players outside me," recalls Bunce. "'He's going for them,' I thought. Wrong! He wasn't fooled by my dummy – he instantly refocused on me and crashed me to the ground, killing the move stone dead.

"As we lay there in a tangle, Lindsay said, 'Shit, Frank, you're having a shocker!' I could but agree with him."

When he returned home Frank copped an earful from his youngest brother Chris, who'd watched the trial on television. "You were bloody terrible," his brother blurted out with alarming honesty. "You'd never be able to foot it with players like Philippe Sella at international level."

Frank limped away to apply ice to his troublesome muscle feeling thoroughly depressed. Right at the moment he didn't think he would ever be able to foot it with Philippe Sella either. However, there would, he assured himself, be better weeks in his rugby career.

Bunce's hamstring tear was mended in time for him to play Auckland's Southpac game against Fiji in Suva. He wasn't altogether certain he appreciated being in the starting line-up as the Fijians ran out on to their national stadium. "They were all so big, you couldn't tell the backs from the forwards. They were monsters. Thank goodness our forwards controlled the game. I wouldn't have wanted those guys running at me all afternoon."

The game for which Bunce is most fondly remembered by Auckland fans is the Otago challenge late in the 1988 season. It was Bunce's tackle on Otago winger Noel Pilcher that was to save the Ranfurly Shield.

As usual, Bunce started the day on the reserves bench, becoming part of the action shortly before halftime when Terry Wright retired with concussion, Bunce taking his place on the left wing.

Pilcher being on the opposite wing, their paths were unlikely to cross, but twice in just over 40 minutes Bunce was to focus on the strong-running Otago player.

The first occasion was following a scrum when Bernie McCahill, operating outside Grant Fox at second-five, took play to the right. Bunce could see the move unfolding and as it involved fullback Lindsay Harris, he contemplated moving across into midfield to cover. "I remember thinking, 'No, I'll stay back on my wing.' The next instant Pilcher intercepted and raced away for a try. If I'd followed my impulse I would have stopped him. It's something I always did after that."

Pilcher's sensational runaway try shot Otago out to a 17-12 lead with two-thirds of this pulsating encounter played. An air of despondency had settled upon the Auckland supporters which deepened as Otago returned to the attack, applying relentless pressure upon the Auckland line.

Bunce thinks it was because of his earlier indecision that he was keeping his eye on Pilcher, obviously an Otago danger man. Suddenly, he could see a desperate situation unfolding for Auckland. Otago, having attacked off a scrum, was cleverly committing individual Auckland backs and when it eventually brought Pilcher in from the blindside wing in midfield, he had a virtually clear run to the tryline. Bunce says he had been shadowing him – "I always had him in my sights" – and crashed him to the turf with a copybook tackle.

Bunce admits that it wasn't until he saw the photograph of his tackle in the *New Zealand Herald* on the Monday morning that he realised how desperately close Pilcher had come to the tryline. He was less than a metre from the goalposts. A try then would have taken Otago to 21-12 and probably 23-12 and would almost certainly have seen the Ranfurly Shield heading south to Dunedin (for the first time since 1957).

No wonder he was treated as a hero when he called in on the Auckland Supporters Club party later. "Good on you, Frank, you saved the shield for us today," he heard someone shout. Frank wasn't to savour many outings as an Auckland rep but this was definitely one of them.

Much subterfuge surrounded Auckland's preparation for the season's final encounter against Canterbury, a match which doubled as a Ranfurly Shield and national championship game. Terry Wright was obviously out with concussion and on the Friday word leaked out that neither John Kirwan nor Lindsay Harris could play either, because of injuries, leaving Auckland without an obvious fullback.

Bunce was blissfully unaware of these developments when Peter Fatialofa picked him up late Friday afternoon and drove on to Joe Stanley's house. It was Evelyn, Joe's wife, who once again broke the news to Frank.

"You're playing tomorrow," she told him.

"No, I'm not," said Frank, "I'm a reserve again."

"You're playing – I'm telling you."

"How does Evelyn always know these things?" wondered Bunce, as the three of them drove across to the Auckland team's hotel. "I'd been through two training sessions and she tells me what's happening!"

With his team so seriously depleted through injury, Trapp finished up with two centres, Bunce and Innes, on the wings and a newcomer from the Colts, a player who had just turned 20, Matthew Ridge, at fullback.

Trapp regarded this line-up as somewhat vulnerable, against such a formidable opponent as Canterbury, so preferred that the enemy should not know of it until they were ready to kick off. Hence the subterfuge. The media recorded on the Saturday morning only that there were injury problems for Trapp, and the starting fifteen was not announced over the loudspeaker until the teams ran on to Eden Park. And then the announcer rattled through the Auckland side so quickly that scarcely anyone comprehended who *was* at fullback.

The late changes didn't affect the Auckland machine which had the game in safe keeping by halftime. Ridge performed competently, as did Bunce and Innes. The victory represented Auckland's 26th consecutive defence of the shield, a record. It was an achievement worthily applauded at the time. Not for another five years, by which time Frank Bunce would be established in the All Blacks and Innes and Ridge celebrated league players, would the shield move on.

A few months into the 1989 season, when it was apparent that Stanley was the only centre Auckland coach Trapp (and his assistant Beegee Williams) was interested in, Bunce turned his attentions to league. Mackie Herewini, son of former All Black Mac Herewini and a former New Zealand Colt who was playing his rugby as a halfback with Otahuhu, approached Bunce and said he had been talking with an agent of the Newcastle League Club in Australia, one Michael Hill, whose name was to feature prominently in 1995 when WRC was making its bid to lure the All Blacks away from the New Zealand Rugby Football Union.

The club was interested in negotiating a contract with Herewini and it was also looking for an outside back. Herewini had recommended Bunce.

"Mackie was the one taking all the initiative and I sort of went along for the ride. I felt I had nothing to lose, because I didn't seem to be getting anywhere in rugby. I'd blown my two opportunities at national level and I was being squeezed out of the Auckland rep scene by Joe (Stanley) and Craig (Innes)."

A meeting at the Hyatt Hotel in Auckland, with two Newcastle officials, confirmed their desire to recruit rugby players. Bunce, flattered once again that a Winfield Cup club should consider him worthy of involvement, expressed a genuine interest. And so the return air tickets offered by the Newcastle representatives were accepted.

It was the second week of May when Bunce and Herewini arrived in Sydney and connected with a flight through to Newcastle. While waiting at Sydney Airport they encountered a member of the Newcastle premiers, Anthony Butterfield, a thickset individual with a badly broken nose. "His face wasn't a great advertisement for league," recalls Bunce.

Somehow, news of Bunce and Herewini's flirtation with league had leaked out and Bunce was telephoned by a newspaperman the day before he flew out of Auckland. "What the hell was I supposed to say?" says Bunce, "when this guy asked me if I was going to Australia to check out a league club? I said no. It was the easiest answer at the time. Any other answer was obviously going to cause complications."

Herewini and Bunce were separated upon arrival, Herewini being sent to the North Nelson Bay club, a feeder club for Newcastle, while Bunce went along to the Newcastle training.

Bunce was fascinated with the training facilities. One machine simulated rock climbing, the vertical face being a challenge for any sportsman. Bunce took it on and performed remarkably well. His gruelling days as a dustman had prepared him well for this. He was told that only one New Zealander had ever fared better at his first attempt at the rock face.

Herewini wasn't going so well at North Nelson Bay, however. The training had found him out and he was distraught. Bunce was sent up to console him. While he was at North Nelson Bay, Bunce was told they wanted the pair of them to play in a match that weekend.

Bad weather caused the game to be abandoned but Bunce insists there was no way he was going to participate anyway. "Our presence at Newcastle had received quite a bit of publicity back home, and NZRFU councillor John Dowling had said that the moment we walked on to the field we would lose our amateur status. If I was going to change codes, I would do it properly, signing a contract first. Getting myself banned from rugby wasn't going to help."

During his stay Bunce found himself scanning the Newcastle sports pages for rugby stories. "There was almost nothing on rugby, it was all league. That's when I realised my heart was still in rugby.

"Newcastle was an excellent set-up, very professional. If that had been what I'd wanted, I would have happily signed up. But training five days a week wasn't me."

Herewini meanwhile decided he'd had enough, so he convinced Frank they should approach Michael Hill and say they wanted to return to New Zealand.

"Certainly," said Hill, "When would you like to return?"

"There's a flight out of Newcastle this afternoon," answered Herewini.

"Oh, that quickly. If that's what you want, we'll arrange it."

"Yes please."

Before he departed, Bunce was presented with a contract by Hill. He was told the club was "genuinely interested" in him. "I said I would go home and think seriously about it."

A few days later Bunce received a phone call from Eric Rush who, in his capacity as a lawyer, said he had a couple of representatives of the Newcastle League Club in his office. "They say they've offered you a contract. What are you going to do about it?"

"Tell them they're not offering enough money," replied Bunce. "Ask them what figure they're prepared to go to."

"Okay," said Rush.

A couple of minutes later Rush's phone rang. It was Bunce again.

"What's happening?" asked Eric.

"Tell them the answer's no," said Bunce. "I'm sticking with rugby."

Bunce says he never seriously considered signing the Newcastle contract. "I'm pleased I went to Australia and checked out their set-up. It was an eye-opener, to be honest. But when it came to the crunch I knew that in my heart I was a rugby person. It's not easy to explain, especially when you've got almost nothing in the bank, why you're rejecting money to stay with a game which is completely amateur."

That's why Bunce was hurt when he read that John Dowling, as chairman of the NZRFU's status committee, was accusing him (and Herewini) of dishonesty. "It would be nice," Dowling said, "if our sportsmen and sportswomen showed the same honesty off the field as they do on. There's such a thing as honesty to your fellow players, to rugby and to sport in general."

"Was I being dishonest?" asked Bunce. "I went to check out the league scene but found it wasn't for me, so I came back to rugby. John Dowling could surely have made more out of that than attacking me in the manner he did."

Bunce said he was caught completely unawares when the newspaperman quizzed him the day before his departure for Sydney.

"What was I supposed to say? Yes, I'm going to Newcastle to have talks about a league career. Where would that have left me? Would John Dowling have come out and praised my honesty? I think not. At the time I said "No." I still think, given the circumstances, that that was the best answer."

4

The Western Samoan Factor

F rank Bunce and Peter Fatialofa forged a strong friendship through the 1980s. Rivals at club level – Fats played for Ponsonby while Frank was a dedicated Manukau man – their careers followed remarkably similar patterns, as members of the Auckland second XV, all too infrequently with Auckland A and intermittently in the national limelight. At various times both had been touted as potential All Blacks.

They regularly socialised together, often pooling their money. Fatialofa occasionally helped out on the rubbish truck while Bunce deployed his nephew whenever Peter Fats needed assistance to move a piano.

By 1990 when Fatialofa was 31 and Bunce 28, they were both pretty much in the same boat. While considered valuable members of the Auckland squad, not least for their input on social occasions, neither was rated a frontline player. Bunce was still in the queue as a centre behind Joe Stanley and had now also been overtaken by Craig Innes, who, as a teenager, had bounded into the All Blacks the previous year. Fatialofa was now only the third-ranked prop after Steve McDowell and Olo Brown.

While Fatialofa had been disappointed at missing All Black selection, particularly in 1988 when he deserved to tour Australia, by 1990 his greater energies were being channelled into Western Samoan rugby. He was a vital part of the Western Samoan revival headed by manager Tate Simi, coach Peter Schuster and former All Black great Bryan Williams as the technical advisor.

The Western Samoans were devastated at being left out of the first World Cup tournament in New Zealand, particularly as their great south seas rivals Fiji and Tonga had participated. There was enormous resolve to have Western Samoa featuring at the second World Cup in the UK in 1991.

From the moment he became part of the great reawakening of Western Samoan rugby, Fatialofa was on the lookout for players with Samoan bloodlines. He knew that for his nation to be seriously competitive at the World Cup it would have to recruit players who had been hardened in the New Zealand provincial system.

One of the players he began targeting after the chance discovery in 1989 of his Western Samoan heritage was Frank Bunce.

Frank's father, Frank senior, had parents who were both New Zealanders but his mother Sifa, who had been born in Niue, claimed a Niuean mother and a father who was half Niuean and half Samoan. That made Frank Bunce one-sixteenth Western Samoan.

That was enough for Peter Fatialofa. "That qualifies you," he assured Bunce. "Come and play for us."

Bunce admits that he initially gave no serious thought to Fatialofa's offer, for several excellent reasons. For a start, he regarded himself as of Niuean heritage, not Western Samoan. Secondly, he wanted to play for the All Blacks, not Western Samoa. Thirdly, around the time Fatialofa first began tempting him he was having grave misgivings about his own worth as a footballer.

"Being so consistently rejected by the Auckland selectors," says Bunce, "eventually began to undermine my confidence. I began to question my own ability – not that I'd ever been an ambitious player. In fact, it was probably one of my most serious shortcomings that I never set targets or goals or set about making them happen.

"I remember reading how Grant Fox used to take himself down to his local sports field and practise drop-outs till he could land the ball on a sixpence and goalkicking till he never missed.

"I regret I never possessed dedication like Foxy to work on my skills. The opportunity was always there, I just never took it. Occasionally I'd do more running pre-season but I never went out of my way to work on specific skills which, I'm certain now, held me back.

"I guess you could blame it on basic laziness. The part of my game that cried out for attention was kicking. I never ever worked on it. To this day, I'm worthless as a kicker. If I have to make an instant clearance, I can get by, but if I try a long wipers kick, with time to concentrate on what I'm doing, it's awful!"

Bunce's limitations as a kicker are well recognised. These days when the halfbacks and five-eighths practise bombs, he's usually deployed to retrieve the balls.

The doubt that pervaded Bunce through 1989, when he was given just two outings for Auckland – one at second-five, the other on the wing – and into 1990 was traceable to the individual who, by now, had become an institution at centre in the Auckland team, Joe Stanley. This was the player Bunce had beaten to selection for the 1986 North Island team. This was the player Bunce had always engaged head on in club matches. "Whenever we clashed, I stood up to the test," says Bunce. "He was difficult to mark because he was so strong but he never exposed me. In fact, I was never badly beaten by any opponent.

"Although injuries had affected my two opportunities at national level, I believed I had always performed with distinction for Auckland. But while Joe had gone on to glory with the All Blacks, I had somehow lost my way. By 1989, I'd resigned myself to being an also-ran. I didn't know whether I was fit enough or fast enough or good enough. I presumed that because I wasn't wanted beyond club level, except as a spare part, I wasn't good enough."

Moving to another province was one obvious solution, but Bunce was loathe to quit his beloved Manukau club, which had supported him so wholeheartedly, and anyway he didn't possess enough confidence in his own ability to go hawking himself around.

He does concede that if he had known then what he was missing out on as an All Black, he would have striven more aggressively to promote himself. "I guess I didn't have a burning ambition to break into international rugby because I didn't think I was good enough. If it happened, it happened, that was my attitude."

Someone who did have confidence in Bunce's ability was Manukau's (and probably Auckland's) greatest fan Margaret Jamieson who was to achieve an almost legendary status by baking cakes every week and presenting them to the club and representative teams' players of the day. They were always Frank's teams.

She was outraged when Bunce missed selection for the 1990 All Black trials and wrote to New Zealand selector John Hart telling him so.

Hart took the trouble to reply, stating in his letter that "the unfortunate thing about selecting teams, whether it be a local representative team or a trial side, is that inevitably someone has to make a final decision.

"Unfortunately, that decision will never suit everybody and in this particular case we have obviously alienated you in terms of your rating of Frank Bunce. For that, I can only apologise.

"In terms of our approach to these trials and the particular need to look for our All Blacks of the future, Frank Bunce unfortunately was one of those who was omitted."

Margaret Jamieson and her husband Merv became Frank's greatest supporters. Initially dyed-in-the-wool Manukau enthusiasts, they followed him when he represented Auckland A and B, switching their allegiance across the bridge when Bunce's focus became the Helensville club and North Harbour.

Their faithful support of a player it took provincial and national selectors years and years to acknowledge is explained simply by them:

"Frank was always special, as a player and as a person. He became our hero."

Wherever Frank has played since 1982 (overseas tours excepted), the Jamiesons have been on the sideline cheering him on. And always Margaret has brought with her a cake – usually chocolate, although occasionally banana as a special concession to Frank – for presenting to the player of the day.

North Harbour coach Brad Meurant decided Margaret's cakes should be shared by all the team, not just the player of the day. So it has become a pattern now for her to present the cake to the team *before* they play. Er, make that two cakes. "Richard Turner told me one wasn't enough, so now it's two cakes every rep match!"

In April, 1990, Western Samoa, captained by Peter Fatialofa, qualified for the second World Cup, doing it in style by defeating Japan, Tonga and South Korea in Tokyo. Western Samoa was through at Tonga's expense, Japan being the other nation to advance. It was a momentous occasion for the Western Samoans who had worked so hard to achieve this status. Now they had to get the best possible team together to ensure they were competitive in the UK in October, 1991.

Fatialofa began pressurising Bunce again. "We were hanging out together and I kept asking him when he was coming across to join us. 'You want to be an international rugby player,' I'd say, 'then come and play for us. Niue hasn't got a team and New Zealand doesn't want you.'"

It wasn't the appropriate time for Bunce to be focusing on World Cup involvement because with Bernie McCahill injured, he got to play in all five of Auckland's South Pacific matches, at second-five.

The first of these, against Queensland at Ballymore, was Bunce's blazer game. His fourteen outings had taken him almost four years. He richly enjoyed being part of the best provincial team in the world, one which took out the Southpac title once again with awesome ease, but if he thought he'd finally secured a permanent place in Maurice Trapp's team, he was mistaken. Once McCahill was restored to full fitness, he claimed back the No 12 jersey. Craig Innes was secure at centre, leaving the hapless Bunce to resume his seat on the reserves bench. He would get only two further outings that season, an NPC game at New Plymouth and a Ranfurly Shield defence in Gisborne.

He was quoted as saying at the time, "I've never liked warming benches. I've found also that I don't like going on as a replacement. You go in cold and it takes a while to warm up. I dread it."

By year's end, Bunce, approaching 29, was beginning to think that maybe Fatialofa and Western Samoa did have something to offer.

Bunce had never been into long-term planning or goalsetting, but as 1991 dawned, he decided it was time to start thinking seriously about his career and to establish some priorities.

His first priority, still, was to play for the All Blacks. That option was appearing less and less likely, especially as he'd missed out on the World Cup summer training squad, but he knew he would never abandon hope.

Then there was the World Cup tournament. Here he was in the fortunate position of being eligible for two countries, New Zealand and Western Samoa. He was reluctant to declare allegiance to Western Samoa for two genuine reasons – he considered himself Niuean and, having not contributed to the island nation's qualifying campaign, he believed he would be accused of "jumping on board for a free trip."

Bunce projected himself through to the next World Cup – the most extensive piece of long range planning he'd ever indulged in – and realised he would be 33 by then and almost certainly out of the reckoning for any country. It was now or never.

Peter Fatialofa was reversing his truck into a property in the Auckland suburb of Epsom, preparing to deliver a piano. It was a Friday in March. His mobile phone rang.

"Yeah, Fats here."

"It's Frank Bunce. I've made a decision, Peter. I want to play for you guys."

"Hey, that's great news. You've made me very happy."

"I'm doing it because I want to go to the World Cup and I'm obviously on the outer with the All Blacks."

"Well, there are trials in Apia next month, then a four match tour of New Zealand – I presume you're available," said Fatialofa.

"Yeah, although I'd prefer you didn't make my decision public until the time of the trials."

Fatialofa was so excited by the news that he didn't deliver the piano until he had placed a call on his mobile phone to Peter Schuster, Western Samoa's coach, in Apia.

"Peter was over the moon with the news, like me. Frank was the trump card Western Samoa needed."

Fatialofa contends he initially nagged Bunce to play for Western Samoa because "he was the sort of quality player we needed in midfield. It was really just a joke for a start, wishful thinking. I didn't think Frank had any Western Samoan blood in him, but when he told me about his grandfather, I thought I better check out his heritage.

"Even when I confirmed that he was one-sixteenth Samoan, Frank didn't think that was enough.

"'Sure it's enough,' I told him. 'You're going to the World Cup, man. You've got quality. If you do your job, why feel guilty?'

"He did more than just go to the World Cup. He returned a hero."

Unlike the Auckland and New Zealand selectors, Fatialofa didn't have any doubts about Bunce's ability.

"When Ponsonby used to play Manukau, I always told my guys, 'Keep an eye on that guy in the number thirteen jersey – he's dangerous.'

We'd come through together with the second fifteen and Auckland, and I knew what he was capable of. It amazed me that Auckland always preferred Joe (Stanley), Craig (Innes) and Bernie (McCahill) ahead of him.

"Frank could swing a game with his powerful running and unsettle an opponent with his dynamic tackling. I knew he was a player who would go right to the top. We were just fortunate that league didn't get hold of him before we did."

Bunce's arrival in Apia for the trials wasn't the first time he'd been to the Pacific Islands in the cause of rugby. About four years earlier he had undertaken a tour of Tonga and Western Samoa with a Pacific Islands team coached by Bryan Williams.

It was an incident-packed visit to Tonga for Bunce. He twice finished up at Nuku'alofa Hospital as a patient. The first time was for an insect bite that caused his ankle to swell alarmingly, the second after his jaw had come heavily into contact with a Tongan player's head. He survived both experiences without serious consequences.

He remembers the game against the Tongan national team being delayed for almost an hour and a half until the King arrived.

The New Zealand players were billeted in villages for the lesser games, Frank and a colleague getting to stay with the head of one particular village. "One morning," recalls Bunce, "I woke to this violent squealing. A large Tongan fellow was strangling a pig. We had it for lunch!"

It was so hot that all the players wanted to do was lie inside on a mat under the fans. One day his host approached a group of children who were heading for a swimming pool. To Bunce's intrigue, they were ordered to go to the rugby field and clear the stones away so the game could take place later that afternoon. "They protested," says Bunce, "because they wanted to go swimming. But they did what they were told."

As he prepared for his trial game in Apia, Frank was warned by Fatialofa to watch out for the player who was marking him, Fereti Tuilagi. From an outlying island, he had a reputation as a deadly tackler.

Bunce was to be grateful for the tip-off. Tuilagi, just 18, was more than deadly – he was demoniac. "He'd obviously decided this was an all-or-nothing opportunity for him," said Bunce, "and that every hit was going to count.

"Because he came in so aggressively, I found him easy to step around, but he flattened our second-five, Keneti Sio, with one incredible spot tackle that sent the ball flying and left Keneti seeing stars. He kept me on my toes, but I was able to get outside him quite easily and set up some good attacks."

Bunce, as one of the trial's star performers, was named in the party to tour New Zealand and found himself looking forward to the involvement with his newly-adopted team. "I had the feeling I might be treated as an outsider," he said, "but right from the start I was made to feel comfortable. Knowing Peter (Fatialofa) and Beegee (Williams) was a big plus, but I found all the guys so relaxed and friendly. I was immediately at ease."

Bunce was to encounter the New Zealand equivalent of Tuilaga in the first tour game, Waikato's Rhys Ellison. However, Ellison's determination to make an impact with his tackling almost had tragic consequences.

It was Bunce that Ellison directed his firepower at on one occasion. "I remembered him from the Palmerston North trial in 1988," said Bunce. "He winded me on that occasion. He has this unusual style of tackling, leading with his head, which I've always thought was dangerous. I think he was taught that method by his cousin Ricki who made his mark playing American Football with the San Francisco Forty-niners.

"Anyway, just as I received the ball from a skip pass he came flying in, head first, and hit me on the hip bone. Because I saw him at the last moment I changed my angle and that obviously cost him.

"Fortunately, my stomach, which was feeling bruised, took most of the impact. If he'd slammed directly into the bone, it could have been a horrendous accident."

An ambulance was driven on to the field and a neck brace applied before Ellison was taken away to hospital. The game was held up for about fifteen minutes. Bunce, terrified that Ellison might have suffered serious spinal damage, approached him and asked, "Are you all right?"

"He raised his eyebrows. I felt he was telling me with his eyes that he felt he would be okay. Thank goodness he made a full recovery."

Ellison's injury put something of a damper on Western Samoa's historic win against a powerful Waikato side which had finished runner-up to Auckland in the NPC the previous season.

Among the stars for Western Samoa were the two Vs – Sila Vaifale, a hard-tackling, hard-running flanker, and To'o Vaega, an incisive centre. Vaifale intrigued Bunce. "He did everything a top footballer shouldn't do, he ate big, smoked, drank, had late nights. Yet he had no fat on him and he was a swashbuckling flanker."

In Hamilton that night Bunce sampled Samoan culture, and loved it. It was, he soon appreciated, quite different from New Zealand teams' court sessions that followed big games.

With the Samoans, first there were prayers, then food and then music and dancing. Samoans, Bunce had already come to appreciate, are naturally musical. They can all sing and harmonise and many of them can play a musical instrument.

When each village's name was called out, its representatives were required to stand and deliver an item. Bunce, being a Kiwi, hoped he would be exempt, but when the call "Niue" went up, he stepped forward, to enthusiastic applause, and performed an island dance. "Fortunately, I wasn't being scored out of ten. It was all in great fun, with a lot of giggling and clapping. It was the Samoan way."

Most visits to New Zealand by World Cup rugby nations are arranged, and paid for, by the NZRFU, but Western Samoa wasn't on the invite list in 1991. It invited itself, organising a challenging itinerary to prepare itself for the World Cup. This meant that while Romania, the USSR and Australia were flown between many of their venues, the Western Samoans travelled throughout by bus.

Asked if his players minded travelling everywhere by bus, Fatialofa assured the interviewer that, "It sure beats walking!"

Notwithstanding the budget restrictions, Western Samoa achieved what it set out to. It defeated Waikato, Taranaki and King Country, suffered a one-point loss to Bay of Plenty and was outclassed just the once, by mighty Auckland. "Auckland virtually represents the All Blacks," said Fatialofa. "They exposed our frailties which is what we needed to know six months out from the World Cup."

Before coach Schuster returned to Apia, he called Bunce aside and said he wanted him to be playing top-level rugby through until the team's departure for the UK in October.

The time had come for Bunce to seek a new union. Although reluctant to abandon his beloved Manukau, he obviously wasn't going to get the concentrated representative play he needed with Auckland, not with McCahill and Innes frontline selections for the World Cup. He'd be lucky to get two outings by October.

Counties was closest for Bunce, who was living in south Auckland, but two factors counted against it – it already possessed, in Craig Adams, an accomplished centre and, under Andy Dalton, the team was obviously struggling to survive in first division.

North Harbour would involve a good deal more travel but as a team it was prospering under Peter Thorburn's guidance and it seemed there could be an opening in the threequarters for a player of Bunce's talent.

Bunce decided to give Thorburn a ring and see if he was interested. Thorburn, the perfect diplomat, said if Bunce joined a club across the bridge he would look at him, and if he was good enough, he'd be in. "I was honest with him," said Thorburn. "I told him I had an established midfield with Cliff Mytton and Scott Pierce, backed up by Iain Wood, but that I could possibly use him on the wing."

That was good enough for Bunce. All he needed to do now was select a club. Because his great mate Eric Rush had joined Takapuna, for much the same reasons – he couldn't get games with Auckland – he thought he'd start there first.

"I knew they'd given Rushy a car, so I said they could have me for the same offer. But they didn't take the bait. They said the Rushy deal was a one-off, but they were prepared to help with petrol. I told them I'd think about it."

The next day Bunce received a call from an old mate who was playing for the Helensville club, Fritz Solomona. "Why don't you come and check us out," he said.

Initially reticent, because of the distance – it was a 45 minute drive from Papatoetoe where he was living – Bunce finally yielded. "I always used to think it was unreasonable that name players moving to Auckland always seemed to join Ponsonby. Why couldn't they help out a struggling club, I used to think.

"Now here I was in an identical situation. Why shouldn't I help an emerging club? So I drove up to Helensville, and I was won over immediately. For twenty-one years I'd belonged to the same club, Manukau. Here was a club that reminded me very much of Manukau."

Bunce couldn't believe what happened after his first training. While the players were showering and changing, the wives, girlfriends and mums set to, to prepare a sumptuous meal. Taking advantage of the sponsorship from Coastal Seafood, they served up fish, mince pies, potatoes and vegetables.

Bunce wondered if this lavish spread was to mark his arrival, but was assured that this was the usual Thursday night fare at Helensville. Many of the players had to travel considerable distances to training, so the committee felt it was in the interests of the players and their partners if they fed them well before sending them home.

Although Bunce's move to North Harbour received ample publicity, no one associated with the Auckland union or representative team made any effort to retain his services. "Graham Henry telephoned me at the beginning of the next season, after he'd taken over Auckland, inviting me to come back," said Bunce, "but it was too late by then."

Bunce's debut with Helensville was memorable, on two counts. Underestimating the drive time from Papatoetoe, he arrived late, to find his team already on the field. It meant he missed the first few minutes, and everyone missed the last few minutes when the referee abandoned the game (against Glenfield, Walter Little's team) because of a brawl among the forwards.

After only two outings for his new club he received a phone call from Thorburn, inviting him to attend North Harbour training at St Josephs School. "Is that the school you can see from the motorway?" asked Bunce. Thorburn assured him it was. The bad news for Bunce was that more than one school was visible from the northern motorway, and he chose the wrong one. After sitting patiently in his car at Takapuna Normal Intermediate School for some time and aware of a total lack of people and activity, he realised his mistake. The North Harbour training session was well under way by the time he, sheepishly, put in an appearance.

"I have a reputation for tardiness, one unfortunately well earned," admits Bunce. "But here I was arriving late through a pure misunderstanding. Peter Thorburn was very good about it."

Bunce was selected to make his North Harbour debut in the national championship game against Bay of Plenty at Rotorua, on the wing, Pierce being retained at centre.

Thanks to North Harbour's captain Buck Shelford, Thorburn's team sneaked out with a two-point victory after trailing 17-3 at halftime. From the wing, Bunce was witness to what he terms the "remarkable influence" wielded by Shelford. "He just took control of the game," said Bunce. "He instructed everyone at halftime what was going to happen, and he made it happen. Because of Buck, I never thought we would lose that game."

It was in a non-championship game against Wanganui five weeks later that Bunce first wore the No 13 jersey for North Harbour. It brought out the best in him.

Of his performance in Harbour's 82-7 victory the *New Zealand Herald's* Don Cameron wrote that, "Perhaps (New Zealand selector) Lane Penn did not have Frank Bunce's name even pencilled in lightly before the game, but Bunce could be judged, in his best position of centre, as the complete star of the show, the one essential international player in the game. Bunce was outstanding simply because he had the genius for making space for his support players."

Bunce honoured Western Samoan coach Schuster's request. By the time he reported for World Cup duty, he had made eight appearances for North Harbour, seven of them in national championship contests against strong opposition. That was one more NPC appearance than he'd managed in five years with Auckland!

He couldn't believe the difference in attitudes between Auckland and North Harbour, even though Eric Rush had tried to explain it to him.

"Life with North Harbour was just so much more relaxed," he says. "Peter Thorburn – and later Brad Meurant – had a way of making everyone feel comfortable.

"Peter, and later Brad, were far more relaxed as coaches than Maurice Trapp and Bryan Williams and, before them, John Hart. They took their match planning seriously and made us study the opposition closely. But they never took away our licence to think and be innovative.

"When you attend Auckland and All Black team meetings, as players you are expected to wear number ones, although they sometimes now allow tracksuits. But you sit there in a tense atmosphere and concentrate. No one talks at the meeting or during the bus trip to the ground.

"With North Harbour, though, no one minds if you talk or laugh. The coach will occasionally tell the players to settle down, but you're free to chat away in the meeting and on the journey to the ground."

Bunce can recall one session with Meurant at which Glen Osborne was reading the morning paper while he (Bunce), wearing dark glasses to camouflage a hungover state, fell asleep.

Bunce also remembers one damp training session with Harbour when Scott Pierce turned up wearing sand shoes. He kept slipping and sliding and eventually pulled out because he couldn't get any grip. "I remember thinking, they would never have stood for that at Auckland. The cheek of the man!

"I suppose it's because of Auckland's great winning record that everything is taken so seriously. North Harbour doesn't have that constraint. It certainly makes for greater enjoyment."

To cap off its World Cup preparations, Western Samoa made a brief visit to Australia in late July for matches against the Barbarians at Manly in Sydney and ACT in Canberra. By this stage, the Samoans had also recruited first-five Stephen Bachop, a veteran of 90 games for Canterbury, and flanker Apollo Perelini, whose lethal tackling had won him the nickname of The Terminator.

The Samoans checked into a backpackers hotel in Manly. The rooms were in serious need of repair, music from the downstairs disco boomed out until late in the evening and the players had to organise their own breakfasts.

"What the hell's this place?" Bunce said to Fatialofa. "I thought we were supposed to be an international team."

"We are," replied Fatialofa, "but we're broke!"

While thrilled to be heading to the World Cup, Bunce quickly appreciated that he was involved with one of the 'poor cousins' of the rugby world.

"The Samoans were so happy go lucky," said Bunce, "that they willingly accepted whatever they were offered. I couldn't imagine Auckland or the All Blacks accepting accommodation like that."

It mattered not. The Samoans still overwhelmed an international strength Barbarians side, winning impressive reviews from the Sydney media who suddenly alerted their readers to the danger Fatialofa's men presented at the World Cup, in the Wallabies' pool.

A female physiotherapist was made available to the Samoans to help them before the game with their strapping. She confessed her initial reaction was that they would be "a typical bunch of islanders – they'll all be out of shape and will get beaten." By the time she'd wrapped several metres of strapping on to many of their bodies, she admitted she'd dramatically changed her attitude. "You guys have incredible physiques," she told them. "There's not an ounce of fat on any of you." By the time Fatialofa's men ran on to Manly Oval, she was convinced they would win.

The tourists lost their second match, in Canberra, but the trip served the purpose of bringing together the squad members, about two-thirds of whom played their rugby in New Zealand, as a team.

Bunce, who initially had some reservations about the team's capacity to be competitive at the World Cup, now believed Western Samoa would emerge as a formidable opponent indeed.

"The more we trained and played together, the better we were becoming. I was amazed at the athleticism of many of the players. They were strong, physical and skilful. Probably the only thing the island boys lacked was discipline and that's something the New Zealand players brought with them. We were a good mix, therefore."

Money was no problem for the All Blacks in 1991, or the Wallabies, or probably any of the Five Nations teams, or France. But it was a huge problem for the Western Samoan Rugby Union which had mortgaged itself to its eyeballs to qualify the team for the World Cup. As the tournament approached, Western Samoa's debt had risen to almost $NZ450,000.

Fatialofa says he will be forever grateful for the efforts made by the union, backed by the government, to win recognition for Western Samoan rugby after the nation had been ignored at the first World Cup in 1987.

"We didn't get to qualify for the second tournament by chance," says Fatialofa. "It was because of a four year plan effected by the union. They sent us on a tour of Europe, we twice played in New Zealand and there were matches arranged in Apia against the major nations."

Qualifying for the World Cup was one thing. Outfitting the players and ensuring they had adequate expenses was something else, a problem not easily overcome with the bank balance seriously in the red.

It was Alan Grey, mine host of Apia's most famous hotel Aggie Grey's, who came up with a brilliant fundraising concept. The players would push a wheelbarrow around Upolu, the main island of Western Samoa, inviting donations.

Knowing the Samoans' passion for rugby, and their excitement at having their team represented at the World Cup, he was positive such a venture would yield a considerable amount of money.

He was right. The wheelbarrow run around the island, which took about two and a half days – and involved four wheelbarrows, one wasn't enough – netted an amazing amount of money, almost $NZ150,000.

The entire World Cup squad was involved, the players…well, most of them, anyway…taking turns at pushing the wheelbarrows. They'd recover between bursts by riding on the truck that accompanied them.

One player who remained on the truck was winger Brian Lima who was nursing a leg injury. And close by him, as Lima's self-appointed minder, was Bunce. "He's pretty crafty, that Bunce fella," said Fatialofa. "Every time I said, 'Your turn to run, Frank,' he'd say, 'No, I've got to look after Brian!' He stayed on the truck, occasionally throwing coconuts to the young boys."

The wheelbarrow income ensured the players were adequately outfitted, although compared with what the All Blacks were issued with, they received only the bare essentials. They were given one pair of boots, one pair of black shoes, grey slacks, white shirt, jersey, track suit and training gear. There was very little in the way of casual gear, Bunce recalls.

Western Samoa's finances very definitely didn't allow for an upgrade on the flight through to London. When the Air New Zealand 747 roared out of Auckland, the All Blacks were in business class, the Western Samoans (and the Fijians) some fifty rows further back in economy.

"It mattered not," says Fatialofa. "Who were we to expect business class travel? We were more than content just to be going to the World Cup."

During the arduous journey through to London, the Western Samoan boys were visited 'down the back' by two of their own, Michael Jones and Inga Tuigamala, a gesture greatly appreciated by Fatialofa and his fellow players.

Bunce didn't doubt, having come this far, that he could produce what was required of him on the rugby field. What he was having trouble with, however, was the team's chant, Manu.

The chant runs to almost 200 words and is accompanied by actions not dissimilar to those involved in performing a Maori haka. Fatialofa says he knows players who have represented Western Samoa for five years and who still can't manage the Manu properly. To ensure his newest recruits didn't shirk on their lessons, he would always summon them, Frank included, to the front during practice sessions.

"Because I was familiar with the haka, I picked up the actions easily enough," says Bunce, "but I struggled with the words."

There followed an amusing sequel when the Samoans were performing their chant in front of the Wallabies in the rain at Pontypool. There on the field, directly opposite Bunce, was the giant lock Rod McCall whom Bunce had befriended at a sevens tournament in Dubai. He glared at Bunce for a while, then took a step forward and shouted at him, "Bunce, you don't know the bloody words!"

The normally easy-going Samoans, having settled comfortably into their Cardiff accommodation, experienced a crisis a couple of days out from their tournament opener against Wales.

The central character was the captain Peter Fatialofa. Normally so jovial, he had become uptight and was snapping at players, criticising anyone who was late and threatening to banish players to the reserves if they didn't improve their attitude. The team had been too long in Cardiff without playing and Fats was obviously feeling the pressure.

Fatialofa picks up the story himself. "There was so much riding on that first game. The Western Samoan Rugby Union had almost bankrupted itself to get us there and it was terribly important we gave it our best shot. In the days leading up to that opening game I felt some of the players, including Frank (Bunce), Stephen Bachop and Pat Lam, were too relaxed. My attitude was that we trained hard and we played hard. We weren't there for a holiday. I warned the guys that if they didn't buck their ideas up they risked being dropped to the reserves."

To get things sorted out, Fatialofa ordered a meeting of all the players, and asked some of the senior members to organise it. He was horrified when he found the venue they'd chosen was the nearest pub. Fats blew a fuse. "Is this your attitude?" he barked. "We're getting ready to play Wales and you want to meet in a pub, along with all the locals. Let's get out of here."

Where they subsequently gathered, a delightfully tranquil, picturesque setting, if an improbable location for a World Cup team meeting, was on the lawn inside Cardiff Castle. Surely no Welshman passing by would have suspected this group of Polynesians, in heated discussion in the shadow of the famous castle, was about to bring his proud rugby nation to its knees.

Bunce says the meeting achieved its aim. "Fats was feeling the pressure, basically, I believe, because he was carrying too much on his own shoulders. He wouldn't delegate. And he didn't believe we were taking the Welsh match seriously enough. Well, we sure were. There was a long time from arrival in Cardiff to the opening match and it was important to relax to get through that challenging period. Fats interpreted it wrongly."

Fatialofa told the gathering that if he was getting on their nerves, they should take it out on the Welsh. The players assured him he was getting on their nerves and that they would take it out on the Welsh. In that they were in unanimity.

Bunce was named at second-five for the tournament opener. The player whose jersey he claimed was Keneti Sio. Before the match Sio went to Bunce and expressed his disappointment at missing selection. Then, with tears in his eyes, he said, "If your heart is not fully there, take my heart."

Bunce's heart was there all right. At the age of 29 the boy from Manukau was about to make his international debut. Against Wales, on Cardiff Arms Park, the ground he considered the most famous in the whole world. Oh yes, he was ready.

The All Blacks have a set routine before matches. The manager usually speaks first at the final meeting, the captain might contribute but, mostly, the talking is done by the coach. That's it. The players remain silent.

How different is the Western Samoan preparation. Not only did manager Tate Simi, coach Peter Schuster and technical adviser Bryan Williams all have their say, but, according to Bunce, "just about every player had his two bob's worth as well.

"We talked of what we could expect from the Welsh. We were unsure of their lineout but we knew they had a recent history of losing, so we felt it was important to get points on them early. We had so much to play for, nothing to lose. Because we were a tiny, unseeded country, we weren't expected to defeat one of the game's traditionally great nations, but I sensed a strength amongst us. Although I was as nervous as hell, deep down I felt we could win this one."

As an aside, the bus ride from the Crest Hotel, on the perimeter of the rugby stadium, into the ground has to be the briefest at any test venue in the world. The playing field is about 400 metres from the hotel lobby! There is a shorter journey – from the Poenamo Hotel to Onewa Stadium, North Harbour's home ground, at Takapuna. It's about 250 metres and some teams, notably Otago, have insisted on journeying by coach.

Bunce was so nervous he ran on to Cardiff Arms Park with his boots unlaced, becoming aware of the flapping laces as he stepped on to the immaculately groomed turf. "Normally, the laces are the last things I attend to before leaving the dressing room. It shows how uptight I was!"

In his anxiety to remedy the problem, he pulled the laces too tight, and cut the blood supply to his feet. During the first injury break he was down on his knees again loosening them.

Bunce's first touch of the ball in an international provided an unmemorable moment. The backline had called a move involving a miss pass. It was developing promisingly until Bunce threw his pass…behind centre To'o Vaega and fullback Andy Aiolupo. "It was the first time we'd tried to move the ball wide, and we lost ground, because of me."

Apollo Perelini was living up to his title of the Terminator. Bunce recalls one sensational hit on the Welsh fullback Tony Clement which left him lying lifeless on the ground. He was to be one of three Welsh players who retired injured.

"Some of the tackling was phenomenal," recalls Bunce. "Obviously the Welsh weren't used to it and it unsettled them. You could sense they were passing earlier than they should, not drawing their man before releasing the ball. Sila Vaifale and Apollo were the big hitters."

Within 20 minutes Bunce felt his team could win. "Knowing you can win and winning are two different things, but our skill factor and our tackling were superior to the Welsh. We weren't entirely sure what they were capable of, but I felt we only needed to take our chances and we were home."

Tries by Vaega and Vaifale gave the Samoans a decisive advantage and although the Welsh, urged on by 50,000 supporters, came back strongly at the finish, Fatialofa's team held on at 16-13 for an historic victory. It was Western Samoa's first victory over an IRB nation and was hailed by coach Schuster as the greatest moment in his country's rugby history.

On the other side of the world, more than 15,000 people had watched the game live on giant screens at Apia Park. Television hadn't arrived in Western Samoa at the time but a special arrangement among TVNZ, Telecom New Zealand and Samoa's Department of Broadcasting made possible the screenings. The public paid $NZ4 per head to attend, this charge helping off-set the cost of setting up the dish/receiver for the transmission.

The nation was in ecstasy at the outcome. And so were the Western Samoan players. The scenes in the dressing room were, in Fatialofa's words, unbelievable. The players were in raptures. There was much hugging, laughing and singing. And more than a few tears.

Bunce thanked the Western Samoan players and management for inviting him to join them, for creating the opportunity to share "this glorious moment."

Although the celebrations carried on long into the night, the players were mindful that in three days there was another test match, against the tournament favourite Australia. And there was training the next day!

The victory over Wales brought its rewards. Steinlager rushed in cartons of its fine product, plus sweaters and t-shirts, while the team's boot supplier Mizuno displayed a far greater interest in the team's welfare than it had before.

Overnight the Western Samoans had become the darlings of the tournament. Television interviewers hadn't troubled the team from 'down under' much in preliminary stages, but suddenly they were a hot number. Television channels were scrambling for interviews, in their eagerness to project the personalities who had brought about the World Cup's massive upset.

Fatialofa, back to his normal self, enjoyed being in the limelight. "It was all a new experience for us – we soaked it up. Western Samoa didn't make much of a splash on the world scene, so here was an opportunity to project ourselves. Our nation has never had so much publicity. They were even publishing maps of the South Pacific in the newspapers to enlighten readers of just where we came from."

The Western Samoans were closer to causing another major upset, against the Wallabies at Pontypool, than the final scoreline of 3-9 might suggest. The game was played in atrocious conditions. It rained incessantly, the gloom was such that the floodlights were on from the start, and it was cold.

In the finish, three penalty goals by Michael Lynagh outdid one penalty goal by Matthew Vaea, but when it was 6-3 and into the final quarter, the Samoans wasted a golden tryscoring opportunity. Winger Brian Lima had stretched the Australians with a powerful run. The Samoans had numbers but one player went it alone and the chance was lost.

"It was a foul afternoon," says Bunce. "Conditions were such that one try was going to win the game. We created the chance and blew it." The pedantic refereeing of Englishman Ed Morrison didn't assist Western Samoa's cause. Still, this was a game Western Samoa had expected to lose, having targeted Wales and Argentina. So things were going to plan.

The Samoans were hugely relieved when the sun shone for their final qualifying encounter, against the Pumas at Pontypridd. Notwithstanding the triumph against Wales, it was a game they had to win to advance to the semi-finals.

Fullback Andy Aiolupo sparked the victory at Pontypridd and he did it with his halftime comments. During the opening 40 minutes, the Western Samoan inside backs had seriously overdone the tactical kicking.

Aiolupo was fuming when he joined the troops at the break. "I'm sick of chasing the ball, sick of chasing high kicks," he exploded. "We're getting good ball and we're kicking it all away."

He glared at his captain, Fatialofa. "How about instructing the inside backs to let us start running with the ball. We can eat these guys."

Fatialofa remembers the occasion well. "I think the importance of the occasion had got to some of our players. Our first half performance was pathetic. We'd wasted good possession and made a lot of errors. We were lucky to be ahead. Andy going off his rocket like that shocked the backs into action. They were a different team from the re-start."

The Pumas didn't see which way the Samoans went in the second half, Fatialofa's boys scoring a series of dazzling tries – the first of which went to Bunce – to extend the advantage from 13-12 to 35-12. All six tries were scored by the backs.

At their first attempt, the Western Samoans had qualified for the World Cup quarter-finals. They were as much relieved at this achievement as they were at knowing there was a week's break before the next encounter, against Scotland at Murrayfield. Three tests in eight days had taken their toll – the players were bruised and mentally drained. But they were ecstatic at making it to the final eight, which automatically qualified them for the next World Cup. Wales and Argentina weren't so lucky – they would have to do it the hard way to get to South Africa in 1991.

If the Samoans thought Wales was cold, they were dismayed to arrive in Edinburgh and find the temperature only a couple of degrees above freezing point.

"It was," says Bunce, "not the sort of climate appreciated by south sea islanders. We felt as though we were a million miles away from home. It was desperately cold all week."

The Scottish hospitality compensated to a degree, although wherever they went, the Manu Samoa boys were invariably assured that Scotland the Brave would prevail in the quarter-finals.

Fatialofa tried to warn his players of the threat presented by Scotland's most experienced campaigners, Gavin Hastings, John Jeffrey and Finlay Calder. "It takes a crafty old dog to recognise another crafty old dog," said Fatialofa, "and I told our guys not to underestimate Scotland's oldies. As it turned out, they kicked our arse!"

Gavin Hastings wielded a massive influence on the game. The Scots used their 95kg fullback effectively as an extra loose forward in the opening exchanges. He several times linked with Calder, Jeffrey and Derek White, the Scottish loosies, to challenge the Western Samoans head on.

Scotland's audacious tactics seized the initiative so comprehensively, the Samoans, with first use of a strong breeze, never recovered. They were ten points adrift at halftime and although a Stephen Bachop dropped goal brought them brief encouragement, the outcome was inevitable.

Bunce had Hastings lined up at one stage for a telling front-on tackle. "But he sidestepped and I finished up tackling air!"

It was an outrage that Western Samoa failed to score a try. On many occasions Bunce, Vaega and Timo Tagaloa managed to go beyond the second and sometimes third tackle but without ever breaching the Scottish tryline.

The Murrayfield crowd thoroughly appreciated their attacking approach and gave them a standing ovation when they did a lap of honour – a "non victory lap," as Fatialofa put it – to wind up their contribution to the second World Cup.

When you're out of the World Cup, you're out. This was the sobering reality for the Western Samoans when they woke the next morning. They had only a few hours to pack and get down to London and Gatwick Airport for the long flight home.

"At least," said Bunce, "we had the plane to ourselves going home."

If there was an air of disappointment amongst the Samoans as they winged their way out of the UK, it instantly dissolved when they arrived back in Auckland.

"We expected only our families would be at the airport to welcome us," said Bunce, "but there was a welcoming throng of hundreds. The reception was overwhelming and we were instantly made to appreciate what we had achieved. We'd gone further than anyone had expected."

There was better to follow, for two days later the team flew to Apia for the celebration of all celebrations. Such was the impact that Peter Schuster's players had made that on the day they arrived in Apia a national holiday had been declared!

Although it was after midnight when their plane landed, the players entered the airport to a heroes' reception, the terminal building overflowing with excited locals.

After a brief religious service at the airport, the players journeyed

Walter had his mother and father with him, and loads of other wellwishers, too, when NZRFU chairman Russ Thomas named him among the All Blacks to tour Wales and Ireland in 1989. New Zealand Herald

Bunce was never fitter than when he worked on the rubbish cart in south Auckland. This photo from 1990, before he broke into the international scene. News Media Auckland

Little in action during his spectacular comeback performance against Scotland in the third place play-off at Cardiff during the 1991 World Cup. In pursuit are Scottish forwards Derek White and Finlay Calder.   Photosport

Little accelerates into a gap in the first test against the Wallabies at Lancaster Park in 1990. Supporting him are Kieran Crowley and Terry Wright with Michael Lynagh the lone defender.

Rugby News

The New Zealand team to the Sevens World Cup in 1993, the only year Bunce represented his country at the abbreviated version of rugby. Back row: Rob Cashmore (physiotherapist), Junior Paramore, Pat Lam. Middle row: Merlin Shannon (manager), John Timu, Frank Bunce, Marc Ellis, Peter Thorburn (coach). Front row: Glen Osborne, Dallas Seymour, Eric Rush (captain), Peter Woods, Stu Forster.

Cantouris Studio

The mighty Dustys Touch team which won the North Island title seven years in a row. Back row: Nick Williams, Malcolm Beazley. Middle row: Richard Barnett, Eric Rush, Frank Bunce, Henry Amosa, Brian Harris (manager). Front row: Mackie Herewini, Vinnie Clarke, Peter Walters (captain), Arthur Clark, Willie Kemp.

Photo Life Studios

Bunce committing French defenders in numbers during the 1994 series in New Zealand. Above: Philippe Sella (13) and Christophe Deylaud (10) await developments as flanker Philippe Benetton effects a copybook tackle at Lancaster Park. Below: Centre Thierry Lacroix (12) and Sella are unbalanced as Bunce powers towards them at Eden Park.   Andrew Cornaga/Troy Restieaux, Photosport

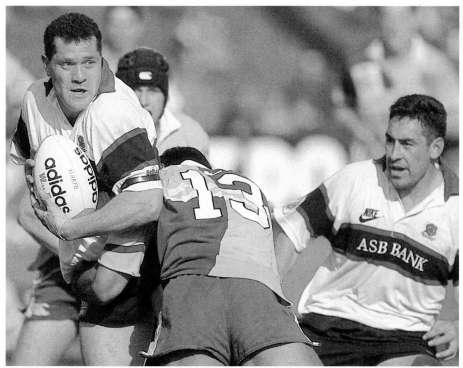

Little and Bunce involved in **NPC** action against Southland at Takapuna in 1995. Rugby News

Frank Bunce and Shem Tatupu swap jerseys following the New Zealand-Western Samoa test at Eden Park in 1993. Bunce had broken into test rugby with Western Samoa two years earlier.

News Media Auckland

Happiness is a new baby. Walter and Tracy are all smiles following the birth of their son Daniel in 1994. New Zealand Herald

Classic Frank Bunce action, for North Harbour against Auckland at Eden Park in 1992. Photosport

by bus through to the city. It was a typical Apia bus with no windows (and if you've ever experienced tropical heat, you'd understand why), which was entirely appropriate because the road into Apia was lined with thousands of cheering fans.

"It was," says Bunce, "one of the most incredible experiences of my life. We took hours to reach Apia because we kept stopping for people to present us with food and flowers and drinks."

When the men of Manu Samoa finally arrived at Aggie Grey's Hotel, there was only time for a freshen up and a quick breakfast before they were on the move again, this time a parade on foot through the capital and on to Apia Park where they were officially welcomed home by the Head of State, cheered on by 15,000 people.

The celebrations went on for days. Bunce's only concern was that he kept running out of clean shirts. But no one seemed to mind. Nor did anyone seem to notice, or care, that the World Cup tournament was still running in the UK. For the happy residents of Apia, all that mattered was that they had *their* heroes among them.

Tate Simi, who has continued to manage the Western Samoan team, says that the promotion of the country as a tourist destination is the most tangible benefit from the World Cup successes. Tourism has improved markedly since 1991 and the level of overseas investment has also increased.

The union secured a couple of major sponsorships following the World Cup and a grant of approximately $NZ100,000 from Rugby World Cup profits helped reduce the overdraft.

"Otherwise," said Simi, "the generosity of the local community through donations has been the main source of revenue."

(5)

Los Mongreles

Rugby, with its conservative traditions, has always shied away from exotic names for its teams, preferring to leave such flamboyancy to those who, prior to 1995, were regarded as belonging to the "professional code" i.e. league.

Not for rugby such sobriquets as the Tigers, the Bulldogs or the Sharks. The occasional Rovers or United represented the only variation to the fundamental labelling of teams.

Rugby approved of mascots and emblems, of course. You had Ferdinand of Taranaki, Mooloo of Waikato, the Waratah of New South Wales, the Red Dragons of Wales, the Irish leek, the English rose, the Argentinian Pumas and so on.

But as for bastardising team names...never! Well, not until Rupert Murdoch began shovelling his millions towards the southern hemisphere nations in 1995, helping accelerate rugby's high dive into professionalism. Getting into the swing of things, the NZRFU approved special brandings for its five regionally selected teams involved in the new Super 12 competition and thus were born the Highlanders, the Crusaders, the Hurricanes, the Chiefs and the Blues.

Where rugby, pre Murdoch, did manage to shrug itself free of conservatism at times was in sevens tournaments, particularly those staged off season in some of the world's more fascinating rugby outposts such as Portugal, Singapore, Dubai and Uruguay.

The Warblers, Bahrain based but usually an exotic mix of players from throughout the world, were prominent at these events, along with other privately organised teams such as the Penguins, the Wolfhounds and the Public School Wanderers. UK players benefited from a rich tradition in sevens and the Middlesex sevens annually drew a near capacity audience (of more than 60,000) to Twickenham, a statistic which was positively mind-boggling to Kiwis.

New Zealand took a long time to get involved in the international sevens circuit, largely because the abbreviated version of the national game was never taken particularly seriously. So cluttered was the New Zealand rugby calendar that the NZRFU could never work out where to fit sevens tournaments in.

In the early days of the world's most prestigious sevens event, at Hong Kong, New Zealand was represented by its premier sevens province which for a number of years alternated between Marlborough and Manawatu.

It wasn't that Marlborough and Manawatu, which now languish a considerable distance behind the country's strongest provinces – and here we're talking fifteens as well as sevens - were such awesome sides, it was more that most of New Zealand's provinces regarded fronting up annually to a sevens tournament, then staged in October, as a great imposition.

New Zealand suffered the indignity of being turfed out of the Hong Kong tournament (believe it or not) in 1982 because its representatives had been performing so disappointingly. There was an obvious political overtone behind the decision. Hong Kong wanted the fully-fledged New Zealand team to participate. Australia and Fiji were sending along nationally selected sides. Why couldn't New Zealand?

Eventually, in 1983, the NZRFU decided to take sevens seriously, although it can't be said that many of its then 26 unions did likewise. Only seven of them bothered to turn up for the national provincial tournament, staged at Feilding in March. Manawatu had to put up a second team to avoid a bye in the second pool.

And when the first official New Zealand team did get to Hong Kong that year, it was embarrassingly knocked out in the quarter-finals by Western Samoa. Coach Bryce Rope declared that New Zealand "had a lot to learn about sevens rugby."

Although the national provincial tournament didn't become a major event until 1987, when the NZRFU found a major sponsor and agreed to pick up the tab for all 27 unions, sevens came of age in New Zealand in 1986 when the national team, still prepared by Bryce Rope, completed an outstanding hat-trick of successes, winning not only at Hong Kong but also taking out the New South Wales and Cardiff tournaments.

That mighty team of '86 included such distinguished footballers as Buck Shelford, Zinzan Brooke, Frano Botica, Wayne Smith, David Kirk and Craig Green.

From that point New Zealand had credibility among the organisers of sevens tournaments and gradually, although certainly not in a flood, invitations were extended to some of the country's leading personalities to appear in overseas tournaments.

The Punta del Este event in Uruguay, staged annually to coincide with the city's fiesta, was one of these. The brainchild of a handful of

Uruguayans from the British Schools Old Boys Club in Montevideo, the tournament was first staged in 1989 with international stars being introduced from 1990.The first Kiwi it invited along was Craig Innes. He joined the great Wallaby loose forward Simon Poidevin and Frenchmen Franck Mesnel, Eric Blanc and Yvon Rousset in an international team that made it to the semi-finals.

In 1991 an Anzac VII was formed through the initiative of Poidevin and Darren Junee. Four All Blacks were involved – Zinzan Brooke, John Timu, Craig Innes again and Walter Little.

Buenos Aires based rugby correspondent Frankie Deges recalls that when the All Blacks flew in, there was a gathering of Uruguayan officials at Laguna del Sauce Airport at Punta del Este to welcome them. As the "stars" emerged, they were identified: There's Simon Poidevin...he's with Zinzan Brooke. The blond fellow must by Darren Junee. Here come Craig Innes and John Timu, who must be a Maori. Who's that with them? It must be Walter Little. "No way," said Gabriel Varela, "that person is obviously a tourist – he certainly doesn't look like a rugby player."

It was indeed Walter Little. And the Uruguayan officials were to have no trouble recognising him as their tournament unfolded. Not only would he become the leading individual pointscorer for the Anzac team as it took out the title but he would win the Player of the Tournament award.

Only two New Zealanders fronted up in 1992 – Eric Rush and, as a late replacement for Terry Wright, Frank Bunce. Operating alongside Junee, John Eales and Jason Little, they helped the Anzacs bag another title, this time with Rush being named player of the tournament.

It was following the '92 event that the Punte del Este organisers expressed a desire to have separate Australian and New Zealand teams involved from the following year.

This recommendation was most enthusiastically received by the 'Anzacs' present. Bob Dwyer, the Wallaby coach, said he would take his country's invitation and forward it to the Australian Rugby Union.

The other invitation was picked up by Eric Rush. He would not be troubling the New Zealand Rugby Union with it. He believed the national body had enough teams to select already. He would bring a team back to Punte del Este in 1993 himself.

He did. And what a team. Headed by Rush, who was rapidly winning fame as one of the world's foremost exponents at sevens, the team also comprised Frank Bunce, Lindsay Raki, Glen Osborne, Junior Paramore, Richard Turner and Ant Strachan. Strachan had the distinction of being the only pakeha in the side but was accepted, according to Rush, "because he had a black man's attitude!"

Seven of them. No manager, no coach, no spares. And no name. Although they did boast a sponsorship from Steinlager.

They lobbed into Uruguay in January in '86 at the same time as the *official* Australian team,who were resplendent in Wallaby colours, and were immediately summoned to a press conference at the Hotel San Marcos where they were staying.

"We are not an official New Zealand team," Rush told the Uruguayan media.

"Then what is your team name?" asked one of the journalists.

Rush looked blank. He hadn't thought about that.

Lindsay Raki leaned forward. "Er, I'll answer that one. We call ourselves the Mongrels."

The media seemed happy about that, even if the Australians looked horrified. Raki's team mates weren't over enthused by the title, but it looked a lot more impressive in print the next morning..."Los Mongreles."

Los Mongreles were introduced to their local liaison officer, Rafael, who appeared a thoroughly co-operative fellow. He inquired what time the New Zealanders would like to train the next morning. They gave a collective shrug. "Oh, about eleven o'clock," said Bunce. "Fine," said the friendly liaison officer, "I will collect you."

This instruction seemed of little consequence when Los Mongreles, delightfully exhausted after an entire evening at large in the fun fiesta city of Punte del Este, arrived back at their hotel some time after 7am the next morning.

The local officials had come to appreciate that the New Zealanders were something special after introducing them to a local pizza parlour, Los Immortales, which was to become their favourite restaurant. Richard Turner startled the management by downing seven pineapple pizzas on his own!

When Bunce's phone rang at 11am next morning, he managed to grunt into the mouthpiece: "Yeah, wozit?"

"Eez Rafael 'ere. I take you to training."

"No mate. Come back in two hours. We're tired."

The faithful Rafael phoned back at 1pm to be given the same message – come back in two hours.

At 1pm he was told to try again at 3 o'clock. At 3 o'clock, he was mercifully released. Los Mongreles, through their spokesman Senor Bunce, assured him they would not be training that day.

What's more, they didn't train the next day. Or the next.

They were too much caught up in the fiesta and had too great an appreciation of Uruguayan beer (and pizzas) to sacrifice partying time for training.

South Americans are 'late' people. They would dine, on average, three hours later in the evening than New Zealanders. And their night clubs seldom swing into life before midnight. "We decided when in South America, live as the South Americans do," said Rush.

On the fourth day – Los Mongreles having not arrived home before 7am any morning, sometimes to greet the Wallabies heading out to training – Bunce said to Rush, "Hey, isn't there supposed to be a famous beach here?" "Yeah, let's go check it out."

There on the beach at Solanas were the Australians, all wearing Speedos.

"Now I'd been warned the previous year," said Bunce, "that only two types of people wore Speedos in Punte del Este – Brazilians and homosexuals. And these guys definitely weren't Brazilians!"

Bunce and Rush spread their towels on the beach and promptly fell asleep. When they awoke, a couple of hours later, they were seriously sunburnt.

When next day Bunce visited the beach, to observe, he looked, according to Rush, like a refugee from Alberia. "He had his track suit on, with the hood pulled over his head and he wore dark glasses. And he had rubbed just about a full bottle of sun tan lotion into himself."

Having observed the New Zealanders' reckless behaviour, Dwyer, himself not averse to a late night beer, dismissed them as serious challengers to the Aussies for the title.

But he was to underestimate the resourcefulness of the Kiwis who swept all before them, defeating the Australians comprehensively in the final, Glen Osborne completing the triumph by taking out the Player of the Tournament award.

"You would never get away with our behaviour in fifteens rugby," said Rush, "but if you're fit to start with, you can manage it in sevens. After all, there's only about eighty minutes of play in an entire tournament. And if you're smart, and control possession, you can slow the game down to your own pace."

Dwyer was astounded that a team of party-goers could sweep aside the pride of Australia who had trained diligently every day.

"I don't understand you guys," he said. "How do you do it?"

When Los Mongreles boarded the plane for the flight back to New Zealand, they had to walk past Dwyer's men who, as official Australian representatives, were travelling in business class.

The last New Zealander on, carrying the gleaming trophy, was Bunce.

"Nice trophy, Frank," said Dwyer.

"I'll swap you for your seat."

"And you know what," said Rush…"he would have, too, the mongrel."

Fielding essentially the same individuals, the Mongrels were to take out tournaments in several far-flung countries over the next few years.

The secret (to being invited back), according to sevens supremo Rush, was to always be polite and to always socialise with the locals.

"Rugby people in places like Uruguay, Dubai and Singapore are in awe of the All Blacks," says Rush, "and when they find them in their midst, they are usually overwhelmed. They presume you are untouchable. So when you mix with them and drink with them, they are enormously grateful and can't wait to invite you back the next year!"

The Mongrels' participation at Dubai had its origins in the prestigious Hong Kong international sevens tournament in 1989. That year New Zealand defeated Bahrain by a record 54-nil in pool play, going on to down Australia (Bob Dwyer's team again) in the final.

"A few of us finished up socialising with the Bahrain players and officials," recalls Rush. "They thought it was Christmas, and they expressed a desire to have us participate in their tournament. We said, simply, 'send us an invitation and we'll be there.' Two months later the invitation arrived."

In Bahrain and Dubai the New Zealanders played as the Warblers, an essentially social organisation funded by a group of squillionaire businessmen. They have distinctly original gear - light blue jersey with pink shorts and pink socks.

It was in Singapore, where the New Zealanders emerged triumphant one year, that Lindsay Raki earned the title of King Mongrel.

Blessed with more than seven players this time, the Mongrels were steadily taking control of the final against a team from Europe.

Raki, not required for the final, was sitting in the Mongrels' dug-out when a gentleman, handsomely attired in a blazer and with a pronounced English accent, approached.

"I wonder if you could assist me, old chap." The question was directed at Raki.

"Yeah, sure thing. What do you want to know?"

"Could you please identify the number two in the New Zealand team. Super player. We think we'll name him player of the tournament."

"Certainly. His name is Lindsay Raki. That's R.A.K.I."

"Thank you so much."

"You're welcome."

At the official banquet that evening the same impressive individual was at the microphone to announce the prizewinners.

After the successful teams had gone forward to collect their trophies, the official advanced to the microphone one last time, to proudly reveal the player of the tournament, a most prestigious award.

And the winner is...from New Zealand (he couldn't bring himself to say the Mongrels)...Lindsay Raki.

While his team mates booed wholeheartedly, Raki, suitably stunned by the announcement, stepped forward to accept his prize. (Number two, incidentally, had been Glen Osborne).

The official realised he had been duped as Raki took possession of the trophy and the microphone and, for the next ten minutes, proceeded to regale the audience.

"Ladies and gentlemen," he addressed them, "I cannot tell you what an honour this is for me. From the bottom of my heart…" and so he droned on, to the chagrin of his fellow Mongrels who conceded that he certainly deserved an award for audacity.

Singapore was the scene of another dastardly act, involving an Australian player who shall remain nameless.

Having consumed an excess of alcohol, this particular player was abandoned at the hotel by his team mates who were heading out for a night's entertainment.

"It's all right," said the magnanimous Kiwis, "we'll look after him."

'Looking after him' involved dragging him upstairs to the seventh floor of their palatial hotel where he was stripped naked and liberally coated in shaving cream. In a comatose state, he was then propped on to a chair and placed in the lift.

Hilarious in-house entertainment was provided over the next ten minutes for the New Zealanders as they arranged their chairs on the seventh floor landing facing the lift. The Ground and Seventh Floor buttons were activated. Down went the hapless Aussie, blissfully unaware of his predicament, to goodness knows what reaction on the ground floor, then back up to the seventh, where the opening of the doors drew riotous applause.

The fifth time the lift came back, the chair was empty. To this day, according to Rush, no one knows what became of the unfortunate Aussie.

On another visit to Singapore the Mongrels were enormously impressed to find a 44 gallon drum loaded with ice and beer at the closing ceremony. While the speeches were in progress the New Zealanders demonstrated great resourcefulness by applying a virtual rolling maul to transfer the drum from beside the main stage into the bushes.

The Singapore officials were perplexed by the drum's disappearance, but the Kiwis were in seventh heaven. They had a limitless supply of cool beer for the entire evening!

Raki's team mates may have acknowledged his enterprise in lifting the player's award in Singapore but King Mongrel was regarded far less charitably later in the year when, in the opinion of his team mates, he cost them victory in the final of the Dubai international tournament. And this was a most serious allegation because Dubai was the only tournament the Mongrels had never won.

According to thoroughly reliable sources, Raki had only 30 metres to run to the goalline to secure victory in the final moments against Queensland, but he was gunned down from behind by the Aussie halfback.

It mattered not that, in the tackle, Raki dislocated his knee. His team mates were dirty on him for costing them a full set of international sevens trophies.

They got even when Raki hobbled into the party later that night.

His fellow Mongrels relieved him of his crutches, snapped them in half ...and threw them in the pool!

It may have reflected a degree of jealousy that Raki had flown into Bahrain, en route to Dubai, in a first-class seat while his team mates were back in economy.

This odd arrangement came about after the Mongrels approached the check-in counter at Hong Kong, expressing disappointment that they hadn't been, as in the past, upgraded to at least business class.

The attendant was most apologetic but explained that the flight was almost completely full. The best she could offer was one seat in first-class.

"That'll do," said the players in chorus. Whereupon they decided the most democratic method of allocating the seat was by spoofing. Spoof they did, and the winner was Frank Bunce.

"Yes-sir-ee!" he shouted.

"Sorry, Frank," said Richard Turner, "you're disqualified for showing emotion," (a serious offence in spoofing).

They spoofed on until a new winner was found – King Mongrel. He showed no emotion whatsoever and duly took his seat up front.

The Mongrels didn't burden themselves with too many team policies. Their motto, which they mastered in four different languages, was: What do you mean, we have to pay!

The annual Middle East rugby celebration, staged in October or November, varied from the others in that it involved two separate venues, Bahrain, where a fifteens mini tournament was staged, and Dubai, scene of the sevens action.

Even for the Mongrels, Bahrain was a challenge because of the demanding social schedule. One night was a pub crawl, another a toga party and then there was always the Warblers' annual dinner. "It was," says Rush, "like Punta del Este without the fiesta."

It was at Bahrain that, for the first time in his life, Bunce became a goalkicker. The circumstances were favourable. "I was the captain and no one else in the team could kick!" His team mates obviously accepted him as a natural as he slotted goal after goal. To his own surprise, he didn't miss once.

Bunce denies that these goalkicking successes went to his head. However, they did result in his volunteering to handle the kicking duties in the opening encounter of the more serious Dubai sevens tournament, much to captain Rush's surprise.

"I don't care what else you do," said Rush, "just make sure the kick-off goes ten metres."

"Sure thing, skip," replied Bunce, who promptly miscued, sending the ball a mere eight metres.

He didn't look at his captain as the referee ordered a scrum on halfway, United States' put-in.

Bunce then proceeded to miss every conversion attempt. When the final try was scored in the corner, Bunce was bringing the ball back to the 22 for one last kick, ever hopeful.

"Gimme that," said Richard Turner, grabbing the ball away from him. To the astonishment of his colleagues, Turner's kick, from the touchline, went straight between the uprights.

Bunce shrugged. "There's no explaining some things," he said.

The postscript to this particular story is that Turner, now fancying *himself* as a goalkicker, had a 100 per cent failure rate in the next game.

When the Mongrels returned to Montevideo in 1994 to defend their title, they had a couple of notable player changes. Glen Osborne and Richard Turner were missing, their places taken by New Zealand sevens representatives Dallas Seymour and Peter Woods.

They had the luxury this time of a manager, although that benefit was tempered somewhat by the fact that the manager was the King Mongrel himself, Lindsay Raki.

Rush recalls that Raki, as a manager, maintained a unique sense of priorities. The day before the team was scheduled to fly home, Rush found Raki in a deck chair at pool side. He wanted to establish that the players' return air tickets were under control. "Bugger off," said Raki, "can't you see I'm into some serious drinking here!"

The Mongrels didn't quite recapture the glory of '93. Losing Rush with a broken rib and Seymour with a damaged achilles tendon in the semi-finals, they were overwhelmed in the final by Waisale Serevi's Fijian Cavaliers.

And that really was the beginning of the end for the Mongrels as a team because, being such talented individuals, they nearly all started winning promotion to the All Blacks.

Bunce had already aspired to international status while Osborne, Strachan and Rush were all to go on and represent their country. "Suddenly we didn't have the time to go charging off all round the globe for sevens tournaments," said Rush. "We had other priorities."

New Zealand was represented at Punte del Este in 1995 by two New Zealand teams – the official NZRFU selection and the Mongrels. "It was a nice touch," said Rush. "The Uruguayans retained a special affection for the Mongrels, as much for the quality of rugby we played as for our willingness to socialise with, and befriend, them as individuals."

Being World Cup year, Rush, Bunce, Osborne and Co. weren't available, but quality players such as Taine Randell, Willie Lose and Rush's brother Robert went along. The link with the original Mongrels was retained because the incomparable Lindsay Raki was back as manager.

Both Kiwi sides were eliminated in the quarter-finals, but Raki took great satisfaction from the fact that the official New Zealand team lost first. It provided glorious material for a stirring team talk. "They're out and we're still going," he reminded his team. Fifteen minutes later, his team was eliminated too.

Rush, who was the regular captain, has only the fondest memories of his involvement with the Mongrels.

"It's the hilarious episodes we naturally talk about," he says, "but the Mongrels trips served an important role in the evolution of sevens rugby in New Zealand. After that first journey to Punte del Este, when we were just seven players having a ball, we made a point of always taking a promising young player along with us.

"In this way we introduced players like Peter Woods, Junior Paramore and even Jonah Lomu – whom we took to Singapore in 1994 – to international tournament play. We socialised extensively but on the field we were serious. The fact that only the Dubai title eluded us demonstrates the quality of sevens we were able to produce."

A swag of Mongrels stars were included when New Zealand despatched its best sevens team to, first, Hong Kong and then the inaugural World Cup tournament in Edinburgh in 1993.

Frank Bunce, Eric Rush, Glen Osborne, Peter Woods and Dallas Seymour were included, but they weren't to enjoy the same successes they had become accustomed to with the Mongrels. Only a few months after their triumph in Uruguay, they were eliminated at the semi-final stage in Hong Kong by Western Samoa (the eventual winner) and knocked out in the quarter-finals at the World Cup (losing to England, which came through to win the event, and South Africa).

It was the only year in which Bunce represented his country at sevens, and he confesses that it was the year in which he performed the poorest at the abbreviated version of rugby. "I have to say," says Bunce, "that I went far better playing sevens for scratch teams like the Mongrels than for highly organised teams like New Zealand. I relaxed more in a Mongrels situation whereas I was tensed up knowing I was expected to perform for New Zealand."

The Mongrels had dared to take on world-class opposition in Uruguay without training, without any preparation whatsoever. They just took the field and allowed natural talent to express itself.

Things were significantly more earnest when the New Zealanders arrived in Hong Kong. Not only was the team equipped with a manager, coach and physiotherapist but also a sport psychologist, Gilbert Enoka from Christchurch.

The players were ordered to report to coach Peter Thorburn's room where Enoka made them lie down on the floor and "visualise" the game they were preparing for. "We had to think our way through the opening seven minutes," recalls Bunce, "focusing on the opposition and what would happen from the moment the ball was kicked off. At the imaginary halftime we were asked to comment on the high points and low points."

Bunce admits to cynicism at Enoka's methods. "They possibly work for some people but they didn't do anything for me. I've never been into that psychological stuff. And I'll tell you who else was sceptical – Todd Blackadder. He's a pretty earthy character in the Andy Earl mould, one of the more uncompromising footballers playing top-level rugby in New Zealand. As we came away from the session in Thorb's room, Todd said to me, 'What a lot of bullshit – rugby's played with the heart, not with the head. Let's get out and do it.'"

One unexpectedly appropriate topic that Enoka embraced in his mind sessions was how to avoid being distracted. "Say, for example," said Enoka, "that a streaker was to run on to the field. Don't pretend not to see. Acknowledge the person, take it in and immediately forget it."

Well, on cue, before the team's quarter-final against South Africa, a female streaker made an appearance right in front of the New Zealand players. "We did exactly what we were told," says Bunce. "We acknowledged her and then put her out of our minds. The advice was obviously good. We went on to beat South Africa easily!"

However, for the first time in eight years New Zealand failed to reach the final at Hong Kong, losing the semi-final to Western Samoa, a team that included a number of Bunce's team mates from the 1991 World Cup.

Bunce says that as a player he didn't enjoy Hong Kong half as a much as on the two other occasions when he was a spectator (both times getting to Hong Kong to play in an associated ten-a-side tournament). "The atmosphere and the social scene is fantastic, but you don't get the opportunity to fully appreciate it when you're playing; well, not when you're a member of a deadly serious New Zealand team which is expected to always reach the final. As a player I much preferred turning out for the Mongrels. And although it's easy to dismiss the Mongrels as purely a social team, we knocked over some of the same international opponents that the official New Zealand team lost to in 1993."

The World Cup of sevens was staged three weeks after Hong Kong in Edinburgh which was as cold as Bunce had remembered it in 1991.

The team had to endure a gruelling journey straight through from Auckland via London, arriving in Edinburgh around midday. To Bunce's horror, Thorburn ordered a training run for 2pm. It would be a light run, said Thorburn, to "dust off the cobwebs."

"Thorbs has got a funny idea of what constitutes a light run," says Bunce, "either that or he imagined there were a lot of cobwebs in the Air New Zealand plane that brought us through! He blasted us and we suffered. I can remember crawling through the down-and-ups and throwing up at one stage."

Bunce says he might have appreciated Thorburn's masochistic

approach a little more had the climate been half decent. "Sevens tournaments are fun events when you can feel the sun on your face. But in Scotland it was a battle against the elements as much as the opposition. I'm certain it was the cold that put paid to the chances of Western Samoa and Fiji, and it certainly didn't help New Zealand (a team comprised of six Maoris, Glen Osborne, Dallas Seymour, Eric Rush, Peter Woods, Stu Forster and John Timu, two Western Samoans, Junior Paramore and Pat Lam, one Niuean, Bunce, and only one pakeha, Marc Ellis."

Bunce remembers the Fijians being perpetually wrapped tight in blankets and crowding around heaters. "The first time they went out to train, they lasted ten minutes. It was just too cold for them."

The New Zealanders were also inconvenienced by the raw climate. Operating out of a tent city set up around the perimeter of the field, they, like the Fijians, existed in blankets until the call-up came for each match. The preliminary warm-up would be undertaken in the tent, followed by furious activity outside on the grass – "before the cold seeped into you," recalls Bunce – before assembly in the dressing rooms. "We had to be ready to go seven minutes before start time. In the circumstances we found it incredibly difficult to engage top gear."

Bunce, and his team mates, were critical of the design of the tournament. There were five matches in pool play (against the Netherlands, United States, Korea, Ireland and France), all of which the New Zealanders won, followed by three further outings in the quarter-finals.

Thorburn concluded from the start that it would be a survival of the fittest, which was why he set his team such demanding training schedules. In the event, he was to lose Eric Rush, Pat Lam and Dallas Seymour with injuries which seriously affected New Zealand's chances.

New Zealand weaved an erratic path through the quarter-finals, losing to eventual champion England before tearing Australia apart 42-nil. That performance seemed to flatten the Kiwis who then went down to South Africa.

The final was fought out between an England team studded with players well versed in the sevens game, and for whom Andrew Harriman was the outstanding performer, and Australia, which rebounded strongly from its calamitous display against New Zealand. England came through to win 21-17.

Bunce was pleased to pull out of Edinburgh. "The event would have been better staged in Hong Kong. I don't think too many players, certainly not those from the southern hemisphere nations, took much pleasure from it. The weather was awful and the format too cumbersome."

The final word came from Lindsay Raki when the players arrived back in New Zealand. After their failure to reach the final at both Hong Kong and Edinburgh, he labelled them The Team of Shame. Plainly, they had missed his input!

The Edinburgh experience so doused Bunce's enthusiasm for sevens that he was never to play the game competitively again. Part of the reason for that, of course, was his commitment as an All Black.

However, there was another version of football that brought much pleasure, and sensational success, for Bunce – the summer game of touch.

He was a foundation member of the Dustys team, formed in 1987 by Peter Walters and Mackie Herewini. The name of Dustys was adopted because Bunce and Walters were dustmen at the time.

This was to be no ordinary touch team. Indeed, during the term of Bunce's involvement, through until 1991, Dustys established themselves as the supreme team, certainly in the North Island and probably in New Zealand. They won the Whakatane tournament, acknowledged as the unofficial national club championship, seven years in a row.

In the five years that Bunce was involved the team won 248 games and dropped just five. Dustys failed to win only one tournament in all that time, an event at Manurewa.

They played in two separate competitions every week, at Manurewa and Otahuhu, and for a time got involved in a third module as well. They never failed to emerge as the champions. Which perhaps isn't surprising when you look closely at the personnel involved.

Bunce and Eric Rush became All Blacks, Richard Barnett, Sam Panapa and Dean Clark represented their country at league, Henry Amosa played for North Harbour and Nicky Williams was a sprint champion. The infamous Lindsay Raki, who was to play more than 100 games for Counties, turned out occasionally also.

More than half the team in any one year, including Bunce, represented Auckland while players such as Rush, Barnett, Herewini and Walters also played touch for New Zealand, being involved in the sport's first World Cup in 1991.

Walters, the captain of this illustrious line-up, recalls Sam Panapa being startled when he joined the team in 1989. "He was the fastest player in the Auckland league team but over forty metres he was the sixth fastest among the Dustys!"

Walters says that the tournaments provided useful pocket money for the Dustys players. Usually the winner picked up a cash prize of about $1200. "Our rivals knew that if we were entered, they were usually playing for second prize money!"

6

From Tokoroa
To Tokyo

I t would have been entirely understandable if Edward and Rewa Little
had cried enough after producing five sons, the first four, Eddie,
Frankie, Kevin and Charlie, having been born in Fiji (like their parents),
the fifth, Lawrence, in Tokoroa.

The rugby world should be eternally grateful that Mr and Mrs Little
decided to extend their family to half a dozen. The odds were pretty
good for a girl – Mrs Little had been hoping for a girl from the time her
first son was born – but it was another boy, Walter, who was delivered
into the world on October 14, 1969.

There was nothing initially to distinguish him from his brothers, all
of whom were to become above average rugby players. They all
represented South Waikato as Roller Mills primary school
representatives, Frankie and Kevin (both midfielders) going on to appear
for Waikato B while Lawrence was to play for North Harbour, King
Country, Waikato and Fiji.

But Walter was to be something special. Very special. If Frank Bunce,
with whom he was to create the most feared midfield back combination
in the world in the 1990s, came up via the Team From Hell, almost
every team young Walter was involved with seemed heaven blessed.

From the first time he pulled on a Tokoroa Pirates jersey, as a
barefooted four-year-old, until he was introduced to the North Harbour
representative squad as a sixth former, Walter was only on the rarest
occasions on the losing side. And many of the teams he featured in were
to etch exceptional records and boast some marvellously talented players.

In 1981 (when he was only 11 and still in the first form) and 1982 he
was a member of the crack Waikato Rangers primary school team –

Waikato Rangers being effectively south Waikato, the city kids playing as Waikato Rovers – which chalked up 19 victories without one setback. Both years the team took out the prestigious Northern Roller Mills Shield, defeating Counties in the final both times, the first time at Pukekohe Stadium, the next year at Onewa Domain.

The second year, the Rangers backline featured, at first-five, Jamie Cameron, who was to be an instant hit for the Wellington Hurricanes when the Super 12 competition kicked off in 1996, along with Little at second-five and Craig Innes at centre. Little and Innes would go on to become All Blacks while Cameron – son of Jim Cameron, who trained horses privately for Peter Thorburn – would make his mark at provincial level for North Harbour and Taranaki.

Little and Cameron were deadly rivals for the first-five position in the Tokoroa Gwynne Shield team when they were at intermediate school, Cameron's kicking, Little recalls, being exceptional for someone of his age. "I didn't have a particularly good kicking game at that stage, so I had to compensate by using my attacking skills." The Tokoroa selector took the easy way out by choosing both of them in his team, using Little on the wing on one occasion. The team won 11 matches out of 11 in 1982.

Little considers that he was one of the earliest professional rugby players in New Zealand. His mother used to offer 50 cents for every try her sons scored. As Walter frequently bagged five and six a game, his money box was soon bulging. When his brothers started complaining that the weekly handout was becoming too one-sided their generous mother increased their rate per try to $1, and sometimes $2, to keep up with Walter!

Rewa Little confesses that no work ever got done at their Grampian Street home on Saturdays once the rugby season kicked off. She had six sons to follow. To facilitate this she secured her driving licence in 1977, when Walter was seven. This allowed her, after preparing the boys' playing gear, to remain on the sideline at Tokoroa Sports Ground from mid-morning through until after the senior match concluded, usually around 4.30pm, after which she would hurry home and prepare herself for another evening's work as a cook.

It was in that year when Walter was seven that Rewa Little rather brazenly predicted to some of the other players' parents, as they stood around at Tokoroa Domain, that she believed her youngest was going to be the best of the crop and was "going to reach the top."

"I said that because Walter was such a clever runner," says Mrs Little, "I felt he was showing all his brothers' qualities, yet he was only seven. My friends remembered my prediction and when Walter became an All Black they were kind enough to say, 'You told us so…!'"

The name Joe Anderson wouldn't immediately spring to mind when outstanding New Zealand rugby coaches are being recalled, but his achievement in guiding Waikato Rangers to victory in five successive Northern Roller Mills tournaments, against the best primary school players from Auckland, Counties, Thames Valley, King Country and Waikato city is quite phenomenal.

Little remembers him as "a big Maori guy" of whom he was initially scared . "All my earlier coaches had taught how the team should develop, but here was someone who was incredibly precise. He knew the requirements for every position. And he was the first person to place me at first-five and teach me what to do."

Anderson, who still lives, and teaches, in Tokoroa says it's not surprising that Walter was apprehensive of him in those days. "Walter was a frail little fellow and I weighed in at about 120 kilograms and wore a thick, bushy beard!"

Anderson, who had played senior club rugby in the Bay of Plenty, says in the early 1970s he "got the bug" for working with players in the twelve to fourteen age bracket. "There were just so many classy footballers emerging from the south Waikato region and I felt it was important to harness that talent."

He took over the running of the Waikato Rangers team in 1975 when the then coach was tragically killed and started his remarkable winning sequence in 1978, drawing players from Morrinsville, Cambridge, Matamata, Putaruru and Tokoroa. It wasn't a region with a large population base, Tokoroa being the most substantial town with 15,000 residents.

Anderson soon identified the particular qualities of players from the various towns. Tokoroa, with a large Polynesian and Maori population, strong, mature footballers with flair, Putaruru produced Maori players with inventiveness and skill while Matamata, a more conservative area, turned out hard-working individuals…"dig deep players," as Anderson describes them.

"That mix created wonders," he said. "There was so much untapped potential, particularly among the islanders and the Maoris. I loved working with them."

The first of the Little boys to come to Anderson's attention was Lawrence who made the Roller Mills team as a form two pupil. A most promising footballer, he was taller and heavier than Walter who was one of the few to win selection while still in the first form.

"I watched Walter playing in the Gwynne Shield (intermediate school) sub-union matches," said Anderson, "and as a first former there, if you didn't have the nous, class and strength, you got blown away. Well, Walter certainly didn't get blown away. He was tiny – he probably weighed only 40 kilograms at the time – but he possessed a lot of class. I felt it was impossible to leave such a talented player out."

Anderson was impressed with Little's instinctiveness. "He possessed tremendous balance and the ability to glide through gaps. If he didn't get through himself, you could be sure he would put one of his team mates away. That gliding talent, it was something Joe Stanley possessed and Walter had it too."

Of the rising stars that Anderson helped shape in the Waikato Rangers team the one he expected would go the furthest was Craig Innes. "I guess I was influenced by the fact that he was such a hard runner. It was difficult to predict Walter's future because he seemed so fragile in those days. He was a touch-and-go player with a lot of class. As it turned out, he developed brilliantly by staying in Auckland and linking up with North Harbour. That was the making of him."

Anderson didn't expose Little unnecessarily during his first Roller Mills tournament in 1981, which was hosted by the Counties union, giving him just one outing. Walter didn't mind. He lapped it all up. "It was all an eye-opener to me," he said. "Just to see Pukekohe Stadium was pretty special. I took great satisfaction from watching our team triumph. We possessed a lot of country boys who were big and strong. There was some incredible talent on display for that age group."

The Waikato Rangers team never wanted for support. In fact, one of its secret weapons was the number of family members and relatives who cheered the players on from the sideline. Anderson recalls that it would not be unusual for thirty-five parents, plus uncles and aunties and nieces, to accompany the team to tournaments. "It was wonderful the way the families followed the players' careers," said Anderson. "They took immense satisfaction from the fact that the boys from south Waikato could foot it with the kids from the big cities."

Walter was billeted with Craig Innes at Devonport on Auckland's North Shore for the 1982 tournament, helping to forge a strong friendship which has survived to this day. Although they lived 50 kilometres apart, their parents would often deliver them to each other's homes, the one in Tokoroa, the other in Matamata. At the Innes property they would usually link with Craig's two younger brothers, Mark and Andrew, and play (often brutal) games of league.

"I can remember Craig and me making a pledge that after we'd finished our schooling," said Little, "that we would return to Tokoroa and play together for the Pirates club, me at second-five and Craig at centre. Things didn't work out that way. I was to play all my club rugby for Glenfield while Craig made his mark for Auckland Marist initially and then Ponsonby. He represented Auckland while I played for North Harbour. And latterly, of course, he's made his mark in league. But we've remained firm friends. He was an enormously talented player, big and strong for his age, with speed and skills. I remember being completely awed the first time I encountered him. He seemed to be running the whole game from fullback!"

They were both to win selection in the Waikato representative primary school team of '82, by far the most meritorious of their three straight successes being a 33-7 demolition of Auckland on Eden Park. Little sparked the victory by fielding Auckland's kick-off, sidestepping a couple of players and racing through to score between the posts. His coach later complained that he hadn't seen what happened. He was still making his way to his seat in the grandstand!

When Little turned out (during the school holidays)in 1983 for a South Waikato Tritons under-14 representative side for a tournament at Taumarunui, the backline this time featured Little, Cameron and Jasin Goldsmith, who was to beat both Little and Innes to All Black honours by a year.

Naturally, the Tritons won the title, downing a much heavier (and highly fancied) Te Awamutu team in the final, in no small measure thanks to Little who drop-kicked a goal and scored a try. On the route to the final, the Tritons had gobbled up Taumarunui by 106 points to nil. In this game, Goldsmith scored nine tries and Cameron collected 32 points.

Walter's primary school education (at Tainui school) having been completed, the decision was taken to enrol him at Hato Petera Maori Boys College on Auckland's North Shore. His Fijian heritage was no barrier; indeed, his brother Lawrence had attended Hato Petera the previous year but, not finding boarding school life to his liking, had returned to Tokoroa to complete his education.

Tokoroa had plenty going for it, not least Rewa Little's cooking. Walter's mother worked as a cook at one of the best restaurants in Tokoroa and the food she consistently served up for her family was, in Walter's words, "wonderful stuff." Roast meals were a favourite but she would regularly prepare island dishes, including a mean chicken curry with a "bite" to it. Whenever Walter went home from boarding school he would request the curry dish.

Whenever he did arrive back in Tokoroa for holidays, particularly during his first couple of years at Hato Petera, it would be to the same greeting from his mother…"Walter, you're so skinny, what have you been doing?"

What Walter *had* been doing was fighting for survival in the dining room at his school, for third formers were a long way down the pecking order. Eight pupils (including two prefects) were allocated to each table in the breakfast room. The food was "terrible" to start with, according to Little, and by the time the older boys had finished their scoffing, there was usually no butter or milk left. "I usually made do with a couple of pieces of dry bread."

Little found leaving home a huge challenge. It was the first time he had been away from his family – and the Littles were a big, close family – and initially he found it "scary" to be alone. "I really felt lost for a while," he says. "I was homesick and rather bewildered in the big city. I appreciated why Lawrence had chosen to return to Tokoroa." However, he recognised that Hato Petera presented him with the opportunity for a comprehensive education, and he resolved to make the most of it. He admits to learning a lot about himself in the boarding school environment. "I learnt I could look after myself, I learnt to live with people from different backgrounds and I learnt to be tolerant of others."

And then there was the rugby, Hato Petera being a school with a strong rugby tradition. Walter rejoiced in that. The school had expansive fields and he loved nothing more than to get out and kick a ball around. The fact that several of his friends from Tokoroa were also attending the school helped him settle in.

His reputation as a rugby player preceded him and although he played only fifth grade for Hato Petera in 1983, operating as the first-five and goalkicker in a team that won the championship, he was identified by the North Harbour under-14 selectors. The North Harbour union was still two years away from functioning as an entity under the NZRFU banner but it was already fielding age grade teams. Walter's under-14 team turned out in Massey club jerseys.

Having worn a Waikato jersey in 1982 and a pseudo North Harbour jersey the next year, Little donned the Auckland jersey in 1984, being plucked from the Hato Petera third grade team to represent the blue and whites at under-14 level, that team winning five out of five. Walter was used at first-five but didn't have to worry about the goalkicking duties.

It was 1985, the year in which North Harbour became New Zealand's 27th union, when things really started to happen for Little as a rugby player, although no thanks to one of Hato Petera's champion athletes whose wayward javelin throw bounced off the grass and pierced Little's foot. "I got a hang of a fright," says Little. "He'd thrown it from the other end of the field and instead of jamming into the turf, it scudded along straight into my foot."

The foot needed extensive stitching, sidelining Little for almost a month and preventing him from playing in the trial match for the Hato Petera first XV. As a result of the experience he remained well clear of the athletic track thereafter! The injury did allow Little to divert his attentions to his studies, which was timely, for this was his School Certificate year. English, mathematics and technical drawing were his strongest subjects, the ones which produced satisfactory marks at exam time. When he advanced to the sixth form the next year, rugby, in Little's words, "poured in" and his studies were put on hold.

There was intense rivalry among North Harbour's schools to become the first champion of the new union. When the first round of the competition was completed, Westlake Boys High was leading from Birkdale, Rosmini and Hato Petera, but the championship round produced a dramatically different result, with Hato Petera, expertly coached by Brother Gerard, coming through to defeat Westlake in a thrilling final.

Little describes the champion first fifteen as a team with "a lot of brute strength but light on individual skill." It was Little's goalkicking – he operated from first-five – that gave the team its narrow advantage in the final which was fought out on a muddy surface in front of a wildly enthusiastic army of supporters. "Whenever we played at home," recalls Little, "the whole school turned out and encouraged us with hakas and singing. Late in the final against Westlake the players were so uplifted by the support we were singing with them."

It was a marvellous occasion for Hato Petera which had never previously won a championship. The players and their supporters celebrated their historic victory worthily.

Little shared in another notable first in 1985. Although only 15, he was a member of the representative under-17 team which had the privilege of playing the first international game in the new North Harbour jersey. The team marked the occasion appropriately by defeating Australia 15-3, an exceptional achievement considering that the Aussies won all their other lead-up matches (against Thames Valley, Waikato and Taranaki) and went on to down New Zealand in the test at Whangarei.

Then it was off to Kerikeri for the northern regional under-16 tournament where Walter found himself up against his old mates Craig Innes (representing Auckland from Sacred Heart College), and Jamie Cameron and Jasin Goldsmith (Waikato representatives from Forest View High School in Tokoroa).

For once, Little wasn't in the starring team. But he thoroughly enjoyed the experience although finding it mentally draining, the teams being required to play virtually every day. He was among the spectators at the final, watching Goldsmith and Cameron's Waikato team outgun Innes' Auckland team.

If there were slim pickings for North Harbour during the tournament, the team had the satisfaction of hearing Walter Little's name read out at first-five when the North Island under-16 team was announced at the after-match reception. He was the only Harbour player to make it. Naturally, Innes, Goldsmith and Cameron were there in the backline, along with a likely lad from Hawkes Bay, John Timu.

The inter-island game was played at Rugby Park in Invercargill, as the curtainraiser to a national championship fixture. The whole experience was treasured by Little who got a great buzz out of flying to the deep south, being billeted at Gore and performing among a team with so many talented footballers. "I remember thinking that if this is what rugby is all about, I'm sticking with it."

His North Island team cruised to victory, scoring six tries to none, North's giant pack including Pukekohe High School's David Dixon who stood 6ft 7in and weighed in at close to 130kg – some weight for a schoolboy. He's now playing gridiron in the United States. Little remembers him as "a monster" and was grateful he was on *his* side.

Timu was the individual star, scoring or creating three tries and being named player of the day. Goldsmith, Innes and Little also excelled and all four of them were to be rewarded with selection in the New Zealand under-17 team to tour Australia the next season. "What a thrill that was," recalls Little. "I'd enjoyed every minute of my trip south and then to be told I was going to Australia, well, what a bonus!"

If Little thought that visiting Invercargill was a big deal, he was positively blown away by his experiences in Australia in May, 1986, as a member of the powerful national under-17 team coached by former All Black winger Ralph Caulton.

Their great adventure started in Brisbane, took in Surfers Paradise and Canberra and concluded, with the international against Australia, in Sydney. All five matches were won, with the team scoring 32 tries while conceding just two.

Little was won over by Australia on the first day. After he and front rower Darryl Wells were introduced to their billet, they were taken to a rugby club where a local match was being played. It being a typically sweltering Brisbane afternoon, Walter was more than happy to accept a cool beer. And another. And another. This, he decided, was what he wanted to do in life – be a touring rugby player.

His enthusiasm for touring ebbed remarkably the next morning when Caulton put the squad through a torturous training session. "I wasn't feeling great after all those beers and I remember thinking, 'If this is rugby touring, maybe I don't want to be part of it!'"

However, Little was to find Caulton an excellent coach, and he was to thoroughly appreciate his tuition – he was particularly good with the backs – and the attacking approach he advocated. "He appreciated that we had great flair in the backline and he was eager to expose it. Which probably helped me get selected ahead of other first-fives who kicked better."

At Surfers Paradise, Little was billeted by a wealthy home owner who lived alongside a canal which he travelled in his own boat. He took a group of the New Zealanders along to the casino, no one seeming to notice (or care) that the Kiwis were only sixteen. Walter had a thrilling time playing the slot machines and the roulette table, giving his modest tour expenses a reasonable boost. Another night his generous host took Walter and a few of his colleagues on a pub crawl!

This was the first overseas trip by a New Zealand under-17 side, reciprocating visits by Australia every year since 1982, and it proved a wonderful investment for the NZRFU.

Rugby News recorded that "the future of New Zealand rugby looks exciting indeed from the performances of the under-17 team in Australia. The positive, fifteen-man approach adopted by coach Caulton is reflected in the tryscoring statistics, the backs accounting for 26 of the 32 tries."

The backline against Australia featured Simon Crabb (later to represent Waikato) at halfback, Little at first-five, Sean Fitzsimons (who would play for Poverty Bay) at second-five, Christchurch's Jason Kilworth at centre with Timu and Innes on the wings and Goldsmith at fullback. Timu was the leading tryscorer while Little, who handled the goalkicking, scored most points.

Rugby News said of Little that he was "a swift passer ...who emerged as a champion utility back, playing all five matches and appearing in four different positions."

Little returned home to share in another Hato Petera triumph in the North Harbour schools competition, his conversion making the difference in the final as his team edged out Westlake (again), 6-4. The school's continued success obviously kept it in the limelight and so it wasn't surprising when the New Zealand schools team featured a Hato Petera player at second-five for the internationals against Japan and Australia. But it wasn't Little. The player the selectors favoured in a backline of awesome strength was Eddie Ryan, who was a year older than Little. Outside him were Craig Innes, Va'aiga Tuigamala, John Timu and Jasin Goldsmith, with Jason Hewett (who would wear the All Black jersey at the 1991 World Cup) and Mark George combining behind the scrum.

The same backline, with Sean Fitzsimons at second-five ahead of Ryan, was (understandably) preserved by the North Island under-18 selectors for the inter-island fixture at Carisbrook. Little, who was a shade disappointed at missing selection for the schools team, particularly as he, Innes and Goldsmith had come through together, took encouragement from the fact that he was taken to Dunedin as a reserve. He enjoyed watching his mates run South ragged, Innes and Co. scoring six tries against none.

Little finally cracked it into the New Zealand schools team in 1987, for the early season tour of Japan. Goldsmith, Ellis, Timu, Tuigamala, Hewett and Crabb were there in the backline and so, too, was Jamie Cameron. The team was led from the side of the scrum by Pat Lam, the pack including two others who were to achieve All Black status, Jamie Joseph and Richard Turner.

It was one of the most powerful school teams ever fielded, one to compare with the mighty Australian schools team that toured the UK in 1977-78 and won sixteen matches out of sixteen, producing ten Wallabies (including the three Ella brothers, Glen, Gary and Mark).

Although Tuigamala, at the time distinctive with an Afro hairstyle, stole much of the publicity in Japan, the player who most impressed Little was Goldsmith. "Operating from fullback, he was awesome," says Little. "He had the physique, and he had skill and speed; in fact, he was the quickest of the whole lot, and when you consider the players around him, that's saying something. He consistently set the backline alight as he roared in from fullback."

Coached most effectively by Chris Grinter (then of Wesley College but now of Rotorua Boys High School), the New Zealanders accumulated 49 points in both tests and returned home with a massive haul of 44 tries from six outings, an average of seven a game. Little was the leading pointscorer with three tries, fourteen conversions and seven penalty goals.

The boy from Tokoroa was enchanted by the Japanese experience, although he concedes that three weeks was probably too long to be there, given the New Zealand players' shortcomings with the language. They were billeted in Fukuoka, Hiroshima and Tokyo but enjoyed hotel accommodation in Osaka and Yokohama where the internationals were played.

Walter diligently strove to adapt to Japanese customs. He remembered to remove his shoes before entering homes, he made certain he slurped his soup (silence when drinking soup in Japan being interpreted as a rejection of it), he always showered before taking a bath, he learnt how to sit cross-legged for meals and how to manipulate chopsticks and he presented each family that hosted him with a gift.

He couldn't believe the intensity of traffic in Tokyo, reckoning that it took at least two hours to travel 20 kilometres, at any time of day. And he was intrigued with the bars that charged an admission price after which all drinks were free. The New Zealanders being New Zealanders drank one particular bar out of beer, after which Walter and his mates were invited to step up to the top shelf. It being free, they didn't feel inclined to disappoint their host, so ventured into previously unchartered waters (or should that be liquors?), suffering dreadfully at training the next morning.

If Little was to find the Japanese experience somewhat unreal, it was nothing to what was in store for him back home. In quick succession he was to be invited to play for North Harbour Maori and to join the North Harbour representative squad. Heady stuff for a 17-year-old.

(7)

Come In
Thorbs

Walter had been back from the schoolboys tour of Japan only a few weeks in 1987 and was adjusting to life as a seventh former at Hato Petera when he received a phone call from Nick Botica (Frano's dad) in his capacity as selector-coach of the North Harbour Maori team.

Nick had watched Walter play for Hato Petera and he had been enormously impressed, he said. He was naming him in his squad and he hoped young Walter would be available to play in the upcoming match against Bay of Plenty. It would, in all likelihood, afford him an opportunity to mark former All Black Arthur Stone and could be most beneficial to his burgeoning career.

Walter was flattered at Nick Botica's invitation. He said he would consider it and phone him back. He knew there was only one impediment to his representing North Harbour Maori. So he telephoned his mother in Tokoroa.

"Hey, Mum," he said, following a little introductory chit-chat, "I've been invited to play for North Harbour Maori."

There was a lengthy silence on the other end.

"...but you're not a Maori, son – you're a Fijian."

"Yeah, but they don't know that!"

Being the sage person that she is, Mrs Little suggested that playing for North Harbour represented impropriety.

"I'm sure there will be many opportunities to play for other teams," she advised. "Don't be impatient, son."

Walter acknowledged his mother's wisdom and duly conveyed the bad news to Nick Botica – he wouldn't be turning out for his Maori team for the simple reason that he wasn't a Maori.

He went back to being a Fijian and enjoying his rugby with the school first fifteen, and to contemplating his future. This was his final year as a student. By year's end he would have to make important decisions about his vocation.

Such lofty matters were put on hold when John Paterson, the manager of the North Harbour representative team, telephoned Brother Gerard Mahony at Hato Petera and asked if Walter's studies could be interrupted while he attended North Harbour training sessions. Coach Peter Thorburn was wanting to involve him in his squad trainings.

Brother Gerard had no objections, but Walter was dumbfounded. "I'd regularly attended North Harbour matches at Onewa Domain because it was only walking distance from the school," said Little, "I'd marvelled at the skill of players like Buck Shelford, Frano Botica, Scott Pierce and Richard Kapa. Now I was being asked to join them. I couldn't believe it."

When Paterson arrived to collect North Harbour's newest acquisition, he was a little startled to find Walter coming away from the Tuck Shop carrying a pie, a packet of biscuits and a bottle of Fanta. "What's all this?" Paterson inquired. "I'm starving," replied Walter. "The food's not great here, so I'm filling up before I train."

Walter expected he would be kept way in the background at his first training session but upon his arrival coach Thorburn summoned the whole squad together and introduced the bright-eyed teenager to them individually. He was completely overawed.

Thorburn says he had Little's talent brought to his attention by Jamie Cameron's father Jim, so he went along to watch him play for Hato Petera. "What I saw impressed me mightily," says Thorburn. "I saw him place a huge right foot kick followed by a huge left foot kick. That immediately had my attention. He was obviously a player with loads of talent, a player with a future.

"I didn't go looking for players like Walter Little so I could boast that I discovered them. Half the art of being a selector is to uncover players, with skill, who in the right environment will develop. I didn't see Walter as a gamble. He was only seventeen but he was smoking and drinking and very mature physically. We brought a lot of young players into the North Harbour squad over the years. Some went on with it, some didn't."

Thorburn involved Little fully in the training sessions and was so impressed with his development that he earmarked him for a North Harbour appearance against New Zealand Combined Services, a game when Harbour would be without several of its regular members (including regular first-five and goalkicker Frano Botica) because of NZRFU and club commitments.

Sadly, Little's chance to become North Harbour's youngest representative was shattered when he seriously injured his knee – the same weekend Thorburn was announcing to the papers the team to play Combined Services. Little was named at first-five.

When he had been back home in Tokoroa on holiday, Little had turned out for the Tokoroa Pirates under-21 side but in jumping high for the ball he had landed awkwardly and partially torn his cruciate ligament. He received some treatment in Tokoroa and more when he returned to Auckland. He believes now that he should have had the knee operated upon because it has continued to trouble him throughout his career.

The knee was mending, and would have been right for the Combined Services match, had Little not turned out for his school against St Stephens College. "I said I was okay, but I wasn't. And when this giant forward (Myles Ferris who was later to represent North Harbour) sat on my knee following a tackle, I was in big trouble. They carried me off and I didn't play rugby again for several weeks."

He recovered in time to take his place at first-five in a potent New Zealand under-19 team (featuring Tuigamala, Goldsmith, Timu and Innes) that overwhelmed Wales 54-9 at Pukekohe Stadium, contributing 20 points as the goalkicker, before turning out for the North Island under-18 side, captained from the wing by Timu, in its drawn encounter with South in Hamilton.

However, it would be another season before the likely lad from Tokoroa would make his first-class debut. In the meantime, there was the important matter of a job to sort out.

His growing status as a rugby player was to involve him in a decent tug-of-war towards the end of 1987. Thorburn was dead keen for him to work in Auckland and play for North Harbour. Glen Ross, the Waikato coach, was eager for him to return to Tokoroa and become available for his representative team. Walter's father had organised a boilermaker's apprenticeship for him in Tokoroa. Meanwhile, an apprenticeship as a motor mechanic was being offered in Auckland by Lindsay Ellery, the coach of the Glenfield club. This offer also included accommodation with Ellery and his wife Trish.

It was the first major decision that Walter had had to make in his life. How to decide? He would discuss the options with his parents, then weigh their comments with his own judgment and instincts.

"I had been away from my home for five years," recalls Little. "There was a strong desire to return to Tokoroa and involve myself with my family. Against that was the opportunity to play rugby for North Harbour, a team that had already taken me in, a team – as I saw it – of the future."

What Walter didn't know was that Peter Thorburn had telephoned his mother and convinced her of the wisdom of allowing her youngest son to stay in Auckland. "He told me that he believed Walter had a big future in rugby and that his prospects were much greater in Auckland than in a small town like Tokoroa. Although I would have loved him to stay here, I could see that there were greater opportunities for him up north."

Thorburn says he felt it was important for Little, at that point in his career, to stay in Auckland where he would win greater recognition. "But also," said Thorburn, "I felt there were some bad influences, away from the rugby field, in Tokoroa, and Walter could have been easily led astray."

Little himself listened to the two sides of the argument. His father (emphasizing the valuable boilermaking apprenticeship) and one of his brothers urged him to remain in Tokoroa. His mother took a more conciliatory line. "I told Walter it was his career at stake – he should make the decision himself, but if he chose to return to Auckland, I would support him one hundred per cent."

Walter weighed it all up. He was reluctant to leave his old home town but he could see his rugby career opening up with North Harbour. The lure north was too strong to resist. Also, he had enormous respect for Thorburn as a person and as a coach.

When Lindsay Ellery telephoned to establish if Walter had made a decision, he was told, "Yeah, I'm coming up to play for Glenfield." Ellery was delighted and a couple of weeks later drove down to Tokoroa to collect his new recruit. Little recalls that "old homesick feeling" wrenching into him as he was driven north. But he knew, in his heart, that what he was doing was for the best.

The decision to base himself 'across the bridge' in Auckland paid immediate dividends in 1988 when Thorburn, impressed with the rugby that Little was playing for Glenfield, and well aware of his potential anyway, named him in his North Harbour squad as the back-up first-five to Botica, who continued to challenge Grant Fox for the No 10 jersey in the All Blacks.

Botica was Little's idol. As a North Harbour supporter, he'd admired his play during the previous couple of seasons. Now here he was training alongside him. "I considered Frano to be the ultimate attacking first-five and I set out to model my play upon his. Peter Thorburn saw me as a first-five and so that was the position I was concentrating upon. I took special notice of everything Frano did. I thought his option-taking was brilliant and I was deeply impressed at the way he would often break out from near his own goalline. He was magical."

The influence has survived, Little claiming that he has adapted a lot of Botica's ideas to the second-five position he now specialises in. He was encouraged wholeheartedly by Botica in those formative days at representative level. "He talked to me and encouraged me," recalls Little. "I thought it was the greatest thing. We'd have question and answer sessions on the technicalities of first-five play. I'd pose a hypothetical question…'If there was a ruck happening here, say, where would you stand?'...and he'd give the answer. He was never dictatorial but he was always happy to advise. We had a wonderful, open relationship."

Little fell in love with the whole North Harbour scene, describing it as being "rather like one great big family." He was chuffed by the manner in which senior players like Richard Kapa and Paul Carlton took him under their wing, advising him on "every little thing," from etiquette in restaurants and hotels to dress codes to acceptable behaviour in social situations to what was required at training sessions and team meetings.

"You think a lot of these things will come naturally to you," says Little, "but for a boy from a little town like Tokoroa there was a lot of growing up to be done."

If Little, at eighteen the youngest by two years in the North Harbour squad, idolised Botica, he was in awe of the team's other international star, the skipper Buck Shelford.

"You can't begin to describe the influence, the mana, he wielded over every player in the team. He was an inspiration to everyone. You just knew that if Buck said, 'Follow me', everyone would, regardless of whether there were red hot coals along the way. Like Frano, he handed out invaluable advice. He'd give precise instructions of what I, as a first-five, was to do in a given set of circumstances. However, unlike my relationship with Frano, which was so relaxed and natural, I found myself totally awed by Buck. I was too shy to ever talk to him. I would just nod. I think the longest sentence I ever uttered in his presence that year was, 'Yes, Buck.'"

North Harbour was a first division union by 1988. It had come a long way in a short time under Thorburn, easily winning promotion from the third division in its debut year, 1985, before making the all-important jump to the premier division two years later, largely thanks to the massive input from Shelford and Botica. For Little, being involved at the top level of New Zealand provincial rugby was "like a dream come true."

His debut in the white, black and cardinal colours of North Harbour came at Pukekohe Stadium on Anzac Day when Botica and Shelford were away at the All Black trial. His delight at scoring a try and kicking three goals was tempered by the fact that Harbour lost the game by a point.

With Botica on national duty, which included a tour of Australia, Little got the feel for representative play with further appearances against British Combined Services and North Auckland but his biggest thrill in '88 came when he took the field as a replacement during the NPC game against Canterbury at Lancaster Park. Although it has to be said that getting to Christchurch was almost as nerve-racking as running on to the field as one of Shelford's men. That's because the day North Harbour flew south young Walter was required to appear in court on a drink-driving offence.

"I kept it quiet," confesses Little now, "but I was terribly worried. I hadn't anticipated being required for North Harbour's national championship campaign and I wondered whether Peter Thorburn would still entertain me as a member of his team if I was convicted."

Little had been stopped in Hobson Street in Auckland city by a traffic officer and after admitting that he had had "a couple of beers" was horrified when he blew into the bag and turned the crystals green. "I saw my world tumbling down at the time," he says. "I felt certain there would be long term complications. And I had convinced myself that Thorbs wouldn't want a player guilty of driving while under the influence in his team."

Good fortune was on Little's side. On a technical fault, detected by his lawyer, the charge was dismissed, allowing the teenage rugby star to walk free from the court. Enormously relieved, he returned home to pack his gear bag, with plenty of time to make the team assembly at the airport.

He admits to being "as nervous as a kitten" sitting in the grandstand while the big game unfolded. North Harbour had yet to beat Canterbury, and the red and blacks were a formidable foe on their own territory. Little has never enjoyed running on as a reserve…"you can't prepare yourself properly"…and he admits to receiving the biggest shock of his life when Thorburn yelled at him, "You're on, Walter," after midfielder Allan Pollock came off injured.

For a while, Little felt as if he was in a dream. "Here I was surrounded by Canterbury guys I'd only previously seen on television, players like Stephen Bachop, Bruce Deans, Shayne Philpott, Albert Anderson and Andy Earl, and inside me was Frano Botica. A heavy tackle brought me back to reality. As play developed, I realised that this was what first division rugby was all about. If I could get a place I would be doing this week in, week out. I decided I liked the atmosphere – it was something I wanted to be part of."

After giving Canterbury a 19-point start, North Harbour clawed its way back to salvage a bonus point from the game. Not a victory, for sure, but another demonstration that the country's newest union was worthy of its first division status. Walter wanted to remain involved, he decided, and he particularly looked forward to Harbour registering its first victory over Canterbury. He would have to wait a long time – till 1993, in fact – for that satisfaction.

After an outing as a second-five against West Coast at Greymouth, Little's rep season effectively came to a conclusion. Botica was back from the All Blacks to fill the No 10 jersey and Walter was sidelined anyway when his knee began troubling him again.

For those who treasure trivia, the Commonwealth Games fundraising match between the Barbarians and Auckland at Mt Smart (now Ericsson) Stadium at the commencement of the 1989 season, is of special significance – it was the first occasion that Walter Little and Frank Bunce played together. Well, in terms of their magnificent midfield liaison of later years, 'together' isn't a truly accurate description because they were well separated in the Baabaas backline – Little was at first-five marking Grant Fox and Bunce was on the wing looking after Inga Tuigamala.

They remember each other only as team mates on that occasion. It would be another couple of years before their destinies would link them together.

Little was thrilled to receive the invitation from John Hart to wear the Barbarians jersey, particularly as he would be playing against the best provincial team in the world. The Baabaas line-up was studded with personalities itself, including Wallabies Andy McIntyre and Brad Girvan, Graeme Bachop, Ian Jones, John Drake and Walter's old schoolboy team mate Jasin Goldsmith.

"It was a great experience for me," says Little. "I got a huge buzz out of playing against and later talking to Foxy. Hart, our coach, was so enthusiastic and encouraged us to go out and have a good time which is how I like to play my rugby."

Having opposed Foxy on that occasion, Little next found himself partnering the great man for North Zone against Central and South in the George Nepia Trophy series, a series that was tried for three years and then abandoned.

Against Central at Wanganui, Little, relishing the opportunity to operate at second-five in front of the national selectors, found himself up against a couple of dangerous midfielders John Schuster, whom he knew, and John Hainsworth. When he first sighted Hainsworth he thought he was a prop. "Then he turned round," said Little, "and I saw he had number thirteen on his back. I remembered they called him The Tractor which seemed entirely appropriate at that moment. He and Schuster were certainly the biggest centre pairing I had been up against. Hainsworth was huge. I didn't bring him to the ground once. I just grabbed a leg and got dragged along. Although we won comfortably, it remains one of the hardest rugby days of my career."

If Hainsworth was The Tractor, Little considered Fox to be The Operator. "It was so completely different to playing outside Botica," he says. "Foxy was so much more precise in his option takings. It was almost like playing rugby by computer. He called all the moves, did all the kicking. He even marshalled our defence. He certainly looked after me, which I appreciated at that stage of my career. I wasn't encouraged to call any moves for which I was grateful." There were times in the years ahead, however, when Little would resent the fact that Fox continued to call *all* the shots.

The national selectors (who that year were Grizz Wyllie, Hart and Lane Penn) obviously liked what they saw in the zonal games because they named Little as a reserve to the shadow test team for the All Black trial in Hamilton, a happening which stunned Little. "It meant I was in the selectors' eye. Gosh, I was only just out of school and here I was mingling with the country's most elite rugby players. Everything was happening so quickly. It was like a dream unfolding."

Grizz Wyllie, as the national coach, prepared the shadow test team. It was Little's first experience of him and he made sure he arrived "real early" for the first team meeting where a count of heads revealed two players were missing. Walter wondered who. All was revealed when room mates John Gallagher and John Schuster, both dishevelled and with their socks and boots in their hands, arrived, claiming they had missed their wake-up call. Kipper had been kipping! Little looked on wide-eyed as Wyllie berated the pair. "I felt later that he was probably just doing it for the sake of us young guys. But I know it sure scared hell out of me at the time!"

Little says he remained "as quiet as a mouse" throughout the meeting, nodding when Wyllie told him that, in the event of injuries, he would be covering both first and second-five (for Fox and Schuster). His first impression of the All Black coach was that he was "a real southern man – he didn't waste words, for sure, and I had the feeling you wouldn't want to cross him."

It didn't bother Little that no players stumbled off injured. He was as happy as could be sitting in the grandstand as a reserve for the best team in the world, occasionally acknowledging his mother and brother Frankie who were among the spectators.

Ten days after the trial and with his star glowing brightly, Little turned in an heroic performance for North Harbour in a national championship game against Auckland at Takapuna...in an unexpected way. He was deputising at first-five for Botica who was injured and was concentrating intently on his role opposite Grant Fox.

But after fullback Paul Feeney had missed his first three kicks at goal, he came to Walter and said, "I haven't got my kicking boots on – you take over." A startled Walter replied, "What if I start missing them? It's a pretty important game." Feeney assured him he would be okay. And he was. After goaling his first kick from almost 45 metres, he landed two more demanding goals, matching Fox's effort, to give North Harbour a more than satisfactory 9-all draw.

"To draw with the champions was a great thrill," says Little who suggests he might not have been so successful if his kicks had been from close range. "Nerves might have taken over then," he says. "Because they were all long-range efforts, I didn't really expect any of them to go over. I went thwack three times, and they were all on target." It was the only game Auckland failed to win in its '89 NPC campaign.

With the national selectors responsible for the New Zealand Colts, Little was a sitter for inclusion in the squad of under-21s who would play three provincial teams before tackling Australia's best in the curtainraiser to the Bledisloe Cup international at Eden Park.

John Hart had been entrusted with the role of reinstating colts rugby in New Zealand after an embarrassing 1988 season when footballers like North Auckland lock Ian Jones were overlooked and a star-studded line-up was defeated by the Aussies at Ballymore.

Hart scoured the country ensuring he had the best material available, then with former All Black flanker Graham Williams as his assistant, he moulded the 22 players selected into a super efficient, spirited team. Outstandingly led by Auckland loose forward Pat Lam, the team swept past Horowhenua, Taranaki and Thames Valley in spectacular fashion before tackling an Australian team boasting such Wallabies-to-be as Jason Little, Darren Junee, Richard Tombs, Paul Kahl and Mark Catchpole.

Many more internationals were to emerge from the New Zealand Colts team – 11, in fact, an amazing statistic. From the backline Matthew Ridge, Inga Tuigamala, Craig Innes (all now playing league), Little and Jason Hewett made it to All Black honours while out of the pack came Mark Carter (another league convert), Jamie Joseph, Lam, Norm Hewitt, Craig Dowd and Richard Turner.

It was a classic contest, New Zealand racing away to a 16-nil advantage in the opening 30 minutes before the Aussies clawed their way up to 12-16 with two fine tries. If the New Zealand supporters – and the game was screened live on television – were anxious at that stage, coach Hart certainly wasn't. "I knew we would outlast them because of our fitness," he said.

The player who sparked a landslide of tries by New Zealand in the final quarter was Little. In scoring one of the most sensational solo tries seen on Eden Park for many a year, he scythed between the Australian five-eighths, eluded the halfback and the number eight, wrongfooted the fullback and carried on to score between the posts after a run of some forty metres.

The *New Zealand Herald* recorded that that was only one example of how Little embarrassed the Australians with his skill. "The visitors just could not keep up with Little's stops, starts and sidesteps as he left flailing Australian arms and legs in his wake."

Little ranks the try among his favourites, because of the critical stage of the game at which it was scored and because of the calibre of the players on both sides. It all came about, he says, because he spied a gap between the Australian five-eighths. "Once I'd probed that, everything happened instinctively."

Little had only praise for coach Hart. "He appreciated he had an exceptional line-up of players, but the important thing was that he drilled us well and encouraged us to use our flair. He brought out the best in all the players. He got Craig and myself, as midfielders, working with the wingers which resulted in the threequarters scoring a packet of tries."

Hart, in turn, nominates Little as the best player in the backline of '89, which is saying something considering Ridge, Tuigamala and Innes were all to achieve All Black status the same year. "He possessed special touches," said Hart. "He had good hands, he was a great defender and he possessed vision. His try at Eden Park was a brilliant effort. It wasn't surprising that he went on from there."

Little underwent minor surgery after the colts game, to remove torn cartilage from his knee. It had troubled him throughout the internal tour and was initially thought to be a ruptured ligament. But as he continued playing a piece of cartilage broke free and "floated around."

During his first training run with the colts, the cartilage popped out. "It was painful," admits Little. "We would twist the knee around for about five minutes until it came back into place. The operation was to remove the broken piece, and the knee was fine after that."

Thorburn used Little at second-five outside Botica for the main thrust of North Harbour's championship campaign. They teamed beautifully together as Harbour enjoyed a rich sequence of success, defeating Waikato, Taranaki, Wellington, Otago, Counties and Hawkes Bay.

And then came Bay of Plenty at Rotorua where a victory would give Harbour a stunning second placing in the championship. "Buck Shelford reminded us in his team talk that because he was from Rotorua there was no way he wanted to lose. We were determined to give him his victory.

"Well, two minutes from time we were ahead by two points when Ron Preston (the Bay first-five) went for a dropped goal. Frano Botica partly charged it down and it deflected across the goalline into my hands. I wasn't sure whether I could force it and win a twenty-two drop-out or not, so I tried to run the ball out. Unfortunately, I was ambushed and conceded a penalty – twenty metres out from the posts. Preston kicked the goal and we lost by a point.

"I ran straight off the field without saying a word to anyone. When Buck came in he threw a can of lemonade at the wall! I blame myself. I should have forced the ball or kicked directly to touch. However, I didn't, and that was that. Peter Thorburn maintained a diplomatic silence."

Notwithstanding that little hiccup in Rotorua, it had been a magnificent year for Little. The decision to play his rugby with North Harbour had paid handsome dividends.

And now the pundits were labelling him a near certainty for selection in the All Black team to tour Wales and Ireland.

Looking Good
In Black

The announcement of the All Black team to tour Wales and Ireland in 1989 was to be made live on television on a Sunday evening by NZRFU chairman Russ Thomas. Because a full complement of thirty players was going and because all the media and most of his mates were insisting he would be involved, Walter Little was prepared for a happy outcome.

What he wasn't prepared for was the stream of visitors to Lindsay and Trish Ellery's home as the big moment drew near.

He was heartened by the arrival from Tokoroa of his parents and brothers Charlie, Frankie and Lawrence. What a lovely surprise and how appropriate to be surrounded by family on an occasion like this. Then a couple of aunties called in. Wow, what a family gathering, thought Walter. Next some of his good friends dropped by. *G'day, Walt, thought we'd come and hear the team announcement with you.* Wonderful, join the party. Then a whole cluster of Glenfield team mates arrived. The club didn't have an All Black on its honours board. *Be nice to be around in case today's the day.*

By the time a bunch of old buddies from Hato Petera squeezed into the rumpus room as well, Walter was beginning to wonder. He assessed the scene. There were about forty people present. He knew something was up, but he wasn't quite sure what, although his suspicions intensified when a photographer from the *New Zealand Herald* arrived...*just in case Walter's name is read out*... followed by a film crew from Television New Zealand.

"By that stage," admits Walter, "I thought 'What the hell's going on!'?" It occurred to him that there were countless people more certain than he was that he would be named in the All Blacks.

In fact, the names of the thirty tourists represented the worst kept secret in New Zealand rugby in 1989. The team had been chosen by the selectors seventy-two hours previously but for some obscure reason the announcement of it was being delayed until early Sunday evening. The three Sunday newspapers had obviously been "leaked" the names, prompting commentator Keith Quinn to speak, with some indignation on television, of the game's tradition regarding team announcements being broken. One could understand him being peeved that secrecy had most certainly not been maintained, although tradition with All Black team announcements never involved television. Genuine tradition was having the team read out by the chairman of the NZRFU at an aftermatch function in the bowels of the Athletic Park grandstand in Wellington following the final trial.

Lindsay Ellery was another to learn in advance, if not the whole thirty names, certainly enough for his purposes. From an "impeccable source" he'd been assured that Little was in the touring party, which accounted for the Ellery house outdrawing the local cinema that evening.

However, nothing was allowed to detract from the player himself hearing the names read out. His focus lasted only until he heard Russ Thomas say…"W. K. Little, North Harbour." Then all hell broke loose. He didn't care about the rest of the names. He was an All Black. For the next short while, he admits, everything was a daze. People were hugging him and kissing him and congratulating him, television cameras were whirring, flashlights were popping, the phone was running hot. He concedes that, a month away from his twentieth birthday, it was undoubtedly the greatest day of his life.

Then it was party time. Host Ellery had stocked up well and says that what followed was "one great Fijian party." Nobody wanted to go home. The new All Black didn't finally get to bed until 6am, and it's reliably reported that when he drifted off to sleep it was with a huge smile on his face.

When a degree of normality returned the next day, and it was only a degree because the phone rang almost incessantly with wellwishers and journalists wanting to speak to the 'baby' of the All Black touring party, Little was able to analyse the balance of the squad that would undertake an itinerary of mouthwatering appeal featuring one match in Canada, seven in Wales, five in Ireland and one (against the Barbarians) in England.

He was delighted to realise that four of the Colts had made it – himself along with Inga Tuigamala, Matthew Ridge and Craig Innes – while North Harbour also had four players involved, the other three being Frano Botica, Ron Williams and the captain Buck Shelford.

Little was to receive a prestigious accolade before flying out with the All Blacks. He would be named New Zealand's Most Promising

Rugby Player of the Year. It took a fair amount of coaxing by the function organisers, the Ponsonby Rugby Club, to lure him along for the announcement. He was a most reluctant participant, insisting he hated social functions of that kind and that there wasn't any point in his attending when obviously the trophy would go to Inga Tuigamala, Craig Innes or Matthew Ridge.

Although he didn't sight any of these players at the dinner, he tried to guess which one of the trio would be the winner, when his name was read out. "I almost fell off my chair," he admits. "I was absolutely dumbfounded. I hadn't prepared any speech and when I was invited to make a response, all I could mumble was, 'Thank you – this is most unexpected!'"

Little had been named at second-five in the All Black touring party along with John Schuster. That pleased him because he had come to regard second-five as his favourite position. He was more than happy to play first-five but because he considered there were limitations to his tactical kicking game, he didn't believe he was equipped to be a flyhalf at the highest level. And, anyway, in Grant Fox and Frano Botica, the All Blacks possessed two of the most accomplished exponents in the world. They didn't need another one.

Well, in an ironical twist, Walter was to make his All Black debut at first-five. Not because coach Grizz Wyllie preferred it that way, but because the team's two specialists, Fox and Botica, were excused the Vancouver stopover to remain in Auckland with their wives who were expecting.

So one of the new kids on the block, Little, wore the No 10 jersey in Vancouver. And another new kid, Tuigamala, was on the wing, both scoring tries and both excelling as the All Blacks romped away to victory. Little compared operating in the All Black backline with being set loose on the motorway in a Ferrari after spending one's whole life driving a Morris Minor. "It was pure luxury," he says. "Bernie McCahill and Joe Stanley called all the moves and Bruce Deans, at halfback, guided every pass straight into my hands. All I had to worry about was distributing the ball or, very occasionally, kicking it."

Little had his own special cheer squad in Vancouver when eight members of the Glenfield club, returning from the Golden Oldies festival in Toronto, made a special stopover so they could take in Walter's debut.

The club's senior team manager, Willie Louie, described it as the greatest day in the club's history. "We couldn't let the game pass without someone being there to see Glenfield's first All Black play," he said.

Little expected, on his first All Black mission, to be consigned to midweek outings. Schuster was the established test second-five, Walter merely the apprentice. As long as he could justify his existence, he was more than happy. "I accept that every touring player should strive to make the test team but as the youngest player in the touring party I didn't consider I was realistically in contention to play against Wales or Ireland. I was perfectly contented just being involved and soaking up all the guidance and advice I could get from the great men around me."

Walter was to underestimate the impact he would make on his first tour. Initially benefiting from a groin injury suffered by Schuster, which allowed him to feature in successive matches against Pontypool, Swansea, Neath and Llanelli, he operated with such panache that many of the correspondents accompanying the team were spiritedly advocating his appointment to the test backline.

As it turned out, the selectors retained the status quo, teaming Schuster with Fox against Wales and Ireland. But it was, apparently, a close-run thing, and in the final week of the tour, when coach Wyllie broke the joyous news to Little, when Joe Stanley was ruled out with injury, that he would be playing outside Fox against the Barbarians at Twickenham, he realised he had come desperately close to test selection. "Grizz...it was a long time before I was confident enough to call him that...said that I'd had a great tour and that in any other circumstances I would have got a test. But he considered that against the Welsh in Cardiff and the Irish in Dublin experience was the safest investment. It wasn't until that discussion with Grizz that I realised I had been a contender for test selection."

Little earned some marvellous reviews for his performances against the always-tough Welsh clubs.

Of his game against Pontypool, Don Cameron (*New Zealand Herald*) said, "Perhaps Botica and Little appealed most of all – Little because he turns what looks like quiet efficiency into quite unexpected riches."

Rugby News reported on the "sensational impact" Little was making.

"The amazing qualities he demonstrated throughout the domestic season - there wasn't a backline in New Zealand he could not penetrate - have become obvious at the higher level," it claimed. "After replacing Schuster against Swansea he sliced through the defence with ludicrous ease. Already comparisons are being made between Little and the great J. B. Smith. Like Smith, he doesn't immediately appeal as a talented sportsman, but once he receives the ball, he rises on to his toes and anything is possible."

Lindsay Knight wrote in the *Auckland Star* that "for such a small man Little has an extraordinary ability to break tackles. He is one of the most significant newcomers and until incumbent Schuster produced a brilliant game against Newport on the eve of the Welsh international, Little appeared to have made the test second-five berth his own."

And former All Black winger Stu Wilson, writing in *Truth*, insisted that the second-five spot against Wales was clear cut. "On present form Walter Little has to be given the opportunity to show his skills at test level."

Little, obviously because of his youth and innocence, didn't detect in Wales the same level of hostility encountered by many of his team mates. He was aware, though, of extreme fanaticism. He recalls walking through Swansea with Ian Jones and Craig Innes and being confronted by all sorts of people, all of whom were adamant that Wales was going to defeat the All Blacks. "Even little old ladies with shopping bags were warning us of the fate that awaited us at Cardiff Arms Park," recalls Little. "They all assured us that their team was the best and that they were going to beat us." It was only the little old ladies who would have remembered Wales' last defeat of the All Blacks – in 1953.

For most of his outings in Wales and Ireland, Little was partnered with Botica. The only two occasions he teamed with Fox were against Llanelli and the Barbarians. And against Llanelli it wouldn't have mattered if Richard Loe had worn the No 10 jersey, so diabolical were the conditions. A wind of hurricane force blew throughout, making orthodox rugby impossible.

Playing into the storm in the second half, the All Blacks were interested only in retaining possession which the forwards did magnificently. They had Llanelli perpetually in retreat as they drove ahead relentlessly, using players running one off the ruck, league style.

Occasionally the forwards would ask for a breather and the backs would take their turn at driving ahead. Even pint-sized Foxy got involved. "At least," says Little, "it was warm in the middle of those rucks."

Fox, Little, Joe Stanley and Craig Innes all took turns at first-five, partly to rest the forwards but more pertinently because it took them away from the biting cold and driving rain. Conditions really couldn't have been more miserable, with wind gusts of 108mph being recorded only a few kilometres from Stradey Park that afternoon.

Little labels Wellington, Toulouse and Llanelli as the windiest cities in which he has played rugby, but says nothing matches that day in Wales.

He had been warned that he would find the Irish physically more demanding than the Welsh but he says he still wasn't prepared for the onslaught when the All Blacks engaged Leinster at Lansdowne Road.

"When they told me the Irish would be physical, I thought, oh yeah, I've encountered some pretty rugged opponents in my time," says Little, "but I got a hell of a shock. They were as hard as nails and so incredibly physical. I remember saying in the dressing room after that game in Dublin, 'Are these guys always like this?' The answer was yes.

"Throughout Ireland, they just kept coming at us. They loved tackling and hurting. They fearlessly put their bodies on the line. They weren't the most skilful players, in most cases, but they all gave one hundred and twenty per cent.

"And afterwards they were the nicest people, more interested in what the Guinness tasted like than whether the referee had made the right decisions. They'd take you to four or five different pubs in one night and as long as you drank Guinness, everything was on the house. What a great place to visit!

"There would be singalongs and a lot of story telling. I'd have to say it is probably the best country I have ever toured. It would be a tragedy if the advent of professionalism meant the end of rugby visits to Ireland."

Playing against the Barbarians, a virtual British Lions selection plus Wallaby ace Nick Farr-Jones, was tantamount to a test appearance, in Little's eyes, especially as the game was played out in front of a capacity 60,000 audience at Twickenham.

Nervousness began to overcome him as the match drew closer and he didn't sleep the night before the game. He tried focusing on a few hundred of New Zealand's sixty million sheep to induce drowsiness but the sheep were always wearing black and white jerseys and kept stampeding towards him.

He was grateful when match day dawned and when all the formalities, which included an introduction to Princess Anne, were over and he could focus on his role as a second-five opposite two midfielders of vast experience and rapidly growing reputations, Jeremy Guscott and Scott Hastings.

Little had heard colleagues say they were surprised at how fast test matches rushed by, and that's exactly how he found this game. "Somehow you had the feeling the game was over before it had started – I couldn't believe how quickly the eighty minutes raced by.

"The pace of the game was the other shock. When you step from club to provincial level the speed increases. The tempo gets faster again when you advance to international level. And test matches, into which category you would place that Barbarians contest, are the fastest of the lot. You quickly appreciate that it's the ability to make instant decisions at that level that separates the men from the boys."

Although the Barbarians led 10-6 at halftime and stayed within striking range until four minutes from time, Little never gave defeat a consideration. "The biggest motivation for the All Blacks," he says, "is the fear of losing. No one wants to be part of a New Zealand team that loses."

Defeat wasn't something that troubled Shelford's men. They proved invincible, winning all fourteen matches and running up record scores against Wales at Cardiff (34) and Ireland in Dublin (23).

Little considers that the investment in the four Colts paid a rich dividend. Innes played both tests, Walter got the Barbarians game and both Tuigamala and Ridge impressed mightily in their mostly midweek outings.

"Ridgey was unlucky in being in John Gallagher's shadow, because Kipper was probably the best fullback in the world at the time, a great impact player."

Little appreciated the fact that players like Joe Stanley, John Kirwan (who was in plaster from the third game but remained on tour), Fox, Bernie McCahill, skipper Shelford and Zinzan Brooke took the time to help the younger players.

"As a newcomer, you don't go along just for the Tiki tour, you go along to learn and to get the feel for international rugby. That's where you rely on the experienced players to guide you."

Two years later when he returned to the UK for the World Cup, Little was to appreciate just how fortunate he, and the other colts, had been to travel under Buck Shelford's inspiring leadership. Things were to deteriorate rather alarmingly. And he would find out what it felt like to be part of an All Black team that lost.

Little reflected on a boomer year as he flew back home to New Zealand. From the New Zealand Barbarians outing at the beginning of April to his appearance against the British Barbarians late in November there had been any number of highlights in 1989 and precious few low points, just the occasional niggling knee injury.

He celebrated his year of achievement by holidaying with brother Lawrence in Sydney, bunking down with two of his other brothers Eddie and Kevin. "It was," he recalls, "an opportunity to put some colour back into my skin. You don't see a lot of sunshine when you make a rugby tour of the UK!"

As he soaked up the scorching Sydney sunshine and contemplated the new season, Little could not possibly have envisaged the sensational happenings that would reverberate through New Zealand rugby in 1990.

First of all, Russ Thomas was sacked as chairman of the NZRFU, the Canterbury stalwart giving way to Eddie Tonks.

That didn't make half as much impact on Little as the sequence of events in May that saw Matthew Ridge, John Gallagher, John Schuster and Frano Botica all defect to league following the Palmerston North All Black trials in which they had all participated.

While their departures were terrible news for Grizz Wyllie and his fellow selectors, they represented encouragement for Little. Suddenly the All Blacks needed a new second-five for the upcoming tests against Scotland.

The losses to league impacted first on North Harbour, and while coach Thorburn searched for a worthy replacement for Botica, he used Little at first-five, eventually replacing him with Little's old schoolboy rival Jamie Cameron, who was only twenty.

Little didn't presume he would bound into the test team. He expected the selectors to resort to older players and set his own target as making the squad of twenty-one.

So he was over the moon when he was named at second-five for the first international against the Scots at Carisbrook. Not so fortunate was his good mate Innes who was relegated to the reserves bench to accommodate a fully repaired John Kirwan. Taranaki veteran Kieran Crowley was brought in to fill the yawning gap at fullback caused through the loss of Gallagher and Ridge. Crowley's recall at 28 was greeted with derision in many quarters, though the player himself took it all in his stride. "Such criticism is water off a duck's back to me," he said. "I've experienced it all before."

Little admits to greater excitement at finding himself in the test team than learning of his original selection in the All Blacks nine months earlier. "It was, for me, the ultimate," he says. "It's what every player strives for. And knowing that I would be operating between Grant Fox and Joe Stanley gave a feeling a reassurance."

Foxy, The Operator, arrived in Dunedin prepared like no other player Little had ever known. He remembered from the Barbarians game that besides taking all the kicks, Foxy called all the shots, which suited Little, in his first major challenge, just fine. As a teenager, he was delighted to have a master inside him outlining every movement in advance.

At the Shoreline Hotel in Dunedin, an All Black retreat almost as familiar to the players as the Poenamo in Auckland, Foxy diligently handed out sheets of paper to every player in the team detailing moves. Walter was amazed. He'd never struck anything like it before.

"It was all so professionally done," says Little. "There were moves for when the backline was moving left to right, moves for going right to left, moves for midfield situations. And everything was detailed. Skip ones, skip twos, cuts…they were all there, in total probably thirty to forty options. And all with names.

"I knew the majority of them from the 1989 tour. A lot were basic moves used by most provincial teams under different names. A few were straight from the Auckland handbook which made sense seeing more than half the test team came from the champion Auckland team.

"It just proved how incredibly well prepared Foxy was. He not only practised his own skills and his goalkicking endlessly, but he put in all this preparation on behalf of the team. No wonder he was acknowledged as a matchwinner.'

Although Foxy was very much The General, and called the shots, Little came to appreciate that Stanley, at centre, wielded a strong influence on the team and was the only individual who ever over-ruled calls by Fox.

"As the new boy, I wasn't canvassed for an opinion, which suited me fine. As I established myself in the position, it started to become a frustration, but at the time it was a dream to be operating between Fox and Stanley. I never had to wonder what I would do next. Foxy always instructed me, and if he didn't, Joe did!"

Fox's preparation didn't finish with the distribution of the team move sheets. He also had a major input at team meetings, and it was apparent to Walter that he must have studied countless videos because he seemed to be able to pinpoint the strengths and the weaknesses of virtually every member of the opposition.

"I was amazed at how he knew so much," said Little. "It was a revelation. Peter Thorburn was excellent at assessing opponents as North Harbour coach but Foxy was unbelievable – he'd done so much homework."

So by the time Little stepped on to Carisbrook on June 16 for his international debut he had stored away in his mind an extensive dossier on both of his midfield opponents - Scott Hastings (whom he'd opposed at Twickenham) and Sean Lineen, the New Zealander who'd gone to Edinburgh and made good.

Walter wasn't sure what model car they drove or the name of their local pub, but, thanks to Foxy, he was confident there was nothing they could do on the rugby field that he wouldn't anticipate.

Hastings, Little and Stanley acknowledged, was a hard runner who was dangerous because of his strength. It was important to stop him before he gathered momentum. "We determined to use defence as an attacking weapon," says Little. "The benefits would be two-fold. It would stop Hastings advancing and the confrontational aspect, applied from the beginning, would help me settle my nerves."

The theory was impeccable. Putting it into practice was something else. And when Lineen dummied and scored between the posts in the sixth minute, Stanley and Little, who'd been embarrassingly upstaged, looked at each other and said simultaneously, "What happened there?"

What happened was that as Scotland attacked from a second phase situation on the New Zealand 22, Lineen and Hastings worked a dummy cut move. Little and Stanley were ready for the cut but not the dummy. They both found themselves advancing menacingly on Hastings while Lineen retained the ball and danced through for a sweet four-pointer.

"We'd talked defensive patterns for three days," says Little. "We thought we had every eventuality covered but they got through us. It was a worry but we got things sorted out. It didn't happen again, that was the main thing."

Displaying great enterprise and resolve, the All Blacks charged in for five tries (to Scotland's three) to win a thoroughly enterprising encounter – staged in sparkling Dunedin weather – by 31 points to 16.

Little thought he was going to mark his test debut with a try. Having run the blindside from broken play, he chipped a kick through towards the goalline to beat Scotland's last two defenders. It was a straightforward sprint for the touchdown but as Walter zeroed in on the ball, someone shouldered him aside and claimed the try for himself. "Lo and behold," recalls Little, "it was Ian Jones. It was his first test and obviously he was more desperate than me for a try."

The Carisbrook victory extended the All Blacks' winning sequence (dating back to 1987) to 47 matches and the 48th was considered a formality when the teams clashed again at Eden Park seven days later, notwithstanding the fact that the Scots had come to New Zealand as the Five Nations champions.

Victory, however, was anything but a formality and the All Blacks had to fall back on Fox's trusty boot to secure a hard-earned victory by 21 points to 18. While Little considered the Scots to be the hungrier team, he says there was no shortage of commitment among the All Blacks when the pressure went on. "We certainly didn't want to be the first New Zealand team to lose to Scotland."

Although the All Blacks were to come in for a lot of criticism over their performance, Little was delighted to have launched his test career with two victories. He felt he had contributed significantly to the Dunedin win but had been thrust into a defensive role at Eden Park.

The Auckland game was to have a sensational sequel when the captain Buck Shelford was dropped, the first such dumping of a test captain since Pat Vincent in 1956. Shelford's axing was to cause a public uproar and spark a Bring Back Buck campaign which survived till long after Shelford had gone beyond his used-by date.

Zinzan Brooke was introduced at No 8 for the first test against Bob Dwyer's Wallabies while Gary Whetton assumed the leadership. Missing, at test level for the first time since 1986, was Joe Stanley, who had voluntarily stepped down because of a persistent viral infection. It meant Little would form the midfield combination with his great friend Craig Innes.

When Grizz Wyllie pulled Little and Innes out of the team room on the morning of the test in Christchurch, they wondered what could possibly be amiss. It had to be something pretty serious judging by Grizz's scowl, Little thought.

"Now listen," he said, when he had them alone. "Dwyer (the Australian coach) has been spouting his mouth off and he reckons you two are the weakness in the All Black team.

"That means they'll be targeting you. If by the end of the game it turns out that you two are a weakness then we've got big problems.

"So don't let those Aussie bastards get the better of you. Okay?"

Little and Innes returned to the team room harbouring a powerful feeling of outrage. "How dare anyone brand Postie and me the weak links?", Little remembers thinking. "We'd played alongside each other from primary school level and were invariably part of our teams' strengths. And that was because we were both excellent defenders. Now here was someone daring to suggest we represented a weakness."

They smouldered away. And by the time they ran on to Lancaster Park their opposites, Tim Horan and Paul Cornish, were marked men. Grizz's words had really fired them up. "There was no way we were going to let Grizz, or the team, down," said Little.

Far from becoming the All Blacks' soft underbelly, Little and Innes emerged as one of their team's special strengths. In defence, they contained Horan and Cornish for the entire eighty minutes while as attackers they set the backline alight, flummoxing the Wallabies with a series of snappy, cut-out passes that sent the All Blacks regularly hurtling towards the tryline.

Innes was arguably the player of the day, featuring in all four New Zealand tries. He created scores for John Kirwan and Kieran Crowley with superb cut-out passes, set up the ruck from which Sean Fitzpatrick went across and grabbed a four-pointer himself right on halftime.

Having improved infinitely on the display against Scotland, the All Blacks were a contented bunch as they unwound in the dressing room (the final score being a resounding 21 points to 6).

Little and Innes were sitting together as their coach sought them out. "Well done, guys," he said. That, according to Little, was effusive praise from the grizzled one. "He never wasted words. To earn anything more than a grunt meant you'd had a monumental influence on the outcome. Postie and I put our arms around each other. It was an occasion to treasure."

When they relaxed in the team room back at their hotel, they made sure they drank a special toast…to the Wallaby coach Bob Dwyer.

"I wonder," said Innes, "what he will do to fire us up for Eden Park!"

New Zealand's victory in the second test, in a game of lost opportunities for Australia, brought up 50 matches without defeat (a milestone achieved only once previously by the All Blacks). But the game was spoiled as a spectacle by a near gale force wind that swept down Eden Park.

The conditions militated against flowing rugby, so tactician Fox determined that it was safer to play a crash-bash game in midfield rather than continually work the ball wide (as in Christchurch) and risk losing sixty metres of ground through one mistake. So Little and Innes became involved in a lot of unpretty, but effective, crunching play in midfield.

Four days later North Harbour took on the Wallabies but not even an audacious 14-man maul – a typical example of coach Thorburn's inventiveness – could swing this game Harbour's way. Fourteen thousand five hundred fans crammed into Onewa Domain (the biggest attendance ever at this seriously inadequate venue) but their hopes of seeing Harbour win its first fixture against a major overseas touring team were destroyed by the power of the Wallaby scrum and the dynamic tackling of Tim Horan.

All great winning sequences have to come to an end at some stage and the All Blacks' stunning 50-match run, which started at the World Cup in 1987, was halted most emphatically by the Wallabies on a bleak afternoon at Athletic Park.

The Dallas Cowboys Cheerleaders (flown in to provide the pre-match entertainment) encountered extreme difficulty in handling the freezing conditions and muddy surface and the All Blacks didn't fare any better, going down by 21 points to 9, with Wallaby hooker Phil Kearns scoring the game's only try.

Many experts have tried to account for New Zealand's dismal showing that day. It certainly wasn't a performance worthy of the world's best rugby team.

Some saw it as symptomatic of the problems that were welling deep within the All Blacks, problems that would manifest themselves much more seriously in 1991. While Little acknowledges that, he says he was too fresh to the test scene to pinpoint the faults at the time. What he did feel contributed enormously to the result was the Australians' determination to salvage the career of their coach Bob Dwyer.

"His critics back in Australia had been demanding his scalp," said Little. "A loss in Wellington meant a whitewash in the series, and inevitably Dwyer would have been sacked. From my observations his players regarded him too highly to let that happen. Rather like Craig and I in Christchurch, they were desperate men when they ran on to Athletic Park, and for desperate men, anything is possible."

With the series already secure, the All Blacks lacked that desperateness. Having gone four years without defeat, there was a sense of invincibility about the team that Little detected. "There was this feeling that no matter what happened, the All Blacks would come through and win. Well, in dreadful conditions and against a resolute opponent, this time they didn't."

Little found the reaction in the dressing room rather unnerving. "A lot of the players, particularly the Aucklanders, had never experienced defeat at top level and they didn't know how to take it. They were stunned. I personally have always considered that a loss now and then strengthens a team, but I didn't have the feeling that every All Black was going to be the stronger for this reverse.

"We had played badly and lost. To my mind, that's easier to rectify than playing badly and winning. It seemed to me that several of my team mates felt they had played badly and should still have won – simply because the All Blacks always won. The symptoms weren't looking good."

It turned into a bleak month for Little. The Wellington reverse was the middle of five successive losing games he played in, the others being with North Harbour which was having trouble getting its act together. Indeed, Harbour, having finished a gallant third in the national championship in 1989, this time slumped to a disappointing sixth placing.

The consolation would have been lifting the Ranfurly Shield off Auckland but Harbour's brave challenge was defused when referee David Bishop disallowed a try by Richard Turner after Harbour had startled Auckland with another of its monster (14-man) mauls.

Photographic evidence revealed Turner grounding the ball (twenty minutes from time with his team trailing 9-18) but Bishop was unsighted, claiming he couldn't see what was happening under the seething mass of bodies.

The North Harbour players having stayed in a motel overnight before the shield challenge, and performed so heroically, the team management decided it would be a good idea to repeat the process before the final NPC fixture against Waikato in Hamilton.

"It was a daft idea from the start," said Little. "We didn't stay overnight in Hamilton but at a motel in Auckland, journeying down by bus on the morning of the game. It was designed to build harmony in the team, but the guys would have been better in their own homes doing what they usually do on Friday nights.

"The end result was a nightmare showing against Waikato who put sixty-two points on us. There was a lot of pressure on me and halfback Paul McGahan to perform, because we'd just been named in the All Black team to tour France. But our team never fired. Passes we would normally hold, we dropped. The Waikato guys suddenly realised they were on to a good thing and started attacking from their own goalline. It was terribly embarrassing. I couldn't wait for the final whistle to sound so I could go home."

There remained one further adventure for Little, and the All Blacks, in 1990 – an eight match tour of France. Little thought he might be the only North Harbour player involved (Shelford being still unwanted by the selectors and Botica now belonging to league) but Paul McGahan, known to his mates as Mad Dog, was named as Graeme Bachop's deputy at halfback.

Shelford and Botica were in town to celebrate Little's and McGahan's selections. They warned that France was probably the hardest tour going because of the language problems, the skill and volatility of the French players and the eccentricities of the referees.

If their forecasts were ominous – and confirmed when a lethal Cote d'Azur selection gave the All Blacks a hiding in the opening encounter – the up side was that with thirty players along for only eight matches, individuals had plenty of leisure time.

Now France being renowned for its epicurean delights, one night in La Rochelle, Walter Little, Craig Innes and John Timu decided to check out the cuisine at one of the town's classier restaurants.

This was no steak-eggs-and-chips night. This was a when-in-France night.

The boys decided grenouille (frogs legs) and escargots (snails) represented the ultimate in entrees, so these were ordered. And in the meantime they sharpened their palates by knocking back several beers each.

Their bravado dipped sharply when the frogs legs and escargots were delivered to the table. They regarded the dishes suspiciously.

"Who's going to be first?" asked Innes.

No one volunteered.

"Well," said Timu, a man of the world, "let's decide this democratically. We'll play paper, scissors and rock."

So with the locals looking on with intrigue, the Kiwi jokers played an earnest series of paper, scissors and rock, till Innes was declared the loser.

"After you," said Walter, who was beginning to think that the pizza house down the road might have been the better option.

Innes cautiously bit into a frog's leg, his mates looking on in awe. "Mmmmm," he declared, "tastes a bit like chicken – not bad at all."

Timu and Little joined in, both conceding that the legs of frogs tasted much nicer than they looked.

"I can't ever see them getting on to the menu at McDonalds," observed Timu. "Frogs legs and chips doesn't sound right!"

The snails were a hit, once the boys had worked out how to manipulate the tongs and prise the creatures out.

Entrees completed, they opted for more orthodox fare for their main courses, requesting steaks "bien cuits."

Bien cuit (well done) was one of the few French phrases the All Blacks mastered on tour. It was shouted at waiters regularly despite which they continued to serve up steaks prepared rare, or at best medium rare.

Little remembers it as one of the great nights of the tour. "It was back to chicken, salad and bread in the team room after that."

On another occasion, in Paris, half a dozen of the players decided to visit the Eiffel Tower. Among them was Inga Tuigamala who, it transpired, had a fear of heights.

He was coaxed into the lift on the assurance that the troops were only going as far as the first level.

"He freaked out," says Walter, "when he looked through the cracks in the floor and saw the ground hundreds of feet below."

When Tuigamala's colleagues announced that they were going to journey up to the second level, and would collect him on the way down, he panicked.

"Don't leave me here!" he pleaded. So they didn't. They bundled him into the nearest lift which he prayed would descend. To his horror, it went up.

"Suddenly we were on the second level," says Little, "which is unbelievably high." Inga froze. He refused to go anywhere near the viewing area, remaining rigid a few steps from the lift.

Eventually his mates returned him to terra firma. "He was not amused," says Little. "He wouldn't talk to us for the rest of the day."

Little played four matches, including the internationals at Nantes and Paris, and was on the winning side every time. He was in the grandstand when the team suffered its two losses, at Toulon and Bayonne.

The test victories were decisive and deeply satisfying. Fox had assured him that defeating France in France provided one of rugby's best feelings.

Although Little had few chances to demonstrate his attacking skills, he didn't mind particularly, because the battle plan, revolving around forward power and Fox's boot, was awesomely effective.

He found that Fox and the skipper Gary Whetton essentially ran the show, in cahoots with Wyllie.

"Everything we practised came off on the field," says Little. "After the two provincial losses we were under extreme pressure to win the tests. And we did that emphatically."

Little says he completed the tour knowing little more about Whetton than at the start. "I knew him as a player but I never got to know him as a person. None of the young guys did. That was because the older brigade in the All Blacks stuck to themselves."

9

Trying To Live With Foxy

G rant Fox was a rugby phenomenon. He achieved legendary status while still playing because of his clinical precision as a kicker of the ball, both for goal and tactically, and for the massive influence he wielded on the teams he represented.

With Foxy, who was seemingly indestructible, operating in the No 10 jersey, Auckland and New Zealand proved nigh on invincible in the latter half of the 1980s.

During the Fox era, the All Blacks claimed a World Cup and went 50 matches without defeat while Auckland almost monotonously pulverised opponents in Ranfurly Shield and national championship matches as well as defeating such celebrated touring teams as England, Argentina and Australia.

There were fifteen players fielded on every occasion, but Fox's influence was massive. So unfailingly accurate was he as a kicker that his teams used his re-starts as an attacking weapon. In addition to which he plotted team tactics and called the moves while shattering just about every pointscoring record in the book.

He was the subject of a This Is Your Life television programme, and it's fair to say most of Auckland and New Zealand's opponents were enormously relieved when he announced his retirement in 1993.

So it borders on the blasphemous when Little declares that he didn't enjoy operating outside the great man in 1990 and 1991.

Now let's be certain we've got this entirely in context. Little appreciated mightily the coaching (and general) advice that Foxy passed on to him. He marvelled at the man's preparation before every international match. He was envious of his ability to land tactical kicks on a ten cent piece and bisect the uprights with his place kicks nine times out of ten. He concedes that he was the greatest matchwinner probably in the history of the game. And he liked him as a person.

But having to operate outside him as an All Black became a source of considerable frustration for Little who felt that he was permanently stifled.

Having made gigantic progress on the tour of Wales and Ireland, when he was mostly partnered with his North Harbour colleague Frano Botica, whose attacking ideals exactly matched his, Little found himself the meat between the Fox and Stanley sandwich when he made the step-up to test level in 1990.

Essentially, if Fox didn't kick the ball or link with his forwards, he threw a skip pass straight to Stanley at centre. Little's chief requirement, in Fox's plan, was to power up the middle and set up second-phase possession.

"And that," he says, "is basically all I did while playing between Foxy and Joe. I was never given the chance to express myself. Foxy didn't believe in us having a go from our own twenty-two, which frustrated me for a start, because I have always seen that as the best attacking zone on the field.

"Fortunately, things improved when Craig Innes came in at centre because that broke up the Fox-Stanley combination.

"I'm not saying I didn't appreciate being there as an All Black. I would have played on the side of the scrum, if Foxy had ordered it. What I am saying, is that by using me as a battering ram, he removed the opportunity for me to express myself. The tactics we employed most certainly did not suit my style of rugby."

Little's frustrations intensified in 1991 when, after a mediocre, injury-troubled tour of Argentina, he was dropped following the first Bledisloe Cup test in Sydney. He was accused of playing poorly but says Fox didn't give him a pass from set play inside the first hour.

The demotion hurt because it elevated Bernie McCahill to the test fifteen where he was retained for the World Cup campaign, Little going along purely as a back-up player.

John Hart, who started 1991 as an All Black selector and finished it as co-coach with Alex Wyllie at the World Cup, concedes that by 1990 Fox had "probably become too dominant" as an individual.

"It was a difficult decision to replace Little with McCahill in 1991," says Hart (speaking in 1996 as the current All Black coach), "but we had to do something to stimulate the backline. That was not all Little's fault, I appreciate. He obviously suffered because of what was happening inside him. Walter, being the quiet person that he is, obviously wasn't standing up to Fox and demanding more involvement.

"Grant had become too dominant. So when we introduced McCahill (for the second Bledisloe Cup test in Auckland) it was with instructions that Fox move all second phase ball on, for Bernie to make the essential decisions. In our judgment, Walter would not have had the confidence to take that responsibility."

Peter Thorburn, Little's coach at North Harbour, was dismayed at the way Little was used in 1990 and 1991.

"They froze him out of the game," says Thorburn. "They used him as a battering ram which was a terrible thing for someone with such innate attacking skills. They should have used Craig Innes for that job. He was physically better equipped.

"Walter is above all else a confidence player. If you've got him in your backline, it's thirty to forty per cent better off straight away. He doesn't even need to know what's going on – you just need to value his ability."

"The All Blacks trained at Onewa Domain before they flew to Sydney. They were sharp, they looked good. I felt they were back to their best and I predicted they would beat the Wallabies. But they went into their shell after a promising start and were well beaten.

"Walter was reportedly dropped because he was not distributing the ball well enough. So I got hold of the video tape and played it several times. You know what – it was the sixty-third minute before Walter received the ball from set play. The next time they gave him the ball the score was 21-9.

"They never used him properly. They just kept asking him to power ahead and set up ruck ball. He's such a good kid, he'd do it all day if asked. But it was a criminal waste of talent."

Things started going wrong for Little in 1991 at the All Black trials in Rotorua. In tackling his good mate Craig Innes he badly twisted his ankle. What's worse, he heard a crack and presumed he'd broken something.

When x-rays revealed nothing but bad bruising, he was relieved and declared himself available for the All Black tour of Argentina.

He wishes now he had withdrawn while the injury mended. For a start, the ankle troubled him throughout, preventing him from producing his best form. And as a destination, he loathed Argentina.

"It was a long tour (nine matches), made longer because of the injury," says Little, who required painkilling injections every time he took the field.

"The language was a problem, the liaison officers were difficult and seemed to get everything wrong and every function was late.

"The tour, in the year of the World Cup, was ill timed. Three games and one test would have been fine. Nine games and two tests became a great bore."

Little simply did not relate to Argentina and says if there was another tour there, he would probably declare himself unavailable.

Back home, the ankle continued to trouble him, despite regular physiotherapy treatment. He had the feeling there was something seriously wrong, but kept playing.

Next up was the first of the Bledisloe Cup double-headers in Sydney. The All Blacks had beaten the Pumas well enough to be regarded as satisfactorily on track for their World Cup campaign (if you disregarded the rumours about certain senior players beginning to lose confidence in coach Wyllie). The hiding from the Wallabies at Wellington the previous August had been carefully filed away under "aberration."

Little was amongst those full of optimism for Sydney. The team had trained strongly in Auckland, the Sydney weather was sparkling and the battle plan was to move the ball wide. Everything pointed to a successful performance.

It was anything but. Less than two months out from the World Cup, the All Blacks had been seriously exposed (again) by Bob Dwyer's Wallabies. The final scoreline of 21-12 flattered the All Blacks.

Wyllie's reputation was rudely dented, causing such alarm in New Zealand rugby circles that chairman Eddie Tonks announced that John Hart would join Wyllie in preparing the team for the rematch (a fortnight later) at Eden Park.

Little was pumping petrol into his car at a garage in Taupo, where he had attended a twenty-first birthday celebration, when a news bulletin on the local radio station made him aware that he and loose forward Andy Earl had been relegated to the reserves for the second test, being replaced by McCahill and Mark Carter.

"That made for a depressing drive home," says Little. "The ramifications were all too obvious. If McCahill succeeded, he would be retained at second-five for the World Cup. The best I could hope for was to go along as the back-up, if they took me at all.

"I saw it all as an Auckland conspiracy. John Hart was coming in as co-coach and suddenly two Aucklanders were being introduced to the team. Funny that! Mind you, I was feeling seedy from the birthday party, so I wasn't in my most magnanimous mood."

After the team had assembled Earl and Little took themselves off for a bitch session. Earl told Little that he'd left his farm to dedicate himself to the All Blacks' World Cup campaign. He considered he'd given his guts in the Sydney international only to be dropped. He said right at that moment he'd rather be back on the farm.

If Little believed he'd suffered enough misfortune that season, he was wrong. During the All Blacks' first training session, at Hobsonville, he aggravated the ankle injury and was forced to withdraw as a reserve (Joe Stanley being brought in to replace him).

A further x-ray this time revealed what had been wrong all along - he had chipped the bone. Suddenly he understood why the ankle had caused him so much discomfort. However, because of the length of time since the original injury, it was considered plaster would not hasten the mending. Strapping and rest were deemed sufficient.

Feeling thoroughly miserable, he checked out of the team hotel and took himself home. Which is where he watched the second Bledisloe Cup encounter of 1991, having first placed a tray of beer in the fridge.

After playing ten tests in a row, it wasn't easy for him watching the boys perform the haka. He found it hard to stomach, knowing he could have been there. He says it made him realise how lucky he was to represent the All Blacks.

As the game unfolded, he found himself piqued with the amount of ball McCahill was receiving. "Foxy was continually shovelling the ball on to him," says Little. "Bernie was calling some of the shots and having the occasional run. It was a dramatic change from what I'd been used to outside Fox. I have to say I was thoroughly brassed off with what was occurring.

"I don't blame Bernie. He's a thorough gentleman, a player I have always been able to relate to. What was happening was plainly a decision of the coaches. Why couldn't they have insisted Foxy varied his tactics when I was operating outside him?"

Because the All Blacks won, by two of Fox's penalty goals to one by Michael Lynagh (who kicked abominably), with McCahill contributing significantly to the performance, Little knew that his prospects of playing a leading part in the World Cup had nosedived. And that was presuming his ankle came right. The immediate outlook was depressing. He returned to the fridge for another beer.

If Little was frustrated at the way Fox treated him in the All Blacks, he certainly didn't have any comparable problems while representing North Harbour. And that's because in 1991, Thorburn used him at first-five. Little, his ankle now strengthened, turned in memorable performances in the national championship fixtures against Wellington and Canterbury.

The Wellington match, at Athletic Park, was important for Little. It was his last opportunity to convince the New Zealand selectors that he was physically and mentally ready for the World Cup tournament. His masterly display from first-five gave them all the reassurance they needed, providing a timely reminder that he was also a skilful exponent in Fox's specialist position.

The game was also notable for the fact that it was the first time Little and Frank Bunce had teamed together for North Harbour, although as with their initial outing together, for the Barbarians in 1989, they were well separated – Little was at first-five, Bunce on the wing, with Cliff Mytton and Scott Pierce between them.

If Little was impressive against Wellington, he was the talk of the nation after his spectacular showing against Canterbury at Takapuna a week later.

Don Cameron wrote in the *New Zealand Herald* that Little "was all bustle and go, slashing through holes that no one else might see, let alone penetrate."

Cameron became quite lyrical after that. "The sight of Little in full flight, the eyes gleaming, the head hunched forward, those flashing legs defying the tackler, those fluent hands ready to flick the ball away when his genius was spent, had the wrinkled ones hugging themselves with delight."

In more mundane style Trevor McKewen wrote in the *Sunday News* that Little's performance against Canterbury was one of the truly memorable individual displays of the 1991 season. "Which begs the question," said McKewen, "will one of the most gifted players in the game be merely a spare part at the World Cup or an integral cog of the All Black machine?"

Thorburn took advantage of Little's rip-snorting play to promote him publicly as the World Cup campaign approached.

"He shows game after game for North Harbour just what he's able to do if given the ball," said Thorburn. "He's a touch and flair player.

"There isn't anybody in the country who can touch him for footwork skills, for balance or for his ability to run second phase ball and breach the defence.

"They are the aspects of his game that have been wasted at All Black level."

If Little's supporters thought they could influence All Black coaches Wyllie and Hart, they were wrong. McCahill was their man at second-five, and that was that.

Hart told McKewen in an interview before the team flew off to the UK to defend its world crown that McCahill ensured "a more effective organisation" in the backline.

"That isn't a criticism of Walter Little." he said, "I've told him personally, it was simply a case of getting the best mix. You can't beat experience when things aren't quite jelling and I think McCahill's experience showed through in that (Eden Park) test in terms of what he brought to the backline."

Little knew when he wasn't selected for the tournament opener, against England at Twickenham, that he was condemned to a mere support role for the whole tournament.

"World Cups aren't like normal rugby tours," says Little. "Every match is a key international and once the leading fifteen players are established, they are usually retained intact. Only injuries or a disastrous performance would lead to a turnaround in selection policy once the tournament is under way."

While pleased to be involved, Little was deeply disappointed at being relegated to the reserves bench because he knew there was no opportunity to push for the starting fifteen. So he resolved to go out and enjoy himself in any games he did get.

His one outing while the All Blacks remained in contention for glory was against Italy on a Sunday at Leicester. Teaming up with Fox again, he was surprised at how ragged the All Blacks had become. Embarrassed by the volatile Italians, they hung on for a 31-21 victory. It was the latest in a now worrying sequence of unconvincing performances by the All Blacks.

In Little's mind, the onfield decline reflected the disintegration of the All Blacks as a team. The wheels had started to fall off in Argentina and by the World Cup there were serious fractures within the team, starting from the top.

"Wyllie and Hart were incompatible, that was obvious," said Little. "How anyone thought they could ever work together, I'll never know. But that wasn't the root cause of the trouble, because individually, as two marvellously well qualified coaches, they were doing their best to ensure the team won the trophy.

"The greater problem, I believe, existed within the team where various factions splintered away. Cliques had been allowed to develop, the most obvious one involving the senior Auckland players.

"We'd lost the spirit of '89. We'd ceased to be a team, in the true sense of the word. Guys were going off and doing their own thing all the time. We were a combination of groups, not one strong unit all pulling together. And that's why we lost."

Little points the finger accusingly at the skipper Gary Whetton who, he says, gave scant encouragement to the newer members of the team. "He'd been part of two magnificently successful teams (Auckland and the All Blacks), with essentially the same players, for so long, that he couldn't really be bothered with the new guys coming through.

"Also, he didn't know how to handle defeat and he wasn't prepared for it. He obviously believed the All Blacks would go on winning forever, regardless. He was in for a rude shock."

One of the few occasions when the All Blacks relaxed as a team came when Hart advised four of the youngest members of the side (Innes, Tuigamala, Timu and Little) that they were responsible for the team's eating arrangements one night in Lille.

When the word came through from the dining sub-committee that number ones were to be worn, manager John Sturgeon became decidedly edgy.

"Hell, I hope they're not taking us to a five star hotel," he said. "Our meal allowance doesn't stretch that far."

When the bus arrived, players and management, resplendent in dinner suits and bow ties, filed on board, intrigued to learn of the destination.

With Tuigamala, one of New Zealand's champion scoffers of hamburgers, involved, the players should have known. They were taken to McDonalds.

Although the menu was incomprehensible to the New Zealanders, being in French, the burgers, chips and milk shakes bore a startling resemblance to those served at McDonald franchises world wide.

Little watched sombrely from the grandstand at Lansdowne Road as the Wallabies shattered New Zealand's World Cup ambitions. He saw an All Black team that for four years had ruled the rugby world beaten for pace, for inventiveness, for urgency (until it was all too late) and for points on the board. Although the forwards won a surfeit of possession in the second half, the best the All Blacks could manage was two penalty goals by Fox, going down 16-6.

The Wallabies had done their homework well. After analysing New Zealand's quarter-final display against Canada, they ruled out halfback Graeme Bachop and five-eighths Fox and McCahill as players capable of making incisive breaks from set play and concentrated their cover defence on centre Innes and wingers John Kirwan and John Timu. To the Aussies' satisfaction, there was no bruising Inga Tuigamala to worry about (he was on the reserves bench with Little) while Timu, the star turn against Canada at Lille, had been replaced at fullback by the old warhorse Kieran Crowley, who hadn't played rugby for a couple of months.

Mission not accomplished. Little was disappointed for his fellow players but contemplative. It was the end of an era, one he felt he had seen coming. Oh well, it would mean a new world champion. More significantly, it would undoubtedly mean a cleanout of many involved with the All Blacks. The 1992 season would be an interesting one as New Zealand rugby regrouped and set fresh goals.

Little didn't immediately think about the play-off for third placing which would now involve the All Blacks. He was focusing beyond the tournament, to the historic town of Rugby where he would play out the northern winter. His girlfriend Tracy was joining him and they would head north once the All Blacks' World Cup commitments were over.

Well, for Little, the World Cup action wasn't over. McCahill, one of the disappointments of the semi-final loss, wasn't wanted for the play-off against Scotland in Cardiff. Nor were Crowley, Timu, Fox (who was injured), Mark Carter and Alan Whetton.

Little was back in business, teaming with Jon Preston and Ellis. With Tuigamala and Kirwan on the wings and Terry Wright at fullback, this was a backline geared for action.

Wyllie prepared the team for Cardiff, which Little interpreted as Grizz's last stand.

"Despite the traumatic events of the previous weekend, Grizz was excellent. He put the Australian loss behind him and got us focused on playing attacking rugby, giving us backs licence to do our own thing.

"He owed it to himself to have the team finish on a high."

Little rates Wyllie as a coach but believes his downfall was that he hung on to too many of the seasoned players too long.

"By World Cup time, the team lacked the enthusiasm that younger, keener guys would have introduced. It's not as if New Zealand rugby doesn't possess those players. The national championship is overflowing with them – talented footballers high on enthusiasm and commitment, players prepared to put their bodies on the line in ruck and tackle situations."

The enthusiasm was certainly rekindled amongst the backs, if not with all the forwards, against Scotland.

Mike Brewer dealt caustically in his autobiography with the attitude of several of the senior forwards in the play-off. "During the game," he wrote, "Steve McDowell, Sean Fitzpatrick, even Richard Loe, who had formed the best front row in world rugby, were hanging around the back of rucks and mauls, looking for a run with the ball, or just a rest. Gary Whetton...had gone to ground once and then just sat there for 10 or 15 seconds, watching play move downfield from him."

Brewer recorded that, for him, it was "the bitter end of an era."

Little was too busy trying to make things happen out back to notice the individual shortcomings of his forward pack.

And it was Little, one of the forgotten men of the campaign, who ensured the All Blacks would return home with a tangible memento of the occasion, albeit bronze rather than gold.

With the Scots, who did most of the defending but, being the doughty lot that they are, hanging on by their finger nails – trailing 6-9 with time running out – something special was required.

Michael Jones created the opportunity with a crunching tackle on Scottish halfback Gary Armstrong that freed the ball.

The All Blacks had frittered away so many genuine tryscoring opportunities their fans had given up hope of seeing another four-pointer at this tournament (the last one was in the quarter-final against Canada) when Little took over, running wide, passing to replacement winger Shayne Philpott and looping outside him to outstrip the defence. It was his first test try – in his 12th test.

David Hands, writing in *The Times,* said it was fitting that Little should provide the *coup de grace.* "How New Zealand have come to omit him from their calculations over the last month only they know but time and again he broke the advantage line, only for the handling of others to evaporate."

John Mason of the *Daily Telegraph* said that Little, paired again with Innes, "all but took charge of a match which was far from being an anti-climax. Little alone found gaps, helped by a deceptive change of pace, body swerve and sheer strength."

And Trevor McKewen's report in Wellington's *Evening Post* captured the feelings of many New Zealand rugby fans when he said, "After the sterile backline displays (by the All Blacks), how Alex Wyllie and John Hart must have wished they had persevered with Little. Four times in the first half he sliced through the (Scottish) defence with disarming ease."

Little was far and away the most effective of the New Zealand backs, turning in an attacking display far superior to anything produced by his colleagues in the preceding matches.

Was it because he was teamed with someone other than Fox? That may be an unfair assumption but at Cardiff Arms Park he certainly produced the magic Thorburn had been arguing he was capable of, given the opportunity.

Little himself was hugely relieved to share in the victory. "We didn't want to go out on a low note," he said. "The young guys, in particular, were determined to restore pride to the black jersey after the setback in Dublin. We tried to inject enjoyment and enthusiasm, commodities we felt were missing in the semi-final."

Having been seriously under-employed by the All Black selectors, Little was thirsting for rugby action when the World Cup wound up. So he was delighted to have negotiated to play the season at Rugby, the town where in 1823 William Webb Ellis did his thing.

Walter absorbed every word on the plaque at Rugby School. *This stone commemorates the exploit of William Webb Ellis who, with a fine disregard for the rules of football as played in his time, first took the ball in his arms and ran with it, thus originating the distinctive feature of the rugby game. AD 1823.*

"Good old, Ellis," mused Walter. "We are eternally grateful."

Unfortunately, the RFU's severe 12-week qualification period for overseas players meant Little couldn't turn out for Rugby's premier side (known as the Lions) until February.

Instead, he played for the second XV (the Wanderers) and had a ball.

"I'd never played for any second team in my life," said Little, "so it was a novel experience. It was all so delightfully relaxed. I loved it."

Accustomed to playing in front of crowds of up to 60,000, he sometimes had to scan the touchlines at Wanderers matches to find any spectators at all. "One day we travelled by coach for more than three hours to some tiny place in the north of England, and there were four spectators!"

He played one game at first-five but mostly operated at centre, running rampant through most defences. "I found I could do what I wanted when I had the ball. I'd usually run thirty or forty metres before anyone even threatened to tackle me."

Largely thanks to their All Black import, the Wanderers were untouchable, winning all their games, many of them by sixty or seventy points. Every player had a turn at kicking conversions.

When Little attempted to introduce planned moves at training (a la Grant Fox) he was regarded with astonishment. "We've never bothered about that sort of thing in the Wanderers," he was told. Which seemed an entirely sensible attitude, Walter thought. No point in breaking with tradition.

Walter and Tracy loved their five months in England. The club provided them with a house and car in return for playing weekends, training (gently) a couple of nights a week and coaching the boys at Princethorpe College.

It left them ample time for sightseeing expeditions and they took the opportunity to visit many of England's more famous scenic attractions.

When it came to socialising they soon realised they were victims of New Zealand's conservative upbringing. Invitations to costume parties meant Come In Costume. They ignored the command the first time and were startled to find Walter's mates arrive dressed as the Ugly Sisters.

"They really let themselves go," said Little. "When they party, they really party. It took Tracy and me a while to get into the swing of things."

The Rugby premier team got just one game out of Little – an important bottom-of-the-table clash against Nottingham late in February which ended in a nine-all draw. Icy pitches – the temperature at Rugby plummeted to minus 11 deg Celsius on one occasion – and circumstances denied him further outings.

He was eager to play in the Cup knockout matches, but a call from Peter Thorburn, telling him to get back for the All Black trials, because Laurie Mains wanted him as a centre, meant a hasty revision of his schedule.

Making It In Midfield

Frank Bunce and Walter Little were little more than casual friends when the 1992 rugby season rolled around. They'd become team mates for North Harbour the previous year after Bunce 'crossed the bridge' in search of regular representative play.

But they'd never operated together, literally. On the three occasions they'd appeared in the same Harbour line-up, Little was at first-five with Bunce out among the threequarters. Their midfield liaison was still to be formed.

Their paths never crossed at the World Cup. While Bunce was establishing himself as one of the game's foremost midfield backs with his displays for Western Samoa at Cardiff, Pontypool, Pontypridd and Edinburgh, Little was confined to the reserves bench at Twickenham, Gloucester and Lille, getting the opportunity to demonstrate his class only at Leicester and (in the play-off for third) at Cardiff.

Bunce, approaching his 30th birthday, wasn't sure what the future held for him when he returned to New Zealand except that with his new found status he was confident he could (finally) command a regular place at representative level.

He wasn't quite prepared for the startling demand upon his services.

First, he fielded a call from an official of the Canterbury Bankstown League Club in Sydney. They were looking for someone to partner Jarrod McCracken in midfield and they'd been hugely impressed with Bunce's performances at the World Cup. They said they were looking for a player "good on his feet."

Bunce was flattered. The Bulldogs were the team he supported in the Winfield Cup. He knew all about McCracken and co. And *they* wanted *him.*

He said he was prepared to visit Sydney to check everything out but would give no commitment at that stage.

Hardly had Bunce put the phone down than the All Blacks' new coach, Laurie Mains, called him. He said he could make no promises but that he was definitely interested in Bunce as a midfielder.

Gosh, me? Okay, Laurie, that's great news. I'm flattered you're interested.

"This gets better," thought Bunce. The Bulldogs and the All Blacks both wanted him. But therein lay an obvious complication.

"I knew that Western Samoa wanted me as well," says Bunce. "I felt a strong allegiance to them because they had picked me up and introduced me to international rugby."

Decisions, decisions, decisions. What to do?

Bunce applied some logic. He knew about the All Blacks, he knew about Western Samoa. What he wasn't too familiar with was the league scene in Sydney. He would check it out, having been invited to travel at Canterbury Bankstown's expense, and then he would be in a situation to weigh all the options.

After a rather lonely night in a Sydney motel, he moved in with Gavin Hill, the former Wellington and Canterbury rugby player who was making his mark at Winfield Cup level.

Hill introduced him around at training. He met the indefatigable Terry Lamb (of whom he was a great fan) and Jarrod McCracken and Jason Williams who, in a quiet moment, told Bunce that if he was serious about playing league he'd be smarter signing with a club in England.

Bunce joined them in training. He was managing adequately until the trainer ordered each player to do two hundred sit-ups.

"Holy shit," said Bunce. "I haven't done two hundred sit-ups in my life."

Determined to demonstrate that rugby players were as resilient as league men, he fought his way doggedly through to No 200, before collapsing in a heap.

That night, at Hill's place, he shared a few beers with the Canterbury-Bankstown coach Chris Anderson, assuring him he would be ready for weight training the next morning.

"Next morning," says Bunce, "I couldn't move. It was all I could do to roll off the couch. There wasn't a chance of me lifting *any* weights. Two hundred sit-ups had found me out. I said I'd see them later in the day."

Bunce was impressed with what he found at Canterbury Bankstown. It was a club, he felt, that he would be happy to belong to. Inevitably, contracts were broached and money discussed. Bunce cannot remember the exact figure offered him by club president Peter Moore but knows it was less than $50,000. When he was asked if there was anything else he wanted, he replied, "More money."

"More money," said the president, "...everyone wants more money."

Bunce was to find great irony in this modest offer when, three years later, the same club offered him $200,000. "I couldn't work that one out," he says. "At thirty-three I was worth four times as much as when I was thirty."

Moore, incidentally, was the official who approached Jonah Lomu after watching him play for New Zealand schools against Australian schools in Sydney in 1992 and offered him, entirely on his own initiative, $100,000 to join Canterbury Bankstown.

"What a buy he would have been at that price," he commented after Lomu's deeds at the World Cup in 1995. "Now he's advanced from six figures to seven!"

Bunce returned to Auckland in possession of a Canterbury Bankstown contract, having been fondly farewelled by the coach. "We'd like to have you back here," he said. "Think it over. We'll be in touch."

Canterbury Bankstown never did get back in touch. Well, not till 1995, anyway, by which time rugby was as professional as league. And if the club had made contact, it would have been to learn that Bunce was sticking with rugby.

"I remembered Newcastle all those years before and realised nothing had changed," says Bunce. "Deep down, my passion was for rugby. Perhaps, for a phenomenal amount of money, I might have been prepared to sacrifice the game I loved. But Canterbury Bankstown wasn't offering a phenomenal amount of money.

"Rugby had so much more to offer – tours to interesting countries, sevens tournaments, a lifestyle. I'd have been playing league purely for the money, and I found the game too cut-throat."

That left Bunce with two options – the All Blacks and Western Samoa.

He delayed a decision until he had spoken with a wide range of people including family and friends, people whose opinions he respected.

One of those, naturally, was Peter Fatialofa, the man who'd badgered him relentlessly until he agreed to play for Western Samoa. It was through Fats that he had achieved international recognition.

Tate Simi, the Western Samoan manager, was another Bunce approached. "He looked upon it as a step up to the All Blacks," says Bunce, "and encouraged me to follow my heart. He recalled that Michael Jones had launched his international career with Western Samoa and said how proud they all were at what he had achieved as an All Black.

"When it came to the crunch, I knew I wanted to be an All Black. When you grow up in New Zealand as a rugby player, the ultimate dream is to play for the All Blacks. Though I owed much to Western Samoa, I knew I had to follow my heart. I declared my allegiance to New Zealand. If Laurie Mains wanted me, I was ready and willing."

Players had until late February to nominate which country they were available to represent. After that date they couldn't change.

Fatialofa says he expected Frank to go. He'd seen Laurie Mains on television saying he was interested in three of the Western Samoans –

Bunce, Stephen Bachop and Pat Lam. All three chose New Zealand.

"None of them ever telephoned," says Fatialofa. "I just read about it in the papers. They're lucky I didn't punch 'em over! Seriously, I could understand their decisions. I'd tried desperately hard myself to become an All Black in the late 1980s.

"I bore no hard feelings when Frank announced his decision," said Fatialofa. "He'd done us a favour by playing for us, helping to make us a respected international team.

"It's obvious some players just used Western Samoa as a stepping stone, but not Frank. He went with our blessings. We were grateful for what he did for us."

Now let's get this straight – these two guys about whom this book *Midfield Liaison* is written are a couple of fancy midfielders, okay? Buncey wears the thirteen jersey and Walt looks good in twelve. Right? Together they've scared hell out of Horan and Little, Guscott and Carling, Sella and whatever that other Frog's name is. Right? But the thing is, they've done it together. *Together.* Buncey's the crunching centre, Walter the clever playmaker at second-five.

So what the hell was going on back at the start of the 1992 season? The All Black selectors, the North Harbour selector, any selector you could think of went to incredible lengths to make sure they didn't play *together.* Not in their best positions, anyway.

For North Harbour's games against North Auckland, Counties, ACT and King Country, Walter was at first-five, Frank at centre. In the All Black trials in Napier they were actually placed together, but Frank was at second-five with Walter at centre (until he was injured).

That's how they were to kick off their All Black careers, against the World XV – Bunce at second-five, Little at centre. That was a horrible failure, so for the next four tests it was Little at first-five (hard luck, Foxy) and Bunce out at centre.

You know when Laurie Mains got it right, when he finally acknowledged that Little in the 12 jersey, Bunce in 13 might actually be the ultimate combination? It was in the third match of the All Blacks' tour of Australia, against New South Wales, on June 28, halfway through the rugby season.

And who was the superstar that day? Frank Bunce. Look what they wrote about him...*But it was Bunce, crash tackling, hard running Bunce, who hurt New South Wales, in all senses...*and what they said of his partner...*Walter Little showed incisiveness at second-five.*

It took that long to establish the midfield liaison that was to do the All Blacks proud (with a couple of hiccups) for four full seasons.

Little, who'd played all his rugby in the five-eighths, had been intrigued when Thorburn contacted him in the UK to say Mains was considering him as a centre. "I didn't regard myself as a centre," he says, "but I was delighted that the new coach was interested in me. I

Canada came to appreciate the potency of Walter Little and Frank Bunce as a midfield duo when they took on the All Blacks at Eden Park in 1995. Walter, back from a major calf injury, has Frank in support as he taunts the fragile defence. Andrew Cornaga, Photosport

ALL BLACKS Y WALLABIES EN PUNTA DEL ESTE

All Blacks and Wallabies together in a powerful Anzac team at the Uruguay sevens tournament at Punta del Este in 1991. From left: Darren Junee, Zinzan Brooke, Walter Little, Craig Innes, John Timu and Simon Poidevin.

Great mates together atop the Eiffel Tower in 1990, Postie (alias Craig Innes) with Walter.

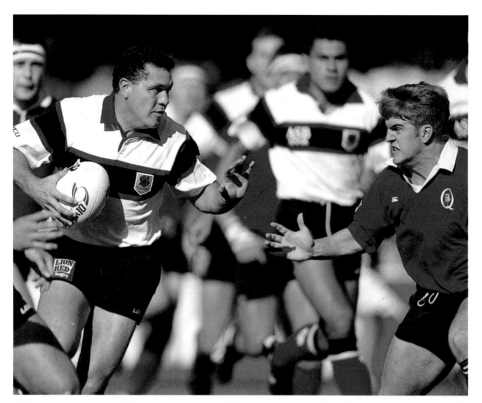

Little about to fend off his great Aussie rival Tim Horan during North Harbour's vital Super 10 clash with Queensland at Brisbane in 1994. A narrow loss cost Harbour a place in the series grand final.

Andrew Cornaga, Photosport

Bunce ambushed by Western Province players during a Super 10 game at Takapuna in 1995.

Troy Restieaux, Photosport

He's not just a pretty face, and a smashing midfield back – he plays the guitar too. Walter putting in a little quiet practice at home.

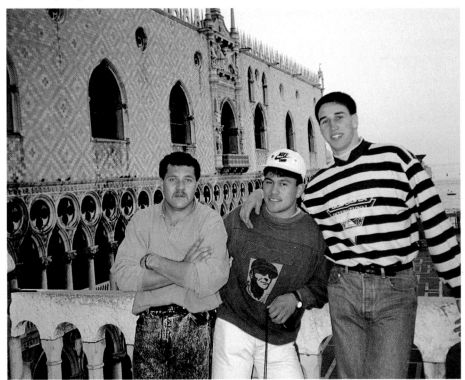

Walter taking in the sights of Venice in 1991 with JT (John Timu) and Kamo (Ian Jones).

Showing off their torsos for *Metro* magazine, for a feature on North Harbour rugby, are, from left: Walter, Warren Burton, Ian Jones, Ant Strachan and Richard Turner.

Kim Christensen, Metro Magazine

One of Bunce's great passions away from the rugby field is motor cycles. So it was entirely appropriate when *Rugby News* posed him on a Harley Davidson for this front cover photograph.   Simon Harper

Bunce defies the attentions of Wallaby centre Jason Little to score a try in the Bledisloe Cup encounter at Carisbrook in 1993.   Photosport

Bunce in one of his rare (80 minute) appearances for Auckland – in a South Pacific championship game against New South Wales at Eden Park in 1990.   Photosport

The All Blacks' tour opener in Perth in 1992 pitted Frank Bunce against his brother Steve. They'd played together for Manukau the previous winter. This time Frank was an All Black and Steve a West Australian representative. One team scored 80, the other nil! Troy Restieaux, Photosport

Trouble for Queensland at Ballymore in 1992 as the All Blacks swing sweetly into attack, with Little directing a pass into the hands of Bunce.

The World Cup was just around the corner when Walter Little married Tracy Wishnowski in 1995. The best man? Frank Bunce, of course.

Maryjane Saunderson and Frank Bunce on their wedding day at Western Springs in 1992, with son Chance.

Clash of the midfield titans: Bunce (in possession) and Little against Tim Horan and Jason Little during the 1992 Bledisloe Cup series in Australia. Photosport

The laidback kicking style of Walter Little, as demonstrated in the 1993 NPC semi-final against Auckland at Eden Park.
Andrew Cornaga, Photosport

Waikato first-five Ian Foster drops in to check out Frank Bunce during the NPC contest at Takapuna in 1993.
Troy Restieaux, Photosport

The Littles at home – Walter with Michael and Tracy with Daniel. *Woman's Day*

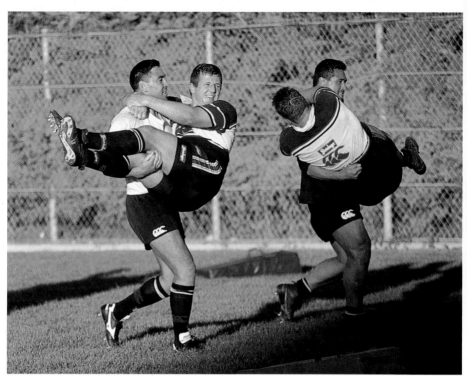

That's one way to impress your captain, by carrying him down the field at training – Sean Fitzpatrick in the safe arms of Frank Bunce.

Andrew Cornaga, Photosport

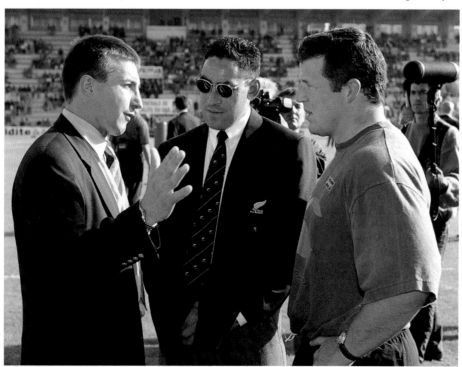

Bunce and All Black captain Sean Fitzpatrick meet the great French centre Philippe Sella, veteran of more than 100 tests, in Toulouse in 1995.

Andrew Cornaga, Photosport

The Bunce family portrait. Frank and Maryjane with, from left, Lauren, Jordan, Janece and Samantha. Andrew Cornaga, Photosport

Not just a midfield liaison, but a strong pairing in private life, too. Walter Little with his best man Frank Bunce on his wedding day in 1995. Little collection

wanted the black jersey back. I wasn't that fussed about the position."

Bunce meanwhile was approached by Mains following North Harbour's early season CANZ series game in Whangarei. "He asked me how much rugby I'd played at second-five, having indicated he was considering Walter for centre. I said that apart from the World Cup, where I'd slotted in between Stephen Bachop and To'o Vaega, I wasn't too familiar with the position. But I was more than happy to give it a go."

Bunce was delighted to be teamed up with Bachop in the main trial at Napier because the pair had developed an excellent understanding during the World Cup. He was even more delighted when their team (featuring Little at centre) won the main midweek trial 44-17 and he was subsequently named in the New Zealand XV (a shadow test line-up) to play the Saracens. A back injury kept Little out of this game.

Bunce appreciated the opportunity to play in Napier. It was where his father had lived until his death in 1991 and where his daughter Samantha had been born (on the day following the funeral). A large number of aunties and uncles lived there and most of them were along to cheer Frank on towards All Black selection.

His main concern when he took the field in the final trial was the presence in the Saracens backline of Marc Ellis, a player who had come north with a huge reputation. "He had youth strongly on his side (he was 20 and Frank 30), and I didn't want him squeezing through the front door ahead of me," says Bunce. "I tried a bit extra because he was there."

Although the Saracens upset the New Zealand XV, Ellis was well contained. Indeed, it was Bunce who made the greater impact. When the All Black team was announced for the three test series against the World XV (to mark the centenary of New Zealand rugby) Bunce and Ellis were both there. And so was Little.

The squad was more notable for who wasn't there. New selectors Mains, Thorburn and Earle Kirton had done some serious culling. Unwanted were test captain Gary Whetton and his brother Alan – who weren't even invited to the trials – and fellow World Cup performers Bernie McCahill, Marc Carter, Jason Hewett, Jon Preston and Shayne Philpott.

Also missing were Craig Innes, who had opted for a league career with Leeds, and Zinzan Brooke, who was disregarded because of his late return from the club season in Italy. He and his brother Robin would come into contention later in the season.

The Mains era was under way. The man who'd guided Otago to NPC glory in 1991 (and who'd won the appointment somewhat surprisingly ahead of John Hart) was given the responsibility of restoring New Zealand rugby to its former glory. He had plenty to work on. Not only had the All Blacks failed miserably on the playing field at the World

Cup (having started as raging hot favourites) but their public relations had been a disaster. They had been embarrassingly shown up by the new world champions, the Australians.

Mains, a good southern man whose qualities as a straightshooter were often to be misinterpreted by suspicious northerners, spelt out his priorities to the new squad.

Cliques would not be tolerated, and any individuals guilty of establishing them would be dismissed from the team. He was prepared to be the first coach to send an All Black home for causing disharmony in the team.

"The principles I applied," recalls Mains, "were a carry over from what I'd done with Otago. I'd always believed the team came before the personal aspirations of any player. I told the players I wouldn't tolerate arrogance, that I expected them as All Blacks always to be humble. I didn't want to make judgments on the previous leaders but I was aware that some of the younger members had been given a torrid time by the oldies."

High levels of fitness – an area in which the World Cup All Blacks had been deficient, in Mains' opinion – would be established. The players' fitness levels would be monitored regularly.

This lead on to tactics. Mains explained that he wanted his team to play expansive, fast-flowing rugby, and the only way this was possible was if his players were superbly conditioned.

Mains' long-term goal (representing a three-year plan) was to win the 1995 World Cup. In working towards that, he explained to his charges, there would be experimentations in both onfield combinations and match tactics.

"It was important to remember," says Mains, "that in creating a new team, to take us through to 1995, Peter Thorburn, Earle Kirton and myself would be introducing players who had never been exposed to rugby at international level.

"Some would make the step up, some wouldn't. We had to find out who could handle it, and that resulted in some experimenting.

"Some players were so good, and became such an integral part of the team, that there was no experimentation necessary. Frank Bunce was one of those. Both Peter and myself, and Earle by the end of 1992, also considered Walter a first choice. Unfortunately, injuries were to curtail his career the next season."

The first backline 'experiment' had Graeme Bachop at halfback, Fox (who was considered fortunate to have survived the World Cup weed out) at first-five, Bunce at second-five and Little at centre.

"Our initial thinking was to use Frank at second-five," says Mains, "where he'd been such a success with Western Samoa in the World Cup. We felt he was a strong man who could take the ball up a bit and allow Walter, at centre, to use his flair. It quickly became apparent they were a more effective combination the other way around."

Bunce thought the original combination had a good feel to it in training. But in the heat of battle it didn't fire and the backline was to be completely restructured for the balance of the series against the overseas stars.

Bunce admits that his inexperience found him out at second-five, where he was up against a formidable pairing in Jeremy Guscott and Tim Horan.

Twice he stopped Guscott without putting him on the deck. Both times the enterprising Englishman doubled around behind Horan to re-ignite attacking moves. Bunce was criticised later for failing to take him out of play. "That's where I was lacking," says Bunce, "in fundamental things like that."

The All Blacks performed dreadfully in what was planned as a centenary showpiece, losing 28-14 after trailing 25-6 late in the second half. The scoreline represented a nightmare start to Mains' career as coach. But he wasn't too despondent because he easily identified the main problem area. His team had dominated the battle for possession but had spent all afternoon turning the ball over to the enemy.

Opposing Bunce in Christchurch was Peter Fatialofa, his World Cup captain.

Peter Fats claimed later he had a particular mission in the game… to clobber Bunce.

"Why?" a mystified Bunce asked.

"Because I wanted people to see me hit you," said Fatialofa. "They'd say, 'Look at that – team mates at the World Cup, now Fats is hitting him. That's because Frank left Western Samoa to play for the All Blacks.'"

"Fortunately for me," says Bunce, "Fats didn't get me in his sights. He had one swing, but it missed! We laughed about it at the dinner that night."

It's amazing how things can turn around in four days. Intensive training, with the emphasis on ball retention, and a new-look backline worked miracles. The All Blacks at Athletic Park were unrecognisable from the error-ridden mob who'd dismayed their fans at Lancaster Park.

Now it's hard to believe, but by Wellington there was only one back survivor from the World Cup semi-final loss to Australia six months earlier – winger John Timu.

Bachop had given way to Ant Strachan (Auckland's second-stringer behind Hewett), Fox had been banished to the reserves bench and replaced at first-five by Little, the midfield places occupied by McCahill and Innes had gone to Eroni Clarke and Bunce, John Kirwan – supplanted by Inga Tuigamala – was keeping Fox company in the grandstand and Greg Cooper was at fullback (the three World Cup fullbacks, Terry Wright, Kieran Crowley and Philpott, being unwanted).

Little was surprised to find himself installed at first-five (marking the famous Springbok Naas Botha), having been initially selected as a centre. He suspected Thorburn had a lot to do with it. "It was a daunting ask," he says, "being asked to take over from Fox. I was familiar with the position but I'd never played there at international level. Obviously they wanted me to clear the ball faster than Foxy had been doing.

"My chief concern was the kicking game. But then I thought maybe I was there because I *didn't* kick."

Little was to have a huge game, attributing much of his success to his North Harbour colleague Ant Strachan. "We got on like a house on fire," says Little. "Ant is such an extrovert, such a cocky individual. He fired up the forwards and called most of the shots, leaving me to concentrate on getting the backline firing. His passing was so sharp, the backline operated brilliantly throughout. I hardly ever had to kick – it was wonderful."

The All Blacks, all efficiency, made such a blazing start they scored five tries in 28 minutes, going on to win 54-26 (the festival nature of the game being tarnished when the World XV's French lock Olivier Roumat was sent off for kicking All Black captain Sean Fitzpatrick).

Bunce didn't enjoy his afternoon so much. Although the backline, generally, sparkled, he rated his own performance among his worst in an All Black jersey. "I missed a tackle that would have cost a try had Greg Cooper not pulled off an intercept and I never felt comfortable."

Satisfaction did come, however, through the successful execution of a move hatched at training and bearing the code name of Coconut (which had everything to do with the fact no white fellas were involved!).

It was a move the All Blacks were to make great capital from over the next few years. The first-five creates the attack by firing a long skip pass to the winger, who the midfielders then double around.

At Wellington, because Clarke wasn't that confident in his first international, he and Bunce swapped positions, with the end result that Clarke scored the try after Bunce had gathered Tuigamala's pass.

"It's a potent move," says Bunce, "difficult to defend against when executed at pace. It never worked sweeter than when Inga was involved because he was especially good at catching the ball and flicking it behind his back without looking.

"Moves like Coconut are spectacular to watch and fun to make happen. It's the way backs should play, with total understanding."

Little being selected at first-five for the clincher in the centenary series at Eden Park had far greater significance than Little being named for the midweek test in Wellington. It meant Fox, the unchallenged supremo of the backline for so long, really had been dropped.

Bunce was looking forward to opposing Jason Little in the deciding test. But the NZRFU intervened, preventing Little (who'd been flown across to reinforce an injury-hit side) from teaming up with fellow

Wallaby Tim Horan. It all seemed very political, with the union ordering South African Jannie Claassens, who'd been having treatment for a hamstring strain, to play, if fit.

A player Bunce and Little did get to oppose was recently deposed All Black captain Gary Whetton, brought in when John Eales was injured and Roumat suspended.

Laurie Mains blew a fuse over his involvement and the All Blacks generally felt his call-up to be inappropriate. Little says that turning out against the All Blacks like that was something "you just didn't do."

Whetton's involvement served to fire up the All Blacks, and from his station at first-five Little says he observed New Zealand's most capped player being used as a doormat on more than one occasion. "He would have had a few souvenirs by which to remember the day."

The decisive victory at Eden Park gave the All Blacks the series, two to one, which, considering the disaster at Lancaster Park, was a satisfactory outcome. It allowed the team of '92 to walk proudly into the third of the centenary dinners. After the Christchurch fiasco, Bunce says he was embarrassed to confront some of the greats of New Zealand rugby who were in attendance. "Here were famous players coming up and congratulating me on my selection in the All Blacks," says Bunce. "But I didn't feel I was worthy of it."

Bunce was certainly worthy of recognition by the time the All Blacks had taken out both tests against the touring Irish, one a desperately close-run affair at Carisbrook, the other a rout in the rain and cold in Wellington.

As the *Rugby Annual* recorded, "Bunce needed to produce heroics at Carisbrook or the unthinkable would have happened – for the first time in 87 years of competition, the All Blacks would have gone under to Ireland. And this was an Irish team which had been whipped by Auckland, 62 points to 7, seven days earlier. When his team seemed to be sliding towards ignominious defeat…Bunce emerged as a matchwinner."

Bunce's two tries (and a scything run by Little which put Clarke across) allowed the All Blacks to escape with a 24-21 victory. The first try was a product of the ingenious Coconut move, the other a gift to Bunce when the Irish defenders, en masse, bought a dummy inside pass to Tuigamala from an attacking lineout.

"I couldn't believe my luck," says Bunce. "Everyone had diverted their attentions to Inga. When I looked ahead, a huge path had opened through to the goalposts. I thought, 'Wow, this is for me!'"

The Carisbrook test provided an important boost to Bunce's career. It was when he first sensed that he was genuinely worthy of the All Blacks. "I'd found it hard to get my teeth into the world fifteen series," he says. "It had taken a while for me to adjust to the greater pace and demands of All Black test rugby. Against Ireland, for the first time, I felt that maybe I did belong."

Little was greatly encouraged by Bunce's form, finding him a terrific asset to the team. "As we had discovered at North Harbour, Frank was an excellent reader of a game and a motivator. He was always lifting us, exhorting us to produce better quality rugby.

"Of course, his other strength was his ability to bring off awesome tackles, often slamming into opponents when they least expected it. His tackles would often give the team a huge lift."

Bunce and Little weren't involved as the selectors effected six changes for the re-match with the Irish, the most interesting newcomers being Olo Brown at prop, Robin Brooke at lock and Matthew Cooper (at the expense of his brother, Greg) at fullback.

The changes worked with New Zealand demolishing Ireland 59-6, a remarkable scoreline considering it had never bettered 24 points in 10 previous contests with Ireland dating back to 1905.

Bunce picked up another brace of tries and although Little had the dubious distinction of being the only back not to share in the 11-try haul, he could reflect that in his four tests at first-five the All Blacks had accumulated 29 tries. In the previous four tests, with Fox wearing the No 10 jersey, only eight tries had been scored.

The selectors had obviously introduced Little to provide attacking impetus and from that viewpoint, their confidence had been vindicated. However, there was some concern that his kicking game didn't match his running and passing skills, with which observation Little concurs.

"I was never a Grant Fox when it came to tactical kicking," says Little. "While I was prepared to practise and develop my kicking game, I had to admit that my natural instinct was always to run with the ball and try and put team mates through the gaps."

Notwithstanding his kicking limitations, Little had begun to feel that first-five was his role. So he was shocked when the 30-strong party to tour Australia and South Africa was announced and he was listed at second-five. The first-fives were Fox and Stephen Bachop.

In five internationals under the new regime, he'd appeared once at centre and four times at first-five. Now he was to specialise at second-five. "I wondered what the hell was going on. I was delighted to be selected for the great adventure but perplexed at the manner in which I was being shunted around the backline."

Mains explains. "We were impressed in most respects with Walter's handling of his duties at first-five, but we felt we needed players who could achieve pinpoint accuracy with their tactical kicking for the important internationals coming up.

"I talked with Fox about how great the All Black backline had been in 1988 and sometimes in 1989 and I was satisfied that he comprehended exactly what I was explaining. He was prepared to return to becoming a ball distributor.

"There was no question that he had been allowed to take control of the backline in a contracting situation.

"Sitting in the grandstand watching the tests against the World team and Ireland, he realised what we wanted and conceded that he was determined to shovel off some of his responsibilities…

"He was happy to allow the backs outside him to play a more expansive game, and to have a go himself occasionally, so we didn't have the opposition defence streaming acrossfield as happened in the World Cup semi-final in Dublin."

It was apparent once the team began training in Australia that Fox had been fully reinstated. But it was a new Fox, his backline colleagues were to discover. He was back in under coach Mains' conditions, and these were that he pass more, that he allow the backs outside him to demonstrate greater initiative (which permitted counter-attacking from their own 22, if they wanted) and that every so often he should tickle up the opposition loose forwards by running.

Little was enthralled. He found it hard to believe that he was operating outside the same player who virtually ignored him in 1990 and 1991. "Suddenly the backline was humming," he says. "Foxy was putting me into gaps, I was putting others into gaps and we were scoring tries, quality tries. I knew then that under Mains, the All Blacks could go all the way."

Fox, Little and Bunce developed a stimulating rapport. Fox, according to Little, still produced his photo-copied sheets detailing dozens of moves. But Little and Bunce were having an input, too.

"I'd suggest a move," says Little, "and Foxy would say, 'Right, let's do it.' Frank basically left it to us, but if things weren't working out, he'd offer a suggestion. I reckon in most games we'd come up with three or four moves that would crack the opposition defensive pattern.

"Among them was the Coconut move which almost never failed us. It netted me a sweet try beside the posts in the opening moments of the third test in Sydney."

Little, appreciating that he'd found his niche at second-five, relished playing alongside Bunce. Their combination had begun to develop excitingly with North Harbour and found full expression in Australia and South Africa where they were linked eight times, including all the major games.

Little says he would instinctively know what Bunce was going to do. "If I took the ball up from set play and wanted to slip it, I'd know Frank would be there. Little things like that become big things and can turn a game. Whenever I found myself in trouble I always knew Frank would be there to support me."

Frank came up against his brother Steve during the tour opener in Perth. They'd played club rugby together for Manukau in 1991, before Frank had made the step up to international level. Now he was an All

Black, a much respected one, and Steve (inside centre for Western Australia) was to spend a large percentage of the afternoon chasing his elder brother around the WACA Ground as the All Blacks ran up 80 points.

The Otago players knew about Mains' ruthless streak as a coach. The others were soon to find out, and suffer.

Determined to elevate the All Blacks to a new strata of fitness, Mains pushed them to extremes.

It started, of course, with the infamous beep test which established each player's VO2 level. Bunce had come through this satisfactorily – his work on the rubbish truck producing a high level of aerobic fitness – while others like Tuigamala scored embarrassingly low.

The real killers, however, were the 150s and the Down and Ups which the players were to come to dread as the tour unfolded. Bunce claims he was more nervous of training than fronting up to any opponent. "The matches were easy by comparison," he said.

For the uninitiated, 150s are what they sound like – a series of sprints of 150 metres. Between each one the players have to jog back to the start line, so it's perpetual motion. The challenge is how many 150s the coach (or trainer) orders. Mains had a nasty tendency to throw in more than the All Blacks felt were beneficial to their wellbeing. It was a good day when the demand was for fewer than twenty.

Down and Ups are more explosive. They involve a sprint of, say, 10 metres out from the goalline, to a point where the players must throw themselves to the ground, touching it with their chest, followed by a sprint back to the goalline. These were usually worked in sets of eight or ten. To the All Blacks' dismay, Mains would never divulge how many, in total, he wanted. He would keep the players guessing.

One day he asked Arran Pene, who as an Otago representative was only too familiar with his agony sessions, what was the most Down and Ups he'd ever done in one session. Pene said eighty, which was not a clever answer. "A smart forward would have said forty," says Bunce. "Laurie promptly ordered us to do eighty Down and Ups, in ten sets of eight. Thank you, Arran!"

The same day that Mains demanded eighty Down and Ups, at training in Adelaide, he also ordered the players to do twenty 150s. During the sprints, Mains commented, "I wonder if Nick Farr-Jones will have the Wallabies doing this."

"I bet he bloody isn't," said Bunce, who concedes that Mains' gruelling sessions made him as fit as he'd ever been.

In the first major challenge of the tour, the All Blacks played New South Wales at Concord Oval. Bunce was wanting to make a big impression, to ensure selection in the first test team. He certainly did that; in fact, he caused mayhem.

Taking exception to New South Wales' best forward Michael Brial being offside at a maul, Bunce charged twenty metres straight into him, leaving him concussed. Bunce's behaviour sparked a major brawl in which two All Blacks, Paul Henderson and Arran Pene, broke bones in their hands.

When the referee (Barry Leask) eventually restored order, he reprimanded Bunce, instructing him to stay in the backs where he belonged!

Bunce was later to give Marty Roebuck, the test fullback, a dreadfully lacerated mouth after crash tackling him. Roebuck and Brial were two of five home team players to leave the field injured, four of them after collisions with All Blacks.

Having scored one of New Zealand's tries, Bunce was obliged to leave the field himself midway through the second half with a strained hamstring. He was roundly booed all the way to the dressing room, prompting the notorious Richard Loe to later declare that he was "proud of him."

In reporting on the carnage at Concord the next morning, the *Sydney Morning Herald* carried this classic headline: ALL BLACKS DEFEAT NEW SOUTH WALES – NOT MANY DEAD.

While the Australians were horrified at what went on, and accused the visitors of brutality, Mains was enormously heartened by his team's display. "That's aggression," he told his players. "That's where I want us to be."

The line-up for Dr John Mayhew next morning included Henderson, Pene and Bunce.

Henderson was first to be treated, having a broken bone in his hand diagnosed.

"What's the verdict?" asked Pene, when the Southlander came out.

"Broken bone – they're sending me home."

"Oh, shit," said Pene. "That's pretty serious. I'm not going to show him my hand then. I'm going back to breakfast."

So while the luckless Henderson returned to New Zealand, having made only two appearances, Pene remained with the touring party, going on to play in eight games.

Wynne Gray, writing in the *New Zealand Herald,* said that Bunce was being likened to the great West Indian fast bowler Michael Holding.

"Holding's prowess as a lethal destroyer won him the nickname of Whispering Death, so silent and deadly was his arsenal. Bunce is earning similar admiration for the manner in which he has dealt with opposing midfield combinations on the All Blacks' tour of Australia. It is hard to recall anyone slipping through his steely defence."

The test series pitted Bunce and Little against Little and Horan, in what could fairly be billed the rugby heavyweight midfield championship of the world.

Little and Horan, at 21, were as good as twins, having grown up as mates and played their rugby together right through the grades to international level. Heroes of the Wallabies' World Cup triumph the previous year, they had been cutting capers against every backline in the world.

They represented a special challenge for Bunce and Little.

"Because they were rated the best midfield combo in the world," says Little, "it provided extra incentive for Frank and me to excel. Every time we opposed them, Frank and I were determined to better them in defence and attack. We knew if we could gain an advantage over them, we had done our bit for the team."

Mains slapped a media ban on the players as the first test approached. No interviews, he insisted. He wanted his men totally focused on the job at hand. So Bunce and Little were surprised when their manager, Neil Gray, advised them, upon their return (from training) to their delightfully situated hotel on the waterfront at Manly, that they were required to report by the sea wall opposite for an interview with Television New Zealand.

"Because our manager was telling us," says Little, "we presumed it had been approved by Laurie."

Sitting on the stone wall soaking up the sunshine, and waiting for John Kirwan to finish an interview (he, too, was following manager Gray's instructions), Little looked up and saw coach Mains staring down from his hotel window. Walter waved, but there was no acknowledgement. "He obviously can't see us," mused Little, whereupon he and Bunce both waved. Still no response.

The response came at the first team meeting following the test. "Obviously," barked Mains, "some of you regard yourselves as bigger than the team. Not only did some players disregard my order not to talk to the media, but two players had the cheek to wave while they were waiting for their interviews!"

Walter and Frank knew it was pointless trying to explain what had happened. And, anyway, they would only have put manager Gray in the cart. So they endured the dressing down...and the extra ration of 150s and Down and Ups at training.

At series end – and what a series it was, with the All Blacks and Wallabies scoring exactly the same number of points and tries - Bunce and Little had yielded nothing to Little and Horan; in fact, the New Zealanders had finished ahead on points, an achievement acknowledged by Mains.

"In my humble opinion," says Mains, "by the end of 1992, Walter and Frank clearly had the edge on Tim and Jason. When our two were together there was not another combination in the world better than them. No one ever outplayed them."

In Mains' opinion you have to go back to the days of Bill Davis and Ian MacRae in the 1960s and Bill Osborne and Bruce Robertson in the

1970s to find an All Black midfield combination as effective.

"Joe Stanley and Warwick Taylor also rank highly but they didn't play that many games together."

After Australia had taken the first two tests 16-15 and 19-17, to claim the Bledisloe Cup, the All Blacks, with immense pressure on them – the prospect of a whitewash in the series was too terrible to contemplate – struck back magnificently to win the third contest 26-23.

Walter Little's try in the opening minutes proved critical. It came from a scrum near the Australian 22, Fox calling a move which was negated because the ball was too slow coming back.

So Little ordered, "Change to Coconut." And the Coconut move it was. Fox threw the long, skip pass to towards the left wing, finding Tuigamala who flipped the ball up for Little, looping outside him. He glided past Horan and on to the goalline for a sweet (and immensely satisfying) try.

This performance was one of the first examples of Mains' men overwhelming quality opposition with their high tempo play. Eighty minutes of all-out action was possible only because of the players' exceptional high levels of fitness.

Bunce had scored in the first test and dotted down legitimately near the finish in the third test, only the touch judge didn't see it that way. He ruled that Bunce had taken out the corner flag first.

By the time Bunce had picked himself up, Timu was remonstrating with the referee over the injustice of it all, for which he was penalised. That allowed the Wallabies to sweep on to attack and, courtesy of a blatantly forward pass which went undetected, the replacement Anthony Herbert (a midfielder who came on for an injured loose forward) scored. So what could have been a decent stuffing at 31-16 finished up a three-point victory.

It was Herbert, one of the more solidly built centres in international rugby (and on again as a replacement, this time for a winger) who had presented Little with a vital intercept try in the Queensland match at Ballymore, a game the All Blacks did remarkably well to win after trailing 14-5 approaching halftime.

Little recalls how Queensland was launching into an attack in its own half when he saw Herbert look towards his outsides before he received the ball. "It indicated to me," says Little, "what he was going to do, so I played a hunch and went for the intercept. After that, it was a case of beating the cover defence."

This Little did by fending off Jason Little with his left hand before transferring the ball across his body to keep Paul Carozza at bay.

The third test victory heartened the All Blacks for their trailblazing journey across to South Africa. The atmosphere would have been funereal if the team had lost three in a row. Even if the opposition were the world champions.

With their flight scheduled to arrive around 1am, the players didn't anticipate there would be much activity at the airport, even though this was the first All Black team to the Republic since 1976, the international sporting sanctions against South Africa having been lifted only a few months earlier.

The All Blacks being the All Blacks were whisked straight through customs and ushered towards the main terminal building where they could hear a hubbub. "What's going on?" Little asked Bunce who shrugged.

What was going on was that an incredible 4000 enthusiastic rugby fans were at the airport to welcome the New Zealanders. They obviously didn't mind missing their sleep to extend gratitude to their greatest rugby rivals for coming back to play the Springboks.

"It was an unbelievable welcome," recalls Little, "especially at that time of the morning. A rugby tour of Australia is pretty low key. You'd be lucky to get six people at the airport, at any time of the day, to greet the All Blacks and most people you engage in conversation around the country are never sure whether you're there for union, league or rules.

"The reception at Jan Smuts Airport let us know we were in for a great three weeks."

Bunce and Little knew they would be marked men after Springbok coach John Williams identified them as "extremely dangerous players – the team's main weapon."

Williams said they were "explosive players with lots of skills and imagination. They not only shut out the Aussies but were on top of them all the time. Little is deceptive and elusive and pretty quick off the mark. Bunce has safe hands and is a good tackler."

Mains, possibly operating on expert medical advice but more likely being just plain bloody masochistic, put the players through what he said would be "a good blow out" to overcome their jetlag twenty-four hours after arrival.

It was, Little remembers painfully, "a real gutbuster," Mains finishing with a stack of 150s and Down and Ups. To add to the players' agony, several of them suffered bleeding noses, a not uncommon happening for players unaccustomed to Johannesburg's rarefied (6500ft above sea level) air.

Bunce was more concerned with the spectators at training who kept saying, "Aren't they small!"

"That was a worry," he said, "especially as we'd been warned of the South African players' size and power. What were we in for?"

Bunce was still concerned about the dimensions of the opposition as he was leaving the warm-up area at Kings Park in Durban, prior to the opening game against Natal, when he came upon Inga Tuigamala, Eroni Clarke and Michael Jones, the All Blacks' three committed Christians, in a huddle praying.

"It was," says Bunce, "the closest I ever came to joining them!"

The All Blacks demonstrated to Natal that size and strength are only part of the essential requirements for success in rugby.

They vividly illustrated to South Africa's champion province that technique, fitness and the capacity to play at a higher tempo for eighty minutes are greater qualities.

Natal hung in well but was swamped in the final quarter, as was Orange Free State in the next game.

The All Blacks swept through the four provincial fixtures, with Bunce and Little earning a special mention in despatches for their play against the Junior Springboks in Pretoria.

Tiaan Strauss, the Juniors' captain (and now playing league for Canterbury Bankstown in Sydney), praised the North Harbour pair for consistently breaching the advantage line. "They were always coming at us, forcing the half gap. They are excellent attacking players."

The first All Black visit in sixteen years created feverish interest in the only test match, which would be watched by a capacity 72,000 fans at Ellis Park, one of the great rugby stadiums of the world.

South Africans conveniently overlooked Australia's triumph at the World Cup in 1991 and recent series win over New Zealand and their own years in the rugby wilderness in none too modestly proclaiming this to be the clash of the game's titans.

Although it was 15 years since the All Blacks and the Springboks had done battle, amazingly two veterans of the '81 series in New Zealand, flyhalf Naas Botha and centre Danie Gerber, survived. They were both now aged 34.

On the eve of the international, Bunce and Little watched a television documentary on Gerber.

"We were just taking it in as we relaxed in our room," says Bunce. "But here was Gerber running around opponents and over opponents, scoring tries, tackling everything in sight, beating teams on his own. He looked like superman.

"And we were marking him the next day. There was an element of anxiety as we tried to get to sleep that evening!"

Gerber scored two tries the next day but, to the great relief of Bunce and Little they came after the All Blacks had established an unassailable lead of 27-10. The men in black held on to win 27-24 for their first victory at Ellis Park in 64 years.

Of special satisfaction to Bunce was the try scored by John Kirwan because it was the direct product of their scheming at training during the week.

Explains Bunce: "We felt we needed to develop something to stop the South African backs pushing us out all the time. So we worked on a move where I ran laterally and JK cut back inside me. We ran through it several times till we were comfortable with it, then stored it away for the right moment.

"Those moments don't always come, especially in internationals, but Inga (Tuigamala) set it up for us with a strong counter-attacking run. He created the ruck and suddenly I was in possession and looking for JK. He was quite a distance away on the right wing, but I could see him coming, and he was screaming for the ball.

"The move worked perfectly, better than it had in training. My running laterally across the field wrongfooted all the defence so that when JK took my pass, he had an unchallenged run to the goalposts."

For Little, the special joy of winning at Ellis Park was in achieving it through the wide-ranging, all-action game that the team had been seeking to develop all year.

"The Springboks were huge guys," says Little. "It took a major effort to bring them down. To have locked horns with them in a battle of strength would have been fatal.

"So we exploited our greater pace and fitness. This was unquestionably the fittest All Black team I had been associated with, and we literally ran the South Africans ragged. They couldn't stay with us.

"I know their three tries in the final stages suggest otherwise, but our guys hit the wall about fifteen minutes from the end. The physical demands of the year caught up with us, quite dramatically. I'm pleased we didn't have to play another ten minutes."

Little singles out for special mention, three members of that backline who have since switched their allegiances to league.

"I thought that John Kirwan, John Timu and Inga Tuigamala were sensational on that tour, three superb players. They all had the capacity to make something out of nothing.

"You'd never get three more explosive footballers in one All Black backline. They possessed so much strength and were all capable of producing moments of magic.

"Laurie (Mains) used Inga's power to blast through opposing defences or set up ruck ball. It's funny, in 1992 I thought Inga was the ultimate in giant threequarters. Now we've got Jonah, and he seems half as big as Inga again!

"John Kirwan was still right on top of his game in '92. He was marvellous value to the team because of his experience. He was our been there/done that player, possessed of so much knowledge. He'd regularly call moves from out wide, and they were always good calls. He'd say, 'Give me the ball and I'll get around him.' Usually he did, because he ran his angles so well."

Back home, Bunce and Little helped guide North Harbour through to the semi-finals of the national championship.

Along the way there were a couple of memorable moments. Against Waikato, Bunce was felled by…guess who?…Richard Loe, who flattened him with a stiff-arm tackle when he tried to step inside him. Bunce, stars floating in front of him, was obliged to go off.

The Waikato tough man (who was banished to the sin bin for 10 minutes) came up with a priceless piece of front rower's logic later: "If I have to be out there tackling threequarters," he told Bunce, "they're going to get it!"

Against Auckland, in a late-season Ranfurly Shield challenge, Harbour would undoubtedly have seized possession of the famous 'log' but for that man Grant Fox who guided (and kicked) Auckland to victory in the second half.

At halftime, the shield was heading across the bridge, nothing surer. Harbour led 13-9 after playing into a substantial breeze. But with its scrum under pressure and Fox goalkicking impeccably, Auckland clawed its way through to victory in an epic contest.

Auckland expended so much mental and physical effort against North Harbour that a week later it sensationally crashed out to Waikato in the first of the NPC semi-finals.

The second semi-final was even more dramatic, Otago and North Harbour going to extra time at Carisbrook after being locked together at 16-all after 80 minutes.

A few minutes into extra time and North Harbour called a rather complicated move, appropriately called Otago. It was unfolding reasonably promisingly when Bunce sighted a gap, abandoned the move altogether, and blew the defence wide open, putting halfback Ant Strachan in for a try beside the posts. Little's conversion had Harbour ahead 23-17 and seemingly on the way to a place in the grand final.

But Otago struck back with a penalty goal before conspiring to put fullback Greg Cooper across in the corner in the final minute for an amazing victory.

Auckland didn't recover from its clash with Harbour, and nor did Otago. In the final a week later, it was blown clean off Rugby Park in Hamilton, losing 40-5.

It had been a marvellous season of rugby, and at the conclusion of it Frank Bunce was named one of the five players of the year in both the *Rugby Annual* and the *Rugby Almanack*.

In November, Grant Fox launched his autobiography *The Game, The Goal*, presenting a copy to Little. The inscription read: "To Walter, it's been a pleasure playing alongside you over the years. The pity is that it probably took too long to talk about what we wanted from each other. Grant."

Tough Times
For Walter

Walter Little and Tracy Wishnowski were high on enthusiasm and optimism when they flew back into New Zealand in April, 1993, having spent a delightful five months in Italy after Walter was contracted to play for the Roma club.

They were a family of two when they departed Auckland but three when they returned, their son Michael having been born in Rome. He was a month old (with an Italian Godfather – no, not that one!) when his famous dad sought to resume his rugby and business careers back in Godzone.

Walter soon found there were major worries with the business, a company in Henderson set up to supply LPG, one of the partners having taken off while he was overseas and the company having incurred considerable debts.

Oh well, that would (hopefully) sort itself out. Walter would concentrate on what he did best – playing rugby. But major problems would arise there too. Injuries would sideline him for a large part of the season and deny him the All Black tour of England and Scotland. It would become a thoroughly depressing year.

There was nothing depressing about his time in Italy though. It ranks among Walter and Tracy's most treasured experiences.

Officials of the Roma club, based, naturally enough, in the Italian capital, had approached Little during the All Blacks tour of South Africa in 1991 and explained how they were wanting to consolidate their standing in the middle of the first division, having battled their way up from second division. They were eager to import a quality midfield player and offered Walter the job.

Little says he saw it as a rich opportunity to broaden his horizons, to experience another culture, to do something completely different. "I knew the rugby wouldn't be too demanding, so I accepted."

He loved Italy – its food, its wine, its people. The rugby was a million miles removed from what he was accustomed to with the All Blacks and North Harbour, but he enjoyed that too, particularly the camaraderie that existed within the Roma club.

"I would have been happy to have stayed for three or four years," admits Little, "but of course I had to return for the New Zealand season, and unfortunately I didn't get the opportunity to go back."

Walter kept running across New Zealanders doing their thing in Italy. Zinzan and Robin Brooke were there, along with John Kirwan, Steve Hotton, Shayne Philpott and Arthur Stone.

The Roma club couldn't have looked after Walter and Tracy better if they had been natives of Italy.

Roberto Corvo, who spoke fluent English – and thus provided Walter and Tracy with an important lifeline when they first arrived in Rome – became like a brother to them. It was he who made all the necessary arrangements when Tracy was expecting. And, of course, it was he who was invited to be Michael's Italian Godfather. The New Zealand Godfather would be Craig Innes.

Robert arranged for Walter and Tracy to attend language lessons three times a week, until they were able to speak Italian, if not fluently certainly adequately enough to shop with confidence and carry on a basic conversation.

Locking into Italian rugby mentality took some time. Walter always considered that, back home, if North Harbour was sufficiently focused and its leading players performed, it could beat any team on any ground.

But not in Italy. The home team always wins. At least, that's the psychology which rather inhibits teams every time they hit the road. And for Walter's club, Roma, well removed from the heart of Italian rugby, in the north of the country, an away trip usually involved a six or seven hour bus journey.

Little's first away trip was to Shayne Philpott's club, Palma. Because he hadn't been in Italy long enough to absorb the away-games-are-always-lost philosophy, he went to Palma full of optimism, played his heart out. And Roma won!

"It was," says Little, "regarded as an astonishing achievement. The club was thrilled with this unexpected bonus."

The next out-of-town excursion was to L'Aquila, which was regarded as a local derby, the equivalent of Auckland against North Harbour. Roma might have succeeded against Palma away but it would never defeat L'Aquila at L'Aquila, Walter was assured.

Well, at halftime, Roma, having played rugby of a sublime quality, was ahead by 35 points to 3. "Our coach was over the moon," says

Little. "You've never seen anyone so happy. Instead of concentrating on the second half battle plan, he kept going on about what an amazing achievement this was.

"The boys were too excited for their own good. They started trying to run the ball from their own goalline and the inevitable happened. We fell apart. I couldn't believe what was happening, with the end result that we lost 46-35!

"A New Zealand team would have been devastated, but the Roma coach was still ecstatic because we'd scored so many points and run L'Aquila so close. I had to keep reminding myself that we were the losing team because everyone was so happy. It was, quite simply, the Italian way!"

For each away trip, one player was responsible for supplying sandwiches and cakes. Walter had observed the Roma players boarding the bus with large boxes of food which they would serve during the journey.

It was only after about the fifth trip that he realised what was happening. The players were doing this chore on a rotational basis, but as the overseas representative, he was being excused

Walter wasn't having any of that. He was part of the team, he would help out with the food. So, for the next excursion, he requested Tracy to bake one of her pieces de resistance, a banana cake.

What was initially greeted with amusement quickly became the Roma team's favourite food. "They didn't really understand about bananas," says Little. "'You mean it's made from those funny yellow things?' they asked me. Once they'd sampled it, they couldn't get enough of it."

Little operated mostly in midfield, occasionally deputising at first-five. The standard, he felt, was about equal to senior club level in New Zealand. His team Glenfield would have held its own with most of the Italian sides.

"It was enjoyable rugby to play because the Italians love to run the ball," he says. "But their Latin temperament would often get the better of them, as when we led L'Aquila by more than thirty points at halftime. If someone erred, another player would blow him up. We had a number of Argentinians in the side and they were pretty emotional too. I was always trying to quieten everyone down."

The moves were always called in Italian which presented obvious problems for Little, although as his Italian improved so did his communication.

In one match, Walter thought he knew what the call was. But what the first-five had uttered and what Walter had in mind were two entirely different ploys.

"He'd called a dummy cut but here was I expecting his pass. Suddenly I was in the clear...but without the ball. It was hilarious because we scored anyway.

"We were so impressed with the new manoeuvre we added it to our repertoire and called it Mistake. It produced tries on a few other occasions."

Tracy went into labour in mid-March and was rushed to a hospital on an island on the River Tiber. Walter was planning on being with his partner when the baby was born but was stopped by an authoritative nurse who, with an open hand extended like a pointsman on traffic duty, ordered, "No men!"

Walter sat anxiously in the waiting room with three other would-be fathers, not knowing what was happening and struggling to make conversation. He was heartened when one of the others was invited into the delivery room but lost a little of his enthusiasm when he later came out and threw up!

Eventually, Walter was allowed in and was present when Michael was born, an experience he describes as "unbelievable."

The Roma club met all the doctor's bills and, the Italians being the great family people they are, made a great fuss over the baby.

"Roberto just did so much for us," says Walter, "which is why we decided to have an Italian Godfather. He's still sending us presents. It's special for Michael that he was born in Rome and that he will have someone there when eventually he travels."

Little hadn't simply made up the numbers for Roma, which completed the season occupying a middle-of-the-table position. He was awarded the Italian Rugby Union's Player of the Year trophy.

Roma was desperately keen for him to return but, mostly because of injury problems, that never eventuated. But the club did pick up another international from North Harbour, Buck Shelford, and Walter's brother Lawrence.

While Little was doing his thing in Italy, Bunce was representing his country at sevens in Hong Kong and Scotland, so they had countless travellers' tales to exchange when they caught up with each other.

They were soon back in business as a lethal midfield combination with North Harbour, at the (storm-lashed) All Black trials in Rotorua and for the All Blacks against the Lions.

Bunce was to play seven internationals for his country in 1993, as well as tour the UK, but the luckless Little wasn't to complete one test in a year he would prefer to forget.

Little's woes began in the season's opening test against Gavin Hastings' Lions at Lancaster Park. This was the occasion when Bunce scored a controversial try in the opening minutes after capitalising on a soaring up-and-under from Grant Fox. Well, Bunce doesn't consider the try was disputable at all, but the Lions and their media went on about it, even claiming in the tour book *So Close To Glory* that the error by the referee (Australian Brian Kinsey) cost the Lions the series.

Bunce insists that his try was perfectly legitimate. "I forced the ball

– no question of that – and was then turned and held up. That's obviously how the referee saw it. The Brits also questioned the last penalty from which Foxy landed the winning goal. I think it was pure frustration showing through because we'd stolen from them a game they could have won."

Late in the game Little collided with Inga Tuigamala while effecting a telling double tackle on winger Ieuan Evans. His knee graunched as he fell to the ground. He knew immediately it was serious.

What he'd done was seriously strain the medial ligament. The doctor's prognosis was not encouraging – rest the knee for four to six weeks. With luck he could be back for the Bledisloe Cup test in Dunedin in mid-July.

Bunce's moment of agony had come two weeks earlier in North Harbour's clash with the Lions at the unusual venue of Mt Smart (now Ericsson) Stadium.

Having effected an important tackle close to his goalposts, Bunce was deliberately slow in clearing the ball. "I deserved a tickle up for killing the ball," he says, "but I got far worse than that."

Dean Richards, the Lions' uncompromising No 8, went searching for the ball rather recklessly and scraped his sprigs across Bunce's head, ripping through an ear.

Bunce is almost apologetic in describing what happened. "Richards, like a lot of the Brits, isn't used to hard rucking. They were trying to match fire with fire and I believe it was poor technique more than maliciousness that resulted in me being rucked. Although the main damage was to my ear, the greater pain was around my ankles, which is an extremely sensitive area when someone is standing on it."

The North Harbour captain Richard Turner didn't see it Bunce's way. He was most unapologetic, taking ruthless retribution on Richards, punching him so powerfully the big Brit was forced to retire injured.

Bunce actually played on, but not before his ear was heavily bandaged.

He confesses that he didn't think there was anything seriously wrong with the ear until he put his hand to it, and discovered all the blood.

North Harbour's physio (David Abercrombie) and doctor (John Mayhew) didn't bother describing the extent of the injury when they treated Bunce. But later, when he went to the dressing room, they insisted on removing the bandages themselves, because they were afraid the ear might come off with them!

"It turned out Richards' sprigs had sliced it clean through. It was hanging by a small piece of skin."

In these days of citings and trial by video, it's hard to believe Richards didn't receive a significant suspension. But neither the NZRFU nor the Lions management at the time deemed his actions serious enough to interrupt his touring schedule. The following week he captained the tourists against Canterbury!

However, the brutal events at Mt Smart did cause a public (and media) uproar and Bunce found his telephone ringing hot, most of the callers being journalists wanting Bunce to make a statement deploring Richards' actions.

One of the callers was a television producer inviting him to appear on a panel condemning foul play. "While I appreciated the tenor of the programme, which was directed at fair play in sport, I didn't think I was the person to be speaking out about thuggery on the rugby field. I'm no saint. I felt it would represent hypocrisy for me to declare my outrage. So I declined."

Ironically, Richards and Bunce were the two players selected from the Mt Smart encounter for drug testing, finding themselves together in a small room waiting for the doctor to arrive.

"It didn't make for animated conversation," says Bunce. "Richards simply said, 'How's things?' He never referred to the incident or asked how my ear was. I might have reacted but I was content in the knowledge that Pod (Richard Turner) had already dealt with him satisfactorily on my behalf."

What Bunce *would* have said if he'd joined the television panel was that he doesn't approve of any player using his feet near another's head. "The head, and I think most New Zealand players feel this, is sacrosanct. Genuine rucking, which is done with a backwards motion, never hurt anyone. But standing on a player's head or kicking at it is, in my book, a serious offence and should be dealt with accordingly. Eye gouging is another disgusting act I feel strongly about."

With Little sidelined Bunce as an All Black was to become involved in many different midfield liaisons in 1993.

The first substitution for Little was Eroni Clarke, the bruising runner of Western Samoan extraction. But after Mains' men had crashed to a humiliating loss in the second test at Athletic Park, he gave way to Lee Stensness, another Aucklander but with more graceful skills.

Stensness operated with such panache against the Lions at Eden Park and the Wallabies at Carisbrook that he appeared destined for a lengthy tenure in the test line-up, but a loss of form on the tour of England and Scotland meant that by year's end Bunce would also team up with Marty Berry and, for the internationals at Murrayfield and Twickenham, Matthew Cooper.

Bunce had never achieved a rapport with Clarke as a midfield partner. "I've never been a fan of Eroni as a second-five. He gets in too close to the opposition and his distribution skills aren't great. He can be a devastating runner but his skills are far better suited to centre or wing.

"Eroni's biggest problem back in 1993 was that he didn't know where he belonged. He was being used all over the backline and that makes it terribly difficult for a player. He and I certainly didn't fire as a pairing which was one of several reasons why the All Blacks took such a hiding in Wellington."

Bunce recalls that every time he handled the ball at Athletic Park "there seemed to be scarlet jerseys everywhere."

"They were more desperate than us, even though our preparation had been excellent. I would label the second test of that series (the Lions won 20-7) as probably the worst performance by the All Blacks in my experience. We offered nothing."

For the Wellington test the All Blacks were quartered at the five star Park Royal Hotel in the central city which seemed like a good idea at the time. But the All Blacks have never been back there. No reflection on the Park Royal which is an outstandingly good hotel, but it was never designed to cater for sporting teams.

Says Bunce: "It was entirely impractical. The players were accommodated on different floors. We ate in the main dining area on the ground floor while our team room was on the top floor. We spent an inordinate amount of time waiting for lifts."

Before 1993, and since, the All Blacks have stayed at the Airport Hotel at Kilbirnie. Although several stars behind the Park Royal, it, like the Poenamo Hotel in Auckland, offers all the facilities a rugby teams wants, on one floor. And it's well removed from the bustle of the central city.

One week separated the second and third tests, and Bunce regards it as the hardest week of his rugby career. "It was the pressure, the unrelenting pressure," he says. "We all knew that another loss would have severe repercussions for Laurie and ourselves.

"The critics came down upon us severely after the forlorn display in Wellington and the talkback shows were malicious. So I made a conscious effort to stay away from the papers and the radios once we had assembled. There was enough pressure within the team."

Bunce lavishes praise on Mains for his attitude in that demanding week. "If Laurie, who was obviously enormously disappointed with the performance in Wellington, had taken a negative approach, he could have destroyed the spirit of the team," says Bunce. "But he was quite magnificent. From the moment we assembled, he was relaxed. We were expecting a tongue lashing and agony on the training field, but there was none of that. He was as lighthearted as I've ever known, even cracking jokes.

"Mind you, he did work the forwards hard in training, because they had given a sub-standard display in Wellington.

"Rather than dwell on the inadequacies of the second test effort, he focused on what we needed to achieve at Eden Park."

Bunce says the mood of the All Blacks was deadly serious from the moment of assembly. "Usually, the players' intensity builds over a day or two. That week, every player was focused from the get-together on the Tuesday.

"When a team loses, the coach invariably takes the blame. But at Wellington we knew we'd let ourselves down. We didn't need Laurie or the media or the public to remind us. We knew ourselves. We also knew what was required in the final test."

The All Blacks were 10-nil down after 23 minutes at Eden Park. If there existed an anxiety among the supporters it certainly didn't apply to the players.

"We were feeling so good," says Bunce, "I don't believe any of the players felt there was any outcome possible other than a decisive All Black victory."

Former All Black Stu Wilson, the comments person on television that day, accused the New Zealanders of being undisciplined when they gave away penalties early on.

Bunce disagrees. "I gave away a penalty for a high tackle on Gavin Hastings. That wasn't indiscipline. That was me trying to make a mark (literally and figuratively) on the opposition. We were taking a more physically aggressive approach, getting stuck into everything."

The turning point came when Stensness, playing the game of his life, placed a delicate chip kick in behind the advancing Lions defence for Bunce to run on to.

"If you allow a ball to roll end over end long enough, it will eventually sit up," says Bunce. "Lee's kick was rolling sweetly as I chased after it. 'It's going to come, it's going to come up,' I told myself. 'Don't rush it …wait, wait, wait.' Finally it sat up. 'Here I am, Frank,' it said. And I scored the try!"

Bunce had expected to confront England's experienced midfield pairing Will Carling and Jeremy Guscott throughout the series but after a disappointing display at Lancaster Park, Carling was dropped for Welshman Scott Gibbs.

Bunce had a healthy respect for Guscott's pace and elusiveness but he had a suspicion that Guscott might be found wanting when the pressure went on.

During the heat of battle at Eden Park he heard Lions captain Gavin Hastings say, "Come on, Jeremy, we need you."

"If you hear something like that coming from the opposition, it gives you an extra boost. Jeremy had gone missing when things got tough."

The All Blacks, finishing with a flourish, topped 30 points to clinch the series in style. They'd saved the best for last. As in Sydney the previous year, they had demonstrated the New Zealanders' capacity to dig deep when the pressure was on.

Bunce recalls a startling lack of celebration in the dressing room. "Everyone was shattered," he says. "It had been an incredibly demanding week. I remember saying to Peter Thorburn, as I sat slumped in a corner, that I was 'absolutely buggered.'

"It's a test match – you're supposed to look like that," was Thorburn's reply.

Little had watched the Eden Park test with mixed emotions. While delighted that the All Blacks had overcome the British challenge, he was bothered by Stensness' accomplished display which he saw as a threat to his future as a test player.

Still, he was heartened to receive phone calls from Mains and Thorburn, both inquiring if he would be ready to play against Australia. Little frustratingly had to admit that he would not be right. The knee was responding to treatment but was two weeks away from full fitness.

Bunce was the ideal person to compare Little with Stensness. "Lee was right on top of his game in 1993 – he was certainly the right selection at the time. Walter's much the better defender. Lee is a calculating player where Walter's an instinctive one. Lee would sum things up before taking a course of action where Walter would just go, sometimes for better, sometimes for worse."

Stensness' excellent form continued as the All Blacks regained the Bledisloe Cup most convincingly at Carisbrook. Another of his exquisitely judged chip kicks produced another try to Bunce, this time after Tuigamala had regained the ball and done all the hard work, dragging David Campese and fullback Tim Kelaher 10 metres towards the goalline.

While the All Blacks relished the opportunity to play in Dunedin, because of the marvellous atmosphere created by the locals, the Australians, who delayed their arrival until late Thursday night, plainly had a complex about the place, which played into the New Zealanders' hands.

Also, the Wallabies with their captain Michael Lynagh injured bravely fielded a rookie teenager at first-five, Pat Howard. He was a natural target for the All Blacks, assisting them by trying to run the ball out from his 22 at one stage. A fatal moment of hesitation and he was pounced on by Michael Jones and soon submerged by black jerseys.

"It wasn't pretty," says Bunce. "The boys gave him a hard time. 'Thanks, Pat,' 'You're not up to it, Pat,' 'Have another run, Pat – we liked that.' Not only did he concede a penalty in the ruck, which Foxy goaled, he would have come out bruised and with his confidence dented."

Bunce was acknowledged as one of the stars of the All Black victory, having unsettled the Australian midfield with his dynamic tackling.

When Little was again checked out by Mains, he was able to give him the heartening news that the knee was repaired and strengthened. He was ready for a return to action.

Mains responded by including Little in the reserves for the final domestic test of '93, against Western Samoa at Eden Park, Stensness being retained at second-five. While it gave Little a much-needed boost, he says now he would have been better off with another fortnight's rest.

Fate was to deal him a cruel blow. Stensness would retire injured – one of several players wounded in what became known as The Battle of the Bandages – and Little would replace him. But in making his first tackle, on To'o Vaega…"or it might have been Alama Ieremia – he was bloody hard, whoever it was"…Little felt something crack in his leg.

It didn't cause any immediate pain and he battled through to the finish, none too impressively. He would play eight matches for North Harbour over the next three months, occasionally experiencing discomfort in the leg, before the extent of the damage was revealed.

The moment of truth came for Little after he'd been enjoying a quiet smoke during an afternoon tea break at work, this a week after he had been included in the All Black team to tour the UK. In getting to his feet, he experienced another 'crack' in his leg, accompanied this time by pain. It was all he could do to walk.

An x ray revealed a spiral fracture in the right fibula, the thinner of the two bones linking the ankle with the knee. The leg would require a plaster cast and six weeks' rest, ruling him out of the tour.

A dejected Little conveyed the bad news to coach Mains. "He said he wanted me along but there was nothing he could do about it. At least they allowed me to keep some of the gear which had been allocated." Marty Berry was called up as a replacement.

The injury capped a thoroughly depressing year for Little. With the LPG business arrangement falling over, and involving substantial debts (which he was still paying off in 1995), he and Tracy found themselves scraping the bottom of the barrel.

He was relying on the modest daily allowances given the All Blacks – in 1993 that was about $55 a day – to survive, but that source of income dried up when he was injured and forced to pull out of the test squad.

The All Blacks Club chipped in with a handout but Little was barely subsisting, at which point the league offers which had tumbled his way (from agents in Sydney) were beginning to look almost irresistible.

Little describes himself as "terribly vulnerable" at this point. Fortunately, because his love for rugby was greater than his desire for a healthy bank balance, he contacted Mains and Thorburn, acquainting them of his now desperate situation.

They acted swiftly and, through the All Blacks Club, organised a job at Lion Breweries, where Little was required to help run the machines in the packaging department. It was a lifesaver for him, especially as he was allowed time off for playing representative rugby.

He was settling into the new routine well when disaster, in the form of his broken leg, struck. Being required to wear safety boots in the factory presented an insurmountable problem with his leg in a plaster cast, so he was obliged to spend the next six weeks at home.

Fortunately, Accident Compensation met 80 per cent of his income and Lion Breweries generously made up the other 20 per cent, so the bills could be paid.

Being left behind when the All Blacks flew out meant obvious disappointment for Little but, reduced to watching live telecasts in the middle of the night, he discovered there were compensations.

He was able to share precious time with his son Michael, now eight months old, while he and Tracy were able to soak up the summer sunshine, something they had desperately missed while concentrating on rugby for five successive winters.

Bunce, blessedly free of the problems that were plaguing Little, flew off to the UK with Mains' All Blacks, not quite sure what he'd let himself in for at representative level.

At North Harbour's end of season dinner there was obvious disappointment that Mike Mills was stepping aside as the back coach but even greater concern that Brad Meurant was contemplating retirement.

"Brad said his commitment to North Harbour was taking its toll on his business (as a plumber) while his tripping around the world in the cause of rugby wasn't fair on his wife Helen.

"The players, who had an enormous respect for him as a coach and a person, dearly wanted him to continue.

"I joined in, assuring him that we wanted him back in 1994. Then, in a moment of bravado, I said, 'If you need a back coach next season, I'll do the job.'

"Brad said he'd think about it. He obviously did because while we were in the UK the word came through that I was the new assistant coach of North Harbour."

Little wasn't the only established All Black missing for the end-of-year tour. John Kirwan had been sensationally dropped, Michael Jones had broken his jaw in a freakish collision at a training session in Auckland and Grant Fox had chosen to put his work (for Carnegie International) ahead of rugby touring.

One other player not selected, but who was to become involved, in extremely controversial circumstances, was Mike Brewer, who would follow the tour in his capacity as marketing manager of Canterbury International.

Bunce doesn't carry a reputation as being among rugby's most enthusiastic trainers. But he's street wise. And he listens. So when coach Mains announced to the players that they would all be tested after assembly in Auckland and their individual ratings would dictate how hard they would work on tour, Bunce listened.

He and Rush resolved to be in the super fit category, so in the fortnight leading up to assembly, they took themselves out almost daily and ran gut-busting 150s.

"Everyone knew Rushy would be in the top group after testing," says Bunce. "But, surprise, surprise, I was there too, turning in my best ever beep test result. No one could believe it."

Bunce smirked once in the UK when Mains, true to his word, made those players who'd scored poorest, regularly run back to the hotel from training and put in extra 150s and Down and Ups.

Bursting with energy, Bunce turned in a smashing performance first up at Twickenham, helping the All Blacks put 39 points on a useful London and South-East combination that featured test stars Rob Andrew, Will Carling, Tony Underwood, Brian Moore, Jason Leonard and Jeff Probyn.

Bunce exerted himself to such an extent that, afterwards, he declared to Mains he was "absolutely buggered."

"I realised later that was not a smart comment to utter near Laurie," says Bunce. "Sure enough, at the next training, Laurie brought it up. There are obviously a couple of players not on top of their fitness, he asserted, because they'd told him they were tired. So he gave us extra work."

Bunce has never been a cold weather footballer, so as the British winter began to set in, he sometimes found himself struggling, never more so than against Scotland A at Glasgow where an icy wind whipping in from the Arctic reduced temperatures to near freezing point.

With his hands frozen, Bunce turned in a shocker. And so did Matthew Cooper inside him. At one stage, during an injury break, 'Doc' John Mayhew told him he had a message from the coach.

"Yeah, what is it?" said Bunce, hugging himself trying to keep warm.

"Laurie said, if you're not going to stop fucking around, come off!"

Bunce's miserable afternoon persisted.

"Right, get him off," ordered Mains.

When Mayhew next stepped on to the field, it was to treat John Timu. Bunce was some distance away. So Mayhew told Timu to instruct Bunce, at the next opportunity, to come off.

Timu's reaction was terse. "Tell him your bloody self!"

Bunce saw out the game at centre, being enormously relieved to hear the final whistle, not because of his dud performance but because he couldn't wait to get under a hot shower.

"Hell, it was cold. I had no feeling in my arms from the elbows down. In those conditions it's very hard to produce good rugby."

Mains was angry at Bunce's display and made it known at the team meeting.

After announcing the team for the Tuesday game (which would precede the test against Scotland), Mains declared he wanted in the foyer at 9am the next day "all those who didn't play today...and Frank Bunce."

"That rather seriously curtailed my socialising," says Bunce, "knowing I had to front for training on the Sunday morning."

Mains answered a knock on his door at 8 o'clock the next morning. It was a forlorn looking Matthew Cooper. "He told me if Frank was being given extra work, he should too, because there was equal responsibility for the breakdown of the midfield at Glasgow.

"I thought that showed great bottle. Together they gutsed it out at training."

Mains didn't spare Bunce, ordering him to operate at lock while the set pieces were being practised.

Mains says he gives Bunce enormous credit for determination that Sunday. "He wasn't feeling great but there was no way he was going to let me break him. In fact, I had the feeling he was enjoying himself!"

"I would have happily played in the forwards the previous day," says Bunce. "At least it would have kept me warm."

Among those who trained that Sunday morning were Mike Brewer.

Bunce confesses that he finds the weather in the UK depressing and would rather tour South Africa or Australia any time.

"Sunshine and firm grounds stimulate you, make you want to play," says Bunce. "But when it's cold all the time, and dark till 9 o'clock every morning, your enthusiasm wanes. We played in some diabolical conditions in Scotland and England at times. We even trained in snow. Once the novelty wears off, it's pure misery."

Regardless of the climate, a visit to England for the All Blacks is always special because it includes a visit to Buckingham Palace and the opportunity to socialise with royalty. On this occasion the players were hosted by the Queen, Lady Di, Princess Anne, Prince Charles and Prince Andrew.

According to Frank, the players were relaxed talking to Charles, Di and Anne, but rather "clammed up" when Her Majesty came into their presence.

"We were broken up into groups, and as she approached I found myself staring at her skin, transfixed by it, because it was so smooth. To my embarrassment she became aware of me staring at her.

"By the time she advanced to our cluster, the sweat was running down my back. Goodness only knows what our small talk was about. I was so completely overwhelmed by the occasion, I can't remember a thing. I felt like Mister Bean, shuffling around and aware at the last moment I had my hands in my pocket. So much for meeting the Queen!"

The onfield highlight of the tour was undoubtedly the spectacular 51-15 victory over Scotland at Murrayfield.

The Scots erred in attaching too great a significance to Scotland A's performance, the one where Bunce and Co. were frozen-fingered. Several players clinched test selection as a result of that performance, including centre Ian Jardine who made the huge mistake of blabbing to a television interviewer how well he expected Scotland to perform.

"He'll keep," Bunce mused as he watched the interview. "Some of these guys never learn to keep their mouths shut.

"They were so enthused by their performance at Glasgow, they forgot about us. The worst thing you can do to a touring team the week before a test is embarrass them. Then they come out blazing, as we did. You're far better letting the touring team think they're doing well."

The All Blacks were in charge at Murrayfield from the start, running in seven tries. Although some critics sought to belittle the performance by declaring Scotland to be a weak opponent, the Scots had been defeated on their home turf only twice in five years.

No, this was a vintage All Black performance. The forwards were aggressive and dominated the set pieces while the backs ran riot, with Jeff "Goldie" Wilson the star of the show in his test debut.

Not only did he score a hat-trick of tries but, with Matthew Cooper off injured, he coolly slotted a wide angle conversion in the final minute to hoist New Zealand's first half-century test score against Scotland.

Eric Rush sat in the grandstand directly behind Princess Anne, one of Scotland's staunchest supporters. Once, he says, when Gavin Hastings, the Scottish captain and darling of Murrayfield, was taken by Inga Tuigamala and buried at the bottom of a furious-looking ruck, Princess Anne winced.

"I knew then things were going well," says Rush.

Bunce was delighted for Wilson who he initially thought was a flashy individual.

"He'd come into the team as a wonder boy, and you're always a little suspicious of them, until they've proved themselves. But Goldie soon showed us he was a very special person, mature for his age, a footballer with great skills. His enthusiasm was infectious. He could play wing or fullback and kick goals, and he chased everything. He was a marvellous replacement for John Kirwan."

Frano Botica had driven up from Wigan to watch the All Blacks play and Frank was able to share a drink with him (and Sam Panapa, another Kiwi who'd played for the mighty Dustys touch team) before heading to the official dinner.

"They do things impressively in the UK," says Bunce. "The Scots arrived at the dinner in kilts, and the haggis was duly piped in. With Scottish rugby having Famous Grouse as its sponsor, we were all presented with gift bottles of their fine product.

"They're a great race of people, the Scots, similar in so many ways to New Zealanders, I feel. We shared a memorable evening."

The next international, against England seven days on, wasn't so memorable, the All Blacks crashing to a humbling 15-9 loss in a try-less contest at Twickenham.

The build-up hadn't been good, with Cooper, the second-five and goalkicker, being forced out with a deep-seated groin injury. His replacement, whose selection didn't enthuse Bunce, was Clarke.

"The fundamental backline weakness we fielded against England was that no one from first-five to centre could kick under pressure.

"Marc Ellis, being groomed as a first-five on that tour, possessed a powerful boot. But it's one thing to kick when you can set yourself, another when the enemy is bearing down on you.

"Marc kicked poorly and neither Eroni nor I could kick at all. So we had huge problems when our forwards were being beaten.

"It was the complete reverse of the Scottish game when the forwards were in charge and the backs only had to worry about which move was being called."

Bunce had the feeling throughout that the All Blacks would pull the game out of the fire. "But we never did. We missed our kicks, the English defended mightily and John Timu put his foot into touch going for what would have been the matchwinning try."

Mains, Bunce recalls, was not a happy chappie. His team had played poorly and lost, tarnishing what to then had been an excellent year for the All Blacks.

Mains was to be condemned for introducing Brewer to the reserves at Twickenham and again for the Barbarians match at Cardiff – slipping him into the touring party ostensibly as a replacement for Cooper – ahead of the team's other specialist flanker Liam Barry. Although he remained in the grandstand for the test, he took the field against the Baabaas, subsequently taking his share of the All Black Company payout for his cameo appearance.

While Bunce appreciated the logic behind the move – Brewer, with his vast experience being better equipped to deal with England's giant loosies Ben Clarke, Dean Richards and Tim Rodber, had he been required to go on – he didn't agree with the principle of it.

And nor did a lot of the players, who voiced their protest through the midweek skipper John Mitchell.

"It was done in the right way, at a team meeting," says Bunce. "John (Mitchell) said he was speaking on behalf of a large number of the midweek players when he said he felt the introduction of Brewer, at Barry's expense, was entirely inappropriate."

Bunce had developed huge respect for Mitchell throughout the tour.

"I'd spoken to him at the 1992 awards dinner where he said he'd always wanted to be an All Black, but at twenty-nine he considered the opportunity had passed him by.

"I said, use me as your inspiration. I was thirty when I first pulled on the All Black jersey. And the next year, there he was, an All Black."

Mitchell, according to Bunce, was a great role model for the young players.

"He took a lot of pressure off Laurie Mains. The midweekers had suffered an embarrassing forty-point loss to Sydney the previous year but in the UK the midweekers, under John's leadership, developed an awesome team spirit. They were determined to go through undefeated, and they did, scoring some exceptional victories."

Introducing The Brown Brothers

Ant Strachan at halfback and Warren Burton at first-five were distinctive individuals in North Harbour's hot-shot backline in 1994 – they were white.

The other five members of the first-choice line-up, that dazzled opponents and fans alike, were of Polynesian and Maori extraction, collectively to become known as the Brown Brothers.

There should be a romantic storyline to the origin of the Brown Brothers tag. Or maybe it was such an obvious title, it just materialised.

Well…er…not exactly. Its origin can be traced most accurately to Port Elizabeth in April, 1994, when North Harbour took on Grizz Wyllie's Eastern Province team in a Super 10 match.

After first use of a gusty wind, North Harbour, expected to win this encounter easily against the weakest of the South African Super 10 sides, was trailing by 10 points, having performed abysmally.

Brad Meurant was a coach in despair as he made his way down on to Boet Erasmus Stadium at the halftime break.

He summoned the backs around him. "Listen, you brown buggers," he said, "when the wind is coming from behind and it's so strong it ruffles your hair like this (at which point he shook his hair about frantically), you kick the bloody ball. You kick for position. Got it? Well, we don't have the wind in this half, so you better start working out how to score tries or we're down the drain."

"Jeez," said fullback Glen Osborne to Eric Rush as the players moved into position for the start of the second half, "Brad's not too pleased with us - us brown brothers better start making things happen."

The 'brown brothers' – Little at second-five, Bunce at centre, Eric

Rush and Peter Woods on the wings and Osborne – did just that, in spectacular fashion. And they did it with "sevens magic", Osborne, Rush and Woods having only a couple of weeks previously represented the champion New Zealand team at the Hong Kong international sevens tournament.

Osborne grabbed two tries and Rush one as North Harbour, producing rollicking rugby in the final half an hour, came steaming through to win 31-21.

The Brown Brothers tag stuck. Thereafter, whenever coach Meurant was naming his team, it went something like this: "Halfback - Strawney (Ant Strachan), first-five – Burts (Warren Burton)…and the Brown brothers!"

Bunce was by this stage the assistant coach of Harbour, something which, he admits, took some adjusting to.

For a start, with his new responsibility he felt it important to start arriving on time, preferably ahead of the other players. His coach was most impressed. "Before 1994, Bunce didn't know the meaning of the word punctuality," says Meurant, "but I can't recall him arriving late for training once after he became assistant coach. I think there's a lesson in there somewhere!"

Bunce considered that as the back coach, his role would be purely to advise those around him on moves and lines to run. "I knew no one would take me seriously if I tried to censure them, so I focused on the backline's tactical approach."

Having talked with his predecessor, Mike Mills, with recently retired All Black ace Grant Fox and with his team mate Eric Rush, whom he regarded as a fountain of all knowledge, Bunce considered he was worthily prepared to step into his new role.

What he wasn't prepared for was the attention his fellow backs would accord him at training. "After we'd finishing working out as a team," says Bunce, "we separated into backs and forwards. Suddenly people were waiting for me to say something. I realised with horror there were still twenty minutes to go. Hell, what do I do now?

"I put a lot more mental effort into my preparation from that point. That's when I turned to Ant Strachan and others in the backline. We all thought along the same lines, having achieved sweet harmony the previous year. It began to work."

Meurant basically left the backs to Bunce, only intervening if he felt they were going seriously off the rails. "Which," says Meurant, "they occasionally did, but only because they got carried away at times. They played some terrific rugby and scored a lot of unforgettable tries, but every now and then I had to rope them in."

North Harbour had promised plenty without delivering anything of great consequence since its arrival in the first division in 1988. It had remained consistently in the shadow of its all-powerful neighbour

Auckland, and had performed with mediocrity in the early-season CANZ and Super 10 series.

All that was to change in 1994. The breakthrough, in Bunce's opinion, came with the victory against Transvaal at Onewa Domain, North Harbour's first significant victory against an overseas opponent.

"It didn't seem a game we were likely to win," says Bunce, "as Transvaal applied intense pressure through the first half. But we kept pulling off desperate tackles and frustrating them. At halftime Brad Meurant said, 'You've weathered the storm, let's go and get 'em.' We scarcely had an attacking opportunity in the first half but when they came, we grabbed them, and won."

Victory the following weekend would have projected North Harbour into the Super 10 final, against Natal in Durban, but Meurant's men were to stumble against Queensland at Ballymore.

It was only a small stumble, Harbour losing 13-10 in agonising circumstances. Knowing that a draw would put them through to the final, they couldn't believe their bad luck when Warren Burton missed a penalty attempt from almost straight in front in the closing moments.

"Burton wasn't a popular lad with the Harbour players the next morning," recalls Bunce. "It mattered not that we hadn't won the game. You accept that your goalkicker will be a champ one day, a chump the next. No, everyone was dirty on him because we had to check in at Brisbane Airport soon after 6am. Had we won, we would have been flying to South Africa, and could have had a good sleep in!"

It was a reflection of North Harbour's strength that Queensland swept Natal aside in the series final. Queensland coach John Connolly paid Harbour the compliment of declaring them the toughest outfit they had encountered that season.

As an aside, Queensland officials might have been happy to concede defeat to Harbour had they known that their two champion midfielders, Tim Horan and Jason Little, would return from Durban on crutches, both with their right legs in plaster.

North Harbour's disappointment at losing to Queensland was quickly forgotten when the team pulled off an historic victory over Philippe Saint-Andre's Frenchmen, 27-23, in front of 20,000 fans at Eden Park.

The highlight was a sensational solo try scored by Osborne, reminiscent of some of John Kirwan's dazzling feats on the same ground.

Slipping into the backline from a scrum near halfway, he slipped past No 8 Marc Cecillon, stepped inside fullback Jean-Luc Sadourny and had enough toe to beat Laurent Cabannes to the tryline.

In this game Bunce finally got to oppose Philippe Sella. *Rugby News* was to score Bunce a seven and Sella a six for their performances. Arriving home more than contented with both his own play and the team's great victory, Bunce was subjected to a critical assessment by his sister

Margaret. "She told me I needed to lose weight and work on my speed before the tests. Cripes, you can't win!"

Little was enjoying his rugby thoroughly. His broken leg was fully mended, he'd strengthened his body through the summer with weight training and he was relishing the opportunity to operate in a provincial team that was firing on all cylinders.

He loved the autonomy the Harbour backline offered. "We'd operated together as a unit for so long," says Little, "that we had a great understanding. If you attacked from your own twenty-two, you knew you would have support."

Meurant recalls that some of the backline's calls, particularly those from Little, bordered on the outrageous.

On one occasion Little nominated a certain move when his team was hard on defence.

"It's a complicated move," replied Bunce. "What chance of success do you rate it?"

"Oh, about eighty-twenty against."

"Okay, we'll go for it!"

On another occasion, in almost identical circumstances, Bunce put the same question to Little. This time the answer was ninety-ten against.

Warren Burton, who'd listened with bemusement from first-five, upon receiving the ball promptly kicked it into touch.

"You can try *that* move further up the paddock," he told Little with a finality in his voice.

Little wasn't surprised when the All Black selectors named him among the reserves for the first test against France at Christchurch because the player in his position at second-five, Matthew Cooper, was the goalkicker.

"John Timu, the fullback, wasn't a kicker, so Cooper was needed – I accepted that," says Little. "At least I was back in the All Black squad. There were six tests coming up. I was confident of being involved in some of them."

From the grandstand, he watched the All Blacks crash to successive defeats against the formidable French, the first a thrashing at Lancaster Park, the second an astonishing rescue act by the French who scored their winning try near fulltime from a spectacular attack which swept almost the full length of Eden Park. Both tests were played on Sundays.

"It wasn't the start to the 1994 international series that Laurie Mains, or the All Blacks, needed," says Little. "All it did was place almost intolerable pressure on Laurie, particularly, to succeed."

The French series introduced Jonah Lomu to test rugby. Unfortunately, he didn't live up to the fanfare that heralded his arrival and, in what was unquestionably a huge psychological blow to him, he was dropped for the remaining tests of 1994.

Bunce had first encountered Jonah at a sevens tournament in

Singapore, Eric Rush inviting the emerging giant to join the Mongrels. "Rushy assured me that this guy was going to be good, and Rushy's never far wrong when he makes a prediction. He'd also taken him to a sevens tournament in Apia and said he was particularly impressed at his attitude. When the chips were down, Jonah apparently really got stuck in. That was a good sign.

"While it was encouraging to have such an exciting attacker coming into the All Blacks, we weren't aware he had never been coached in defence.

"It's damned hard to go from schoolboy loosie to test winger in less than twelve months, which was what the selectors were asking of Jonah. And he was up against Emile Ntamack and a bunch of crafty French backs who could expose any opponent.

"I don't think anyone really thought about Jonah's defence. It was glossed over because everyone believed he would trample Frenchmen underfoot every time he received the ball.

"As it turned out, he was seriously out of his depth. He didn't have a clue what to do when the French were running at us, and there was no time to instruct him on the field."

Matthew Cooper hadn't produced his UK form against the French and it seemed inevitable he would be replaced for the first test against the Springboks (just six days away).

The All Blacks were still assembled at the Poenamo Hotel on the Monday morning when manager Colin Meads announced the team to play South Africa. Little was never one to anticipate a selection especially where he was personally concerned. But on this occasion he felt surprisingly optimistic, providing the selectors introduced a specialist goalkicker who didn't play at second-five.

So when the name of Shane Howarth, the Auckland fullback and goalkicker, was the first read out, Little felt a surge of relief. That opened the way for his recall in midfield alongside Frank.

But to his dismay, it wasn't Walter Little featuring at second-five. It was Alama Ieremia, the powerful Wellingtonian who had only that year declared his allegiance to New Zealand, having previously represented Western Samoa.

Little was shattered. "I couldn't believe what I'd just heard. My jaw dropped. The selectors had tried Lee Stensness and Matthew Cooper in my position and rejected them both and now they had gone for Ieremia.

"I was still amongst the reserves, but it was obvious the selectors didn't want me. And right at that moment, I didn't want them. This could be the moment, I said to myself, when I leave the All Blacks. I've been here too long – it's time to check out some of those league offers."

After the meeting Little went directly to his room, packed his bag, and walked out of the Poenamo. There were tears in his eyes as he drove home to be with his heavily pregnant partner Tracy.

Tracy was horrified when she realised what Walter had done. She immediately telephoned Peter Thorburn.

"Send him straight down to my office," said Thorburn.

Thorburn was waiting for him. "He sat opposite my desk crying. They were tears of hurt. I understood why he was so distressed – it was a combination of many things. Being consistently rejected by the All Black selectors hurt most of all, but he was seriously short of money and Tracy was eight months pregnant. He couldn't see any light at the end of the tunnel.

"He'd acted out of pure frustration because there isn't a vindictive bone in his body. He's never got nasty with anyone.

"I told him he had to return to the Poenamo, otherwise his team mates would brand him a quitter, and to use Tracy's pregnancy as an excuse.

"And I offered him some reassurance by telling him that you never know what is around the corner."

Little remembers that day (July 4, 1994...Independence Day, funnily enough) vividly.

"Peter was almost like a father to me, someone I could go to when I was down and out. I think if it had not been for Peter that day I would now be playing league in Sydney.

"I was surviving, at the time, on the All Blacks' daily allowance of about $60 a day. It didn't stack up too impressively against the money the North Sydney League Club was offering .

"Peter convinced me that walking out of the All Blacks' camp was not the right thing to do. He said that while everything might appear bleak at that moment, you never knew what was around that corner.

"I returned to the Poenamo with a different attitude. I would stick it out, although I wondered how many corners I might have to turn before anything would change."

Bunce, unaware of Little's traumas, was meanwhile fixing his focus on Pieter Muller, the powerful Natal centre who would be his direct opponent at Carisbrook. Muller and winger James Small were the most capped Springboks in the touring party.

He'd developed a respect for him in South Africa in 1992 and he was to enjoy their private tussle at Carisbrook, injury sadly forcing Muller (who now plays league in Australia) out of the tour before the second test.

"I'd rate him my hardest opponent," says Bunce. "Jeremy Guscott might have been more elusive, but I found Muller to be similar to myself – hard, abrasive, eager to unsettle his opposite number. At Carisbrook, we were giving each other plenty of stick, mouthing, jostling, elbowing. Towards the end of the game, I tripped him. When he regained his balanced, he came after me with a clenched fist. Just when I was readying myself for a confrontation, play swept towards us, and there were more important events to concentrate on.

"His replacement, Japie Mulder, wasn't half the footballer. Muller's injury was a serious loss to the South Africans.

"I enjoy playing against the Springboks, because while they give it, they take it. And they never complain. Afterwards, they're great mates, which is what rugby is all about."

The series opener was a hard, uncompromising contest in the classic tradition of New Zealand-South Africa test matches, with rival props Johan le Roux and Richard Loe trying to outdo each other in nastiness.

South African correspondent Paul Dobson suggested that "it may be an idea, if just before the match Richard Loe and Johan le Roux were sent to an adjoining paddock, there to do their ill-mannered things to each other, with a herd of bemused fighting bulls looking on."

Bunce watched with fascination at one stage as the Springboks' 110kg prop Balie Swart was pinned at the bottom of an All Black ruck. "It's one of my regrets as a back that I can't get in and ruck away players who are killing the ball." Swart was dealt with rather basically by the All Black forwards for doing just that, emerging war-torn and having to retire with concussion.

Thanks to Howarth, who was on debut, kicking more accurately than Andre Joubert, the All Blacks escaped with a 22-14 victory. It was a game that could have gone either way, but New Zealand had drawn first blood.

The omens weren't favourable for an All Black victory in Wellington. Tradition dictated that the team winning the first test in series between New Zealand and South Africa always dropped the second. At least, as Laurie Mains began his preparations he had to acknowledge that that was how it had been since 1949, a long, long time ago. And since then there had been series in 1956, 1960, 1965, 1970, 1976 and 1981. And always the pattern was the same.

In a determined bid to rewrite history, Mains called in Murray Mexted, who had been a central character in the protestor-marred '81 series.

Mexted described the Springboks' explosive opening to the second test. "Because their rugby tradition is as strong as ours, because defeating the All Blacks is their ultimate, they will come at you like a tidal wave from the opening whistle. You must be prepared for the onslaught."

Bunce shuddered. And he shuddered again when he watched video clips of the opening stages of the second test of 1981. "Mex was right, they would be coming at us with everything. We had to be prepared."

Mains then said he would be introducing the players to a word that they could use to lift themselves when things got tough.

"When your energy levels are drained," said Mains, "when you are wondering whether you can lift yourself for one further assault, this is a word that will provide the necessary inspiration."

Bunce wondered what the word could possibly be. He acknowledged that his vocabulary wasn't perhaps as extensive as some others, but he couldn't, for the life of him, think of any word in the English language possessed of the magical qualities Mains was describing.

The word, said Mains, was Buck.

Of course. That would do it – Buck, the great North Harbour captain, the man who had led All Black teams by example in the late 1980s.

The mere mention of his name caused ordinary players' bodies to steel. Bunce and Little had been privileged to play under him for North Harbour. They, probably more than any of the other All Blacks, appreciated his mana, his power. When he said 'Follow me,' everyone followed.

Bunce wasn't aware of any player calling "Buck" to his team mates during the Wellington test, but that was probably because the All Blacks, after weathering the early onslaught that Mexted had prepared them for, were always in control.

"But players said it to themselves at desperate moments," says Bunce. "It was a most inspirational word."

Johan le Roux's infamous earbiting episode overshadowed New Zealand's achievement in winning the second test, which Bunce considers an injustice because he believes the Athletic Park performance (even though the final score was only 13-9) represented one of the most satisfying and technically efficient displays of his international career.

"You wouldn't get a better defensive display, and the forwards crowned their mighty performance with a pushover try," he says. "There was no way we were letting the Springboks breach our tryline that day. The best they managed were three penalty goals."

Bunce didn't see out the game. In fact, he didn't see much at all after clunking heads with another player prior to halftime. He tried smelling salts, water and ice during the break but still had no wide-angle vision.

When he took another blow about ten minutes from time, his vision was seriously impaired. "The stands started moving," he says. "The Springboks were desperate as they strove to avoid the defeat that would put the series beyond reach for them. It was crucial we kept them out. So I went off."

And who ran on to replace him, for seven minutes of tense action, but Walter Little. It was his first test appearance in one week short of 12 months.

Bunce was irked by the media in '94. "With few exceptions," he says, "they wrote us off after the defeats by France, then claimed we were lucky to beat the Springboks in Dunedin.

"When we won again in Wellington, making us the first All Black team ever to go two-nil up in a series against the South Africa, they branded the Springboks a poor side. A lot of the media were John Hart sympathisers and they never really gave Laurie a fair go – they made an art form out of belittling his achievements."

All Black manager, Pinetree Meads, won legendary status as a player, not least for his deeds in three separate series against the Springboks (in 1960, 1965 and 1970), out of which he formed many lifelong friendships.

On the field, Meads was as uncompromising as any individual who ever wore the All Black jersey – arguably the most feared footballer of his day - but once the final whistle blew he regarded his opponents as drinking companions.

He retained that philosophy when he entered administration, and it was concerning him in 1994 that the All Blacks and the Springboks scarcely knew each other as individuals. Opportunities for socialising had been almost nil.

So following the Wellington test he set out to remedy that. Having co-ordinated events with the South African manager Jannie Engelbrecht, he ordered the All Blacks into their bus and took them to the Boks' hotel, the Park Royal (the one they'd found unsuitable the previous year).

"It was," says Bunce, "a marvellous get-together with the South Africans, an opportunity to meet them personally. Had Pinetree not organised that evening, chances are the Springboks would have departed New Zealand with us knowing hardly any of them.

"They had some characters in their team. James Small was a real extrovert – he kept referring to Chester Williams as Benson.

"Their favourite tour joke was to dip team mates' shoe laces in a liqueur and set fire to them. None of their hotels burnt down, so obviously the joke never got out of control!"

The third test at Eden Park was a fizzer, a lifeless 18-all draw. While the quality of the rugby produced was disappointing, the All Blacks were well satisfied because they were the series winners. "And completing a series victory over the Springboks is very special," says Bunce. "I don't care what the critics think."

Little watched the third test from his now all too familiar seat among the reserves and concluded, because the series had been won, that the selectors would make no changes for the Bledisloe Cup test coming up in Sydney.

But when he turned out for his club side Glenfield against Mahurangi the next day, he was intrigued to notice All Black selector Earle Kirton among the spectators. "I was hoping he couldn't tell that I was fairly seriously hungover from the test dinner," says Little. "If he was wanting to assess my form as a second-five, his presence was wasted, because I played at centre, outside my brother Lawrence."

Little figured he was back in the reckoning when Laurie Mains then telephoned North Harbour coach Brad Meurant with a special request to play him midweek against Marlborough in Blenheim.

Meurant was reserving Little for the NPC clash with Canterbury on the Saturday but was happy to assist the New Zealand selectors.

As things turned out, Meurant was obliged to find a replacement second-five for the Canterbury game because Little impressed sufficiently in the 78-7 romp in Blenheim to win back his test slot. It was Ieremia's turn to sit on the reserves bench.

"It was a pleasant surprise to hear my name read out," says Little. "It proved that you don't know what's around the corner. I said a quiet thank you to Peter Thorburn.

"The worst thing is to be out of contention. But now I was back in the test line-up it gave me the chance to secure the position for the World Cup."

Little relished the change of roles. Instead of doing "gut-busting" training sessions on the fringe of the test team, suddenly he was involved again, talking tactics and plotting, along with his midfield mate Frank, how to place pressure on the Wallabies' dangerous twosome, Tim Horan and Jason Little.

Bunce and Little are slightly at variance as to why the All Blacks performed so tentatively in the opening 40 minutes of the Bledisloe Cup encounter (staged in an electric atmosphere midweek under lights at the Sydney Football Stadium).

Bunce considers it was symptomatic of a general relaxation of fitness levels among the All Blacks that year. "Laurie eased off in '94, which wasn't entirely his fault because it was almost a purely domestic year. Laurie used to work us to a standstill when we were touring, but you can't accommodate much fitness work in three days before a home international.

"That season we were essentially left to motivate ourselves regarding fitness. I don't have to go into great detail to explain that some people do that better than others!

"Anyway, although we intended to operate an expansive game plan against Australia, individually we probably choked a little sensing we might not have the fitness reserves to sustain a madcap tempo for eighty minutes."

Little can't exactly pinpoint why the All Blacks were so ineffective up till halftime, except to acknowledge that the Wallabies started explosively and controlled possession for most of the opening spell.

"Our guys seemed a bit scared to let themselves go," says Little. "We were kicking a lot instead of running. I believe we were fit enough but we weren't performing."

Mains kick-started the All Blacks into life at halftime. He told them they'd trained harder than they had played the first forty minutes. "For goodness sake," he implored them, "play some rugby."

Bunce and Little looked with dismay at the scoreboard – 17-6 to Australia. "Right," they agreed. "Let's start making things happen. Let's run everything."

The following forty minutes produced entertainment on a magical scale. If rugby was always like this, no other sport would ever get a look in. The All Blacks, unrecognisable from the fifteen who'd laboured through the opening spell, came at the Wallabies in waves.

The world champions, unbeaten in 1994 and seemingly impregnable, found their defensive lines being shredded as the men in black, transformed, launched attacks from every point on the field.

Michael Jones was denied a try when a forward pass was called but when Shane Howarth weaved his way through for a superb try, the All Blacks were poised for the kill at 16-17.

Still the All Black attacks continued till finally, with the Aussies stretched to breaking point, Goldie (Jeff Wilson) wrongfooted his illustrious opponent David Campese and set sail for the goalline.

Goldie's colleagues were clenching fists, poised to punch them in the air when Australia's hardly-ever-been-heard-of halfback George Gregan arrived at motor scooter speed and launched himself into such a perfectly executed (side-on) tackle that he caused the ball to spew forward from Wilson's grasp.

Little couldn't believe the try had eluded Wilson. "Goldie's such an emotional guy – and shows it – that he was probably doing too much, rather than simply scoring the try. He was devastated by what happened, crying in the dressing room afterwards, but he learnt an important lesson from it."

Although the All Blacks were intensely disappointed at their failure to regain the Bledisloe Cup, knowing that the loss would jeopardise Mains' prospects of retaining his job through to the World Cup, there was one shining bright light out of the Sydney experience.

"We'd discovered the style we would play in 1995, the style that would take us to the brink of glory at the World Cup," says Bunce. "We had the personnel. With improved fitness and a wholehearted commitment to the all-attack game, we were ready to take on the world. However, the public, more concerned that we'd lost three of our six test matches for the year, didn't see it that way. Most of them were screaming for Laurie Mains' head."

Mains wasn't too optimistic about surviving. He told the players before they departed Sydney that whatever happened, he would always be available to share a beer with them. "I hoped he wouldn't go," says Bunce. "I had a feeling if he did, I'd go with him."

Mains did survive, with nothing to spare, and before the year was through would set in motion a tactical plan that would see the All Blacks re-emerge as the most dynamic attacking team in international rugby.

Bunce and Little, and the other North Harbour test player Ian Jones, flew home on the Thursday and the next day journeyed down to New Plymouth for an NPC clash with Taranaki.

"We were still suffering from the effects of the Bledisloe Cup game," says Bunce, "and training, in the rain, in New Plymouth on the Friday was an agony.

"Once into the game, however, we took off. Playing carefree rugby, even running the ball from our own line, we scored a bunch of tries, after which Pod (Richard Turner) suggested we should tighten the game up for a while.

"The theory was good, but Taranaki, which had an excellent record at home that year, began matching us. So I suggested to Pod we revert to what we were doing at the start."

North Harbour finished with 62 points and 10 tries, another example of the team's exceptional attacking skills.

The secret of the Harbour backline, according to assistant coach Bunce, was that it contained a group of players of like mind who got on "famously" together.

"If the spirit's right, the performance will follow. We were a group of skilled footballers dedicated to running rugby. In Brad (Meurant) we had the perfect coach, someone who gave us licence to pursue our own approach but who was ready to kick us in the arse if we slipped up."

Another of Harbour's milestones in a season of shining achievements was the defeat of Auckland by 35 points to 31. Harbour had already exorcised the Eden Park bogy against France and now Meurant's men overcame another major psychological barrier by registering their first victory (in 10 attempts) against the mighty Auks.

Auckland led 17-nil at one stage and appeared to have secured the victory when Junior Tonu'u scored after a spectacular 90-metre move four minutes from time.

"We knew time was running out when play restarted," says Little, "but we were a team on a high. We believed anything was possible if we could get the ball."

The opportunity was created through a quick lineout and a gigantic reverse pass from Strachan direct to Bunce in midfield. When Liam Barry exploded on to Bunce's pass, Auckland's first line of defence was broken.

Barry slipped a pass inside him to Little whose acceleration instantly carried him clear of the Auckland stragglers. Ahead were two defenders, wingers Eroni Clarke and Waisake Sotutu. Because the move had developed so quickly and unexpectedly, Clarke and Sotutu were unsure of themselves.

Little remembers being confronted with two options. "Either I threw a pass...and I was aware of a team mate out to the right...or I went alone. The player out to the right was obviously a major distraction for the Auckland defenders, because the moment I shaped to pass they both went with the dummy.

"I think I sidestepped to the left and there were the goalposts directly ahead, beckoning me. It was a wonderful feeling to plant the ball and know we'd finally beaten Auckland."

Little was to experience the extremes in emotions in the week that followed.

On a glorious high following the historic victory, Walter celebrated so enthusiastically that it took several minutes of shaking and shouting before his partner Tracy's mother could wake him the next morning.

When he finally came around, it was to learn that Tracy, a week overdue, was in North Shore Hospital, soon to give birth to their second child. It was a relieved, if rather seedy, Walter who made it to the hospital in time for Daniel's arrival at 9.30am.

Walter's elation was shortlived, for two unexpected events jolted him.

First, he heard on the radio that he had been cited by the NZRFU for allegedly stomping on Auckland flanker Mark Carter's hand, which required him to attend a judicial committee hearing in Wellington.

A couple of days later a close and devoted friend, journalist Maurice Dick, collapsed and died while playing Golden Oldies rugby for the Glenfield Grizzlies. Dick had commenced the research for what was to be the definitive book on Walter's career.

"He lived for rugby," said Walter, "and wrote energetically and enthusiastically on the North Harbour scene. He'd followed my career from the moment I joined the Glenfield club and was determined to produce a worthy biography."

Walter wore a black armband as a mark of respect for Dick, who was fifty-nine, when he next turned out for North Harbour.

The NZRFU's citing irritated Little because, to him – and to Mark Carter as it transpired – it was a nothing incident, and he learned of his supposed offence not by a letter or a phone call but through the media.

"The incident happened in a ruck situation on the hard cricket block of Eden Park," he recalls. "As I stepped back I was aware of putting my foot on something soft. Knowing there were no soft patches there, I looked down and realised I'd accidentally trodden on Mark's hand. I immediately stepped clear.

"Somehow, the NZRFU interpreted what I'd done as a deliberate stomp and summoned me to headquarters which meant I had to arrange for a lawyer to defend me and, at considerable expense and inconvenience, get to Wellington for the hearing.

"My lawyer contacted Mark Carter who said he couldn't remember the incident and was happy to make a statement to that effect, which we conveyed to the NZRFU.

"It mattered not. I was found guilty of stomping and suspended for one match. I didn't mind that – it allowed me to have a weekend's rest, which is always appreciated at the thick end of the season.

"But the whole episode I found positively bizarre."

North Harbour continued on its rampaging way, hoisting 35 points against Waikato and 43 against Wellington before crushing Canterbury (a team it hadn't beaten before 1993) 59-27 in the semi-finals.

A victory over Auckland in the final, on Harbour's home turf at Takapuna, would have set the seal on a perfect season.

It wasn't to be. In a grizzly affair, from which Eric Rush and Robin Brooke were ordered off and several others received suspensions following NZRFU citings, Auckland's forward might carried the day, Zinzan Brooke's pack strangling the life out of the Harbour eight.

Bunce regretted the game wasn't staged at Eden Park. The offer had been made by the Auckland Rugby Union but Harbour officials felt the home ground support at Onewa Domain was too important to sacrifice.

"I appreciated why our administrators held out for Onewa," says Bunce, "but I honestly believe Eden Park would have suited us better. The more expansive nature of the stadium would have encouraged our backs, and it's not as windswept as Onewa."

While the NPC title eluded North Harbour, the team's outstanding exploits throughout '94 were recognised when Meurant received the Player of the Year trophy at the first NZRFU Steinlager awards dinner in Wellington.

Bunce, representing Lion Breweries at the function, congratulated Meurant.

"Well deserved, mate," he said. "It's a pity you forgot to mention the assistant coach in your acceptance speech."

"Oh shit, Buncey, I did too. I feel terrible about that."

"Don't worry, mate. It's your night, not mine."

Fit For Anything

T he All Blacks' World Cup campaign began at a camp at Queenstown in October of 1994. Outwardly, it was glorious junket for the players and their wives and girlfriends who posed for photographers on jetboat rides and lake cruises and as survivors of death-defying white water rafting.

The involvement of partners was an important aspect of that initial assembly when manager Colin Meads and coach Laurie Mains spelt out the severe demands that would be placed upon the players over the next seven months, leading into the World Cup tournament in South Africa.

It was important also, the managers determined, for themselves to understand how the players were feeling at this time. What was their reaction to the events of the '94 season, the one which had produced an unflattering 2-3-1 test scoreline?

The players were broken up into work groups, each one a mix of tight forwards, loosies, inside backs and dashers.

"It was quite remarkable," says Bunce, "that every group came up with the same conclusion – we had let ourselves down through a lack of fitness. We had been committed to a high intensity game, but we hadn't established the necessary fitness base to make it happen.

"With perhaps a few exceptions, we had let ourselves down. We hadn't done the extra work. It wasn't altogether surprising because we had been left to our own devices, and rugby players never push themselves as hard when they're training privately as they do in a team or camp situation. When the agony sets in, you flag it!"

Bunce says he pondered the wisdom of the players' honesty at that session because he was only too familiar with Mains' brutal group training sessions. "I wondered what we were letting ourselves in for!"

Just what they were letting themselves in for became apparent when Mains pledged to have the All Blacks at least twenty per cent fitter than any other team at the World Cup. "It's a big call," he declared, "but I believe we can achieve it."

The players' fitness levels were established at Queenstown, by a panel headed by the director of the Human Performance Centre at Otago University, Martin Toomey. They were then set personal training programmes. But that wasn't the end of it – their fitness would be monitored locally through until the Taupo camp at the beginning of February.

Mains gave the World Cup squad members a chilling final message as he farewelled them from Queenstown. "Players who don't adhere to their training programmes and who fall below the standards we have set, be warned – we (the selectors) won't hesitate to go elsewhere."

The other significant factor to come out of the players' deliberations, and which coincided with coach Mains' philosophy, was that they were all totally committed to a high-intensity game.

Other World Cup teams would be bigger and quite possibly stronger but the All Blacks would run them ragged through their fitness, their efficiency and their skill levels.

January has traditionally been a month when Walter has indulged himself in swimming, sunbathing, barbecues and family get-togethers with the occasional run thrown in as a gesture towards the rugby season still a couple of months away.

In 1995, though, it was a full-on month for training. Not only was he faithfully adhering to his World Cup squad training schedule, but North Harbour's new coach Chas Ferris was making things happen.

Walter joined the Harbour contingent for a camp at Whangaparaoa and enjoyed participation in his first triathlon, one involving a 500m swim, a 10km bike ride and a 5k run.

Things were going impressively for the North Harbour contingent, until a certain speed session at Onewa Domain under sprint trainer Keith Roberts.

Little was stepping out nicely in company with Slade McFarland when he felt an alarming tear in his calf. "Oh, no!" was his instant reaction.

"I thought maybe it was just a twinge, but the pain was excruciating and got worse and worse. I knew then I'd blown the opportunity to participate in the Taupo camp."

Dr John Mayhew advised Little there was no point in even trying to get to Taupo. He'd torn the calf, good and proper, and it would take several weeks to repair the damage which was being compounded by fluid from his "wonky" knee draining through into the calf area.

Little has mixed emotions about missing Taupo. "When I heard what Laurie and his trainers had put the guys through, I was relieved to have missed it. But deep down, I wish I had been there to tackle the pain barriers. It's those things that build a team."

Taupo was to become a watershed in New Zealand rugby. Bunce claims that although most of the players had diligently applied themselves to their personalised programmes and arrived at the camp in excellent shape, "no one was prepared for what eventuated.

"I know that Laurie wasn't intending to push us as hard as he did. But when the players responded, he kept going. It finished up as a virtual commando course. Laurie had this ruthless streak, which I'd observed while touring, and it expressed itself in unabashed fashion at Taupo."

They were long days: Swimming at 7am, breakfast, team meeting, fitness testing and training all day, with a break for lunch, and evening functions.

The 3km time trial, on a grass track, with a "must finish" time of under 15 minutes was a challenge.

Jon Preston, who was to prove himself probably the fittest individual at Taupo (but who would miss World Cup selection) was first home, in 10m 46s, ahead of Eric Rush, Simon Culhane, Stephen Bachop, Andrew Mehrtens, Glen Osborne, Marc Ellis, Graeme Bachop and the first forward, Ian Jones.

Bunce came a satisfactory twelfth in 12m 12s, a long way ahead of the stragglers. Last home, with seven seconds to spare, was Waisake Sotutu. And only a few paces ahead of him was Jonah Lomu.

No one observing at Taupo would ever have predicted that Lomu, four months on, would be the sensation of the World Cup. Taupo exposed his physical limitations, particularly the dreaded 150s. He became the sideshow.

Bunce, well familiar with 150s by now, knew that it was important to start them strongly and to settle into a rhythm that would be maintained till the finish. One thing you didn't do in running 150s was waste energy. The call on the Saturday afternoon at Taupo was for twenty-two 150s, a fearsome number considering the amount of energy already expended that day.

Lomu, according to Bunce, "didn't care" after the first ten. "We'd turn for the next sprint and pass Jonah still jogging back, a pained expression on his face. In some circumstances, it wouldn't have mattered. But with Laurie playing the executioner role, we were to all suffer.

"Because Jonah wasn't performing, we were all penalised, Laurie ordering two more 150s.

"Lee Stensness went berserk when he heard that. He hated 150s. He never kept count and was always asking how many to go. When you told him he'd swear away. When Laurie announced we were doing two extra because of Jonah, I thought he was going to explode."

Taupo, and the subsequent camp at Christchurch, combined with personal training, produced a stunningly fit World Cup squad. Bunce hadn't been this fit since 1992 when he was working on the rubbish cart.

The camps weren't exclusively to build fitness. They also focused on individual skills, tactics and areas, such as lineouts, where the All Blacks had experienced difficulties in the tests of '94.

"You can only play rugby effectively at high speed if all the basics are adhered to first," says Bunce. "A major emphasis at those camps was on getting the forwards to clear the ball from rucks swiftly so the backs could operate at maximum velocity."

Back in Auckland, Little was fighting his own battle, striving desperately to return to full fitness so he could rejoin the World Cup squad. He was encouraged that Mains was regularly in contact with his personal trainer, Peter White. "Laurie obviously wanted me. After the disappointments of 1993 and 1994, that was reassuring, but I had to get that blessed calf muscle right."

Maintaining his fitness levels through swimming and working out on the exercycle, he finally ventured back on to the track. The calf felt secure enough, so he risked a few 150s. The first couple, at threequarter pace, were completed satisfactorily but on the third he felt the calf tear again.

"I was so depressed," says Little. "I thought right then there was no chance of me making the World Cup. It was one of my gloomiest days."

It was back to the physiotherapist, the pool and the exercycle, with Little fighting a seemingly hopeless race against time. It was now late February, barely three months before the World Cup opening ceremony in May.

Mains summoned Little to Christchurch for the final camp. Even though he couldn't participate, Mains wanted him involved. "I was just a spectator, hobbling around the place. I felt bad standing by as the players went through more agony."

The second calf injury hadn't been anywhere near as serious as the original, to Little's immense relief, and, with concentrated treatment, the leg was soon sturdy enough for him to resume training.

His first squad session with North Harbour was approached tentatively. "My calf was heavily taped and I made certain I was thoroughly warmed up. But during the grids, you wouldn't believe it, I stepped into a hole and sprained my ankle! My right ankle. Oh, God, would I ever come right!"

When physiotherapist David Abercrombie found Little back in his waiting room, he presumed the worst. If it was the calf again, he could kiss the World Cup goodbye. But no, it was an ankle. How delightfully different.

"I had two limps when I arrived at David's," said Little, "...one on each leg!"

Repairing a sprained ankle was straightforward and Abercrombie soon had Little back running, with sufficient confidence that he declared himself available for North Harbour's Super 12 clash with Otago at

It's captain Frank aboard a Vespa at Catania, Sicily in 1995, the only occasion he ever captained the All Blacks. His beefy mates are Norm Hewitt, Bull Allen and Richard Loe. **Bunce collection**

North Harbour's famous Brown brothers: Back row – Eric Rush, Glen Osborne, Frank Bunce. In front – Walter Little, Peter Woods. Bunce collection

Look out, Walter's comin' through! And having the devil of a job containing him are the Canadians at Eden Park in 1995. In support is Andrew Mehrtens, who marked his test debut with a 28-point haul. Troy Restieaux, Photosport

Frank and Maryjane Bunce, representative rugby centres. Frank has worn the No 13 jersey for Auckland, North Harbour, Western Samoa and New Zealand, Maryjane for Auckland. Andrew Cornaga, Photosport

Only special people are given All Black jerseys, and Dame Kiri Te Kanawa definitely falls into that category. Bunce, applauded by Mike Brewer, makes the presentation in Johannesburg during the 1995 World Cup. Dame Kiri was in South Africa for a series of concerts. New Zealand Herald

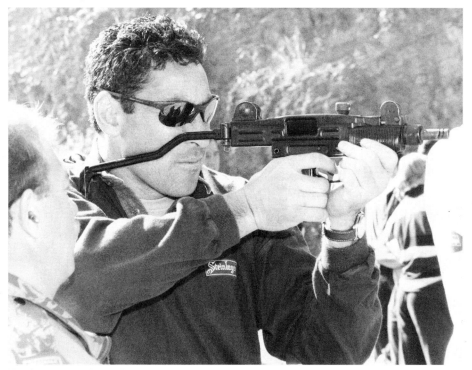

That's one way of stopping a Springbok! Bunce tries his hand with a 9mm Uzi rifle at the Police College in Pretoria in 1995. New Zealand Herald

Little set upon by Jonah Lomu during an NPC game in 1994...before the rest of the world knew about the Counties giant. Troy Restieaux, Photosport

Bunce testing his Italian on Paolo Vaccari during the international at Bologna in 1995. Photosport

Frank Bunce, assistant coach, giving the message to his fellow backs at a North Harbour training session in 1994. Photosport

Carisbrook on March 25.

"The best that could be said," according to Little, "is that I got through the game. I was in agony. The calf hurt, the ankle hurt, but I survived. With Laurie Mains watching, it would have been disastrous for me not to have played."

Although the calf remained sore, Little performed impressively for Harbour against Western Province a week later, *Rugby News* acknowledging the "individual brilliance" that yielded him two tries.

Although Little's focus was on loftier events than Harbour's immediate representative programme, it saddened him that the glamour provincial team of 1994 failed to achieve a single victory in its Super 10 campaign.

With Ferris struggling in the coach's role, the team would go on to lose nine matches in 1995 and only just scrape into the NPC play-offs.

Little was included in the North Island team for the resurrected inter-island fixture set for Carisbrook and he arrived in Dunedin full of enthusiasm, but the calf was so painful, he couldn't train.

"I was given until the Thursday to come right," says Little, "but by then I could hardly run. I was lame. There was the danger of further damage, so I pulled out. The injury was really starting to bug me. You want to be part of the action, but you are continually frustrated."

Little wasn't risked in Hamilton the next week when the Harlequins (effectively the All Blacks) gave the first serious indication of what could be expected at the World Cup by putting 96 points on a none-too-feeble Waikato team.

He was fearfully apprehensive before the All Black team to play Canada was named. The selectors had used Lee Stensness and John Leslie at second-five in the North-South game and given Marc Ellis a run in the No 12 jersey in Hamilton.

It was one of his sweetest moments when he realised the selectors had placed their faith in him, pairing him in midfield with Frank Bunce. The old firm was back in business.

What an intriguing selection it was – Glen Osborne at fullback (John Timu having committed himself to a league career in Sydney), Andrew Mehrtens ahead of Stephen Bachop at first-five, Josh Kronfeld in as the openside flanker ahead of Michael Jones (who wouldn't be going to South Africa because he didn't play on Sundays) and Marc Ellis on the wing.

No Jonah Lomu. No Zinzan Brooke (after he'd seriously damaged his achilles tendon in Hamilton). No Shane Howarth.

Little felt a little guilty about his selection. "The others had done all the work while I'd been standing around. It was unfair on them. But the selectors had shown faith in me, now it was over to me to reward them."

He admits to "a mild feeling of terror" in training before the test when he finally chose to commit himself 100 per cent. "I knew if the calf gave way again, I was doomed, but to my delight, it felt strong. For the first time in three months, I strode out with confidence."

Little can remember few more totally satisfying afternoons than the 73-7 lashing of Canada at Eden Park.

Having boldly chosen to play without strapping, he was delighted to come through eighty minutes of intense action pain free. That heartened him, as did the All Blacks' enterprise and commitment to the all-action game – "a sneak preview of what was to come in South Africa" – and he was chuffed with his new five-eighth partner, Mehrtens.

"It was my first time with Mehrtens," says Little, "and I loved it. It reminded me of my days outside Frano Botica.

"The guy is so talented and the backline buzzed thanks to him. He's my kind of partner. Where Grant Fox played the percentage game, Mehrts will have a go even in a thirty-seventy situation. It had to be sixty-forty before Foxy would try anything. They're both superboots but Mehrts has dazzling acceleration.

"Foxy was a master tactician whereas Mehrts still has a lot to learn about reading a game. But, boy, he sure compensates for that with his pure brilliance."

Although the fifteen players who disposed of Canada so effortlessly were virtually assured of World Cup selection, there was still a worrying final trial in Whangarei to follow.

Little was matched against Lee Stensness, a player with a considerable public following, particularly in Auckland.

The selectors were suspicious of Stensness' defensive qualities, deliberately setting him up in Whangarei against a team guaranteed to dominate possession.

His World Cup prospects evaporated as he flunked tackle after tackle, one of them permitting Little to charge in for one of the winning team's 10 tries.

One player who didn't flunk the challenge at Whangarei was Jonah Lomu. Making life a misery for the player who'd been preferred for the test against Canada, Marc Ellis, he demonstrated in emphatic fashion that he was an explosive force the All Blacks couldn't do without.

Little was thrilled when his North Harbour colleague Ant Strachan made the squad of 26, but he felt sorry for Stu Forster, and for Stephen Bachop, who'd been there for the whole campaign. Overall, he believed the selectors had picked the best combination for the style they wanted to play.

There was one important event to be completed before Walter could fly off to the World Cup – his wedding to Tracy.

The occasion had been deferred from February because of the training camps and was slotted in one week before the team flew out to South Africa.

The ceremony took place in the chapel at Hato Petera College with the reception following at the Fairway Lodge. The best man was Frank Bunce and, to Walter's great astonishment, he not only remembered the wedding ring but turned up on time!

There should have been a stag night, but that was kiboshed once Laurie Mains got to hear about it.

"Listen, I don't want you guys drinking too much," he said. "We've got a big campaign coming up. You can do your celebrating *after* the World Cup."

The stag party went ahead, but was seriously toned down from what was originally planned, much to the relief of Walter who was in trepidation of what 'mates' like Eric Rush and Glen Osborne had in store for him.

Bunce, thrilled simply to be involved in New Zealand's World Cup campaign, was flattered when management advised him that he had been promoted to the selection panel for the tournament (a position he was to retain for the end-of-year tour of Italy and France), completing a high-powered team featuring Brian Lochore, Colin Meads, Earle Kirton, Laurie Mains and Sean Fitzpatrick.

Not many New Zealand rugby players other than goalkickers get to claim world records but Bunce was the proud possessor of a world mark – which still stands – by the time the All Blacks had put Ireland away 43-19 in their impressive World Cup opener.

Bunce scored a try (through charging down a clearing kick by Brendan Mullin), to go with the four he'd scored against the Irish in 1992. That made five which, remarkably considering the Irish have been playing internationals since the turn of the century, is the most against them by any individual.

Bunce was instantly advised of his achievement by Hamilton based rugby statistician Geoff Miller who, throughout the World Cup, faxed invaluable information through to Mains.

Typical of Miller's bulletins, compiled after the most painstaking research, was the revelation that whenever the Irish called a short lineout they almost invariably threw the ball to the same player. It allowed the All Blacks to negate Ireland's short lineouts at Ellis Park.

If the All Blacks had deliberately created a smokescreen, they couldn't have arrived in South Africa less heralded. All the media focus prior to the tournament was on reigning champion Australia, Five Nations champion England, the always dangerous French, particularly following their series triumph in New Zealand, and host nation South Africa, competing at a World Cup for the first time.

The All Blacks, unbelievably, were the fifth favourites with the bookmakers, until, that is, they swept the Irish aside and introduced to the rugby world such dynamic new international footballers as Jonah Lomu, Andrew Mehrtens, Josh Kronfeld and Glen Osborne.

The media seized upon Lomu, who'd seemingly toyed with the Irish in scoring two tries and swatted countless opponents aside to make another for Kronfeld.

It was Little who had created the opportunity for Lomu's greatest moment, flinging him a giant pass on the All Blacks' 22. It wasn't something that had been practised. "Different tactics work against different teams," says Little. "The Irish defence was up flat so I skipped Frank and threw the pass directly to Jonah, to give him room to move. It was part of the team plan to work the ball to the wingers with room to operate. We were to use that tactic a lot at the World Cup."

Little doubts that any other winger would have created a try 80 metres away given the same circumstances. "It was Jonah's lethal mix of power and speed that made it possible. When the try was scored, with Jonah leaving a trail of green jerseyed defenders behind him, I remember thinking, 'Wow, we can do this from anywhere on the field – he's so lethal.'

"It's amazing how much speed Jonah has got. Back at the camps when we were sprinting, he positively exploded out of the blocks. One giant stride and he was about four paces ahead of the rest of us. He's also got an innate ability to beat an opponent which is a natural thing, because no one has ever coached him to do it. One on one, it's a safe bet that Jonah will always win."

Bunce regards the Irish as the most physical team encountered at the World Cup. "Oz (Glen Osborne) couldn't believe what he'd struck. He reckoned they were madmen. Individually, they don't rate with other teams, but collectively, with fire in their bellies, they're dangerous because they operate for eighty minutes with such incredible passion.

"No team in the world plays above its weight like Ireland. Regardless of your size, they'll take it to you forever. It was a great effort by our team to get on top of them that evening."

Bunce says that unlike the Irish, New Zealand's next opponents, the Welsh, did all their talking before the game. "They claimed they were stronger, fitter and better than us – and this from an Australian coach. Well, they certainly didn't possess the intensity of the Irish, and it didn't surprise me when Ireland beat them later to advance to the quarter-finals."

Two handsome victories behind them, the All Blacks advanced to Bloemfontein for what would be a stroll against the Japanese.

With an impressive sequence of 25 consecutive test match appearances behind him, Bunce was rested in Bloemfontein, thanks to Laurie Mains. "At a team meeting," says Bunce, "Laurie thanked several of us for volunteering to step down so the back-up players could get a run against Japan. I was on the selection panel and I said to Sean Fitzpatrick later that I obviously hadn't been invited to that meeting. Obviously Laurie had volunteered our services for us. It was a shame to break the sequence of test appearances, but it was in the best interests of the team."

Bunce and Little watched with fascination as the back-up boys ran up an unbelievable 145 points (including 21 tries, 20 of which Simon Culhane converted), to the humiliation of the Japanese.

They were less fascinated when Mains ordered the Dirty Dirties to commence training immediately the players had cleared the field. In front of a fair-sized audience, he ordered them to do twenty 50m sprints and ten 150s.

It was a costly session with both Bunce and Mike Brewer straining calf muscles. "That wasn't the brightest thing Laurie did at the World Cup," says Bunce. "There's always a risk of damaging muscles after you've been sitting cold in the grandstand for a couple of hours."

Alcohol being particularly bad for torn muscles, Bunce was obliged to spend his evening in Bloemfontein drinking nothing stronger than orange juice which meant that when the players assembled at 6am the next morning, he was feeling dangerously healthy.

"Now I know how Eric Rush feels all the time (Rush being a non-drinker)."

The reason for the early departure was because the All Blacks were being treated to two days relaxation at an exclusive game reserve before commencing preparations for the quarter-finals.

From Jan Smuts Airport, the team was transferred to an Air Force base near Pretoria for a flight aboard a military aircraft to a remote landing strip from where they would be ferried in helicopters to the game park.

Before take-off, the players were given a briefing by an Air Force officer, who explained the unusual configuration of the plane, of which certain features were top secret. For that reason, photographs were not permitted. As a treat for the All Blacks, a refuelling demonstration had been arranged. Two jets would come alongside their plane during the flight and fuel up. The flight would take approximately one hour during which sandwiches and drinks would be served.

"Are there any questions?" the officer asked.

Osborne's hand shot up.

Yes, sir?"

"What's in the sandwiches?"

Their plane touched down in the middle of nowhere. "It was," says Bunce, "all top secret – we had no idea where we were. The helicopters that transported us to the game park were surely the most modern in the world."

The meal that evening, a braaivlais (barbecue), was at a private ranch, with the injured players, which included Bunce, Brewer, Rush, Zinzan Brooke and Blair Larsen, coming later after receiving their treatment.

They were to be transported in a ute with a canopy. It was apparent once under way that their driver had been drinking. For those up front, it was an exhilarating 10-minute thrill ride. For those under the canopy, with nothing to hold on to, it was sheer hell, as the crazed driver powered ahead like Ayreton Senna.

"It was frightening," says Bunce, "as we broadsided around corners and became airborne at times. Blair (Larsen), who was trying to nurse a painful leg injury, became very angry. He banged on the cabin window, but to no avail. If the driver didn't slow down, he was going to whack him when we reached our destination.

"Well, the driver didn't slow down. And when we finally stopped, Larsen climbed out and went straight up to the driver and decked him. Don't mess with Kiwi policemen! Zinzan was upset and Blair later apologised, but I must say at the time I felt the driver, intoxicated as he was, deserved all that he got."

Bunce's lion-spotting adventure was hampered when the kombi van that he and several other All Blacks were in ground to a halt in fading light with a flat tyre. What should have been a straightforward tyre-changing exercise became a major event when the jack wouldn't work.

"About six of us had to lift the van," says Bunce, "while the driver's assistant kept a lookout for lions. It took ages until we realised the driver was trying to put the wheel on back to front!"

Notwithstanding that distraction, the players loved their brief safari and arrived in Pretoria, to prepare for the quarter-final clash with Scotland, refreshed.

Bunce required daily physiotherapy treatment, including acupuncture, to get him on the field in Pretoria.

The Australians had sensationally crashed out of the tournament against England by the time the All Blacks ran on to Loftus Versfeld Stadium.

Little recalls there were two factors motivating the All Blacks that Sunday afternoon – "the obvious desire to advance to the semi-finals and the fear of becoming the first All Black team to lose to Scotland."

In a match of notable milestones – Sean Fitzpatrick's 100th game for the All Blacks and Gavin Hastings' final international appearance – the All Blacks came away with a 48-30 victory after an erratically brilliant display.

Little, the player of the day, grabbed two tries and Bunce one while Lomu gave further demonstrations of his exceptional pace and power, prompting Hastings to tell the press conference later that "he's a hard bastard to tackle – the All Blacks are lucky they don't have to try and put him down."

That the All Blacks switched off after 60 minutes, after leading 45-16, incurred the wrath of coach Mains and manager Meads. "We received the biggest bollocking of the tour," says Little, "for relaxing and letting them back into the game."

A special visitor to the All Blacks' dressing room after the game was

Dame Kiri Te Kanawa, who was in South Africa for a series of concerts. "She seemed as genuinely delighted to meet us as we were to be introduced to our country's most famous singer," says Walter. "It was a magical moment when she sang Po Kare Kare Ana for us."

The week leading up to the semi-final clash with England in Cape Town represented the ultimate in match preparation for the All Blacks.

"We had been expecting to play the Wallabies," says Bunce. "Their demise meant our focus went on to the English players, most of whom we remembered from 1993 at Twickenham. The game promised a fascinating clash of styles – their forward strength and Rob Andrew's boot against our enterprise. They were extremely cocky after beating Australia and were saying their way was the winning way."

Knowing they possessed the fitness levels to run England ragged and the skilled individuals to deal with any situation – which certainly didn't apply at Twickenham in '93 – the All Blacks spent the week familiarising themselves with the enemy.

"I think I probably watched the video of the England-Australia game eight times," says Bunce. "Rugby players as individuals don't usually do different things. Most players have a limited range of skills - once you've identified them, you are in a position to close them down.

"We felt we had all the England players tagged. We recognised the Underwoods as dangerously fast but not great defenders, we saw Will Carling as the strong setter-upper with Jeremy Guscott the runner and one player who could initiate counter-attacks.

"Andrew, we knew, tended to kick first and run second from flyhalf while Mike Catt didn't appear the bravest of tacklers at fullback.

"Ian Jones studied the lineouts so intently, I reckon he knew their calls better than the English jumpers.

"Our overall assessment of the English, which we'd discussed months previously back in New Zealand, was that they were a clinical side, a team that played almost by numbers.

"And we knew, because of their inherent arrogance, fuelled by success in the Five Nations championship and their unbeaten run at the World Cup, nothing would change.

"There was more chance of Pinetree Meads switching to gin and tonics than of the Poms being daringly inventive or impulsive in a World Cup semi-final. So we felt we understood our opponents totally when we ran on to Newlands.

"Conversely, we had a sugar bag full of surprises in store for them, because we knew that the Brits' formality didn't prepare them for dealing with unorthodoxy, not in situations as serious as this."

The kick-off to the left, with the forwards lined out to the right, was just the first of countless surprises the All Blacks had in store for Carling's men, Carling's own knock-on yielding the scrum from which a rampant Jonah Lomu scored the first of his four tries, trampling the hapless Catt in the process.

That was after two minutes. From the restart, the All Blacks were in again, thanks to the audacity of Little who daringly launched into attack from deep in his own 22.

"I was supposed to kick for touch after Robin Brooke pulled down the ball for us," says Little, "but I could sense they were shellshocked from Jonah's try and plainly weren't anticipating another onslaught.

"Jeremy Guscott was hanging back, which left the gap for me. I've always considered the best place for a second-five to launch an attack was from inside his own 22, so I went for it. I was a bit lucky to get away from Guscott, but once clear, the try was always on.

"Oz's pace and Josh Kronfeld's finishing meant we were twelve points up in four minutes."

The rest is history. The All Blacks rocketed out to 25-nil after 24 minutes, which included a Zinzan Brooke dropped goal from 40 metres – not even the All Blacks were prepared for *that* – extending the advantage to 35-3 before England staged a gritty, late revival. The final scoreline was 45-29.

Not the least of Bunce's memories of the great afternoon at Newlands was a late tackle on Will Carling. "For no easily accountable reason Will is hated 'Down Under' and so many New Zealanders had told me to 'Get Will Carling' that I decided this was the occasion to honour them. I pushed his face into the turf, giving it a good screw as I did so. 'And that's from New Zealand,' I think I said to him."

For Bunce, the performance at Cape Town will remain one of the fondest memories of his career. "I guess we would have been happy to have won by a point to qualify for the final," he says, "but the satisfaction of that contest came in the near perfect execution of everything we'd planned."

Both teams flew back to Pretoria the night of the game. The difference was that the All Blacks were allocated seats in business class. And they were first on.

"I can't believe how much room there is up here," said Eric Rush, in an exaggerated voice as the English players filtered past.

"We milked it for all it was worth," says Bunce. "It completed a thoroughly satisfying day."

In contrast to the perfect build-up for Cape Town, the All Black preparation for the final in Johannesburg became a nightmare.

Initially, it was people going to extreme lengths to distract the All Blacks through the night...car horns being tooted, car alarms being set off, telephones ringing at the weirdest hours.

Bunce was rooming with Lomu. Receptions and telephone operators were specifically requested not to put through calls to the team's leading celebrity but, to Bunce's and Lomu's frustration, the phone never stopped ringing.

"Sean Fitzpatrick received abusive calls," says Bunce. "It was unbelievable – the distractions continued for the whole week."

The All Blacks were determined to survive these deliberate attempts to unsettle them, but there was one, crippling, act of sabotage that knocked the ruling favourites for the world crown for six – food poisoning.

"It was something we had anticipated," says Bunce. "Well, our coach did. He warned us that people would go to extreme lengths to stop us winning. And it seems as though he was right. Laurie wanted to fly in our chef from Cape Town, but the hotel manager in Johannesburg wouldn't hear of it. We were given our own dining area but we might have been better eating with the other hotel guests.

"No one can pinpoint how we were nobbled, whether it was the food, the tea or coffee, or the water at training, but almost the entire team was ravaged."

Both Bunce and Little suffered diarrhoea, Little far more severely. Approximately two-thirds of the touring party were laid low, a situation the team management chose to keep secret from the South African camp.

So devastated was the All Black camp that they could not have fielded fifteen fit players had the World Cup final been staged on the Friday.

The final training session, a light one when the attention is on matters tactical rather than physical, had to be abandoned, to Mains' dismay, because more than twenty of the players were still confined to their beds.

Jeff Wilson was the worst hit. He finally dragged himself from his bed on the Saturday morning, having been unable to control his vomiting for 48 hours.

While a few came through unscathed, many, including Little, entered the final, the most important game of their lives, with energy levels seriously depleted.

"I know some people have accused us of sour grapes for even mentioning the food poisoning," says Little, "but if you had inspected our barracks on the Friday, you would have marvelled at the fact we even managed to field a team the next afternoon."

The All Blacks fought valiantly, forcing the Springboks into extra time, with the Webb Ellis Trophy being decided on one Andrew Mehrtens drop kick that didn't go over and one Joel Stransky drop kick that did.

"We desperately wanted to win for New Zealand," says Little, "and after our performance in Cape Town we were superbly confident we would defeat the Springboks, but on the day, they deserved their victory.

"They tackled like men possessed, effectively closing down the player they identified as their greatest danger, Jonah Lomu.

"I believe we should have varied our tactics when our original battle plan wasn't working, but that's with the benefit of hindsight, and there were never more than three points in it at any stage."

Little had created a matchwinning opportunity for Lomu in the second half, but referee Ed Morrison ruled the pass forward.

"To this day," says Little, "I don't reckon that pass was forward. The referee wasn't in line to judge it, and I swear it was all right. Jonah was away, with only Andre Joubert to beat, and we know what happens when he's in a one-on-one situation. Another day, I'm sure the same referee would let that pass go."

A lot of tears flowed in the dressing room afterwards. "When you know you've given your best shot and lost, you accept defeat," says Little, "but in the circumstances that existed that afternoon, our emotions were jangled. Should we have varied our tactics? Could we have done more to win?

"There remains a belief among the All Blacks, I know, that the world crown went to a team that, nine times out of ten, we would defeat comfortably. But they won that afternoon and there's no doubt that the victory was a marvellous boost for the whole country. A South African victory almost seemed to be preordained."

If the All Blacks were crestfallen at allowing rugby's most treasured prize to slip from their grasp, they were enormously heartened to discover the level of public support for them back home, returning to a heroes' welcome, once they finally got out of South Africa. Because of a serious botch-up in travel arrangements – no flight reservations having been made for the All Blacks – they were obliged to remain a further three nights in Johannesburg.

Professionalism was rearing its ugly head by the time the All Blacks returned to New Zealand, and the players were soon to discover that it would be not only the NZRFU that would be slipping enticing contracts in front of them. A Sydney-based organisation, WRC, was making a spirited bid to hijack the world's leading rugby players. Further distractions were coming the players' way, but that story will be dealt with in a later chapter.

Four internationals remained to be played in 1995, the first couple home and away Bledisloe Cup fixtures. If the revitalisation of New Zealand rugby under Mains was to count for anything, the All Blacks had to defeat the Wallabies (who'd flopped at the World Cup) and defeat them in style.

"After the monumental effort that had gone into the World Cup campaign, and Laurie's endeavours to develop a spectacular, new high-speed game," says Little, "it would have been a most depressing anti-climax if we had failed against the Australians. However, the guys were determined to restore pride to All Black rugby."

Although it took a long time for the All Blacks to recapture their World Cup magic in Auckland, they came through to win well enough against Bob Dwyer's Aussies (thanks to Andrew Mehrtens' goalkicking) before demolishing them in the rematch at the Sydney Football Stadium a week later.

If anyone had any doubts about Lomu's matchwinning qualities, they were explosively demonstrated in Sydney when the 120kg winger was either scoring tries or creating them for his colleagues. New Zealand's dominance was far greater than the 34-23 scoreline implies.

For Bunce and Little, there was the satisfaction of putting it over Tim Horan and Jason Little again. Both contributed massively to their team's double triumph.

In Auckland, it was Bunce's scorching break from his own half that set up Lomu for New Zealand's only try while in Sydney they both excelled.

Rugby News wrote of the "twinkling feet" of Little in the movement that led to Mehrtens' try and the "awesome power" of Bunce who scored two tries.

Little has only the fondest memories of the first half of the '95 rugby year, but the balance was to be somewhat tarnished, not least because of the intrusion of professionalism.

The players' preoccupation with their contracts was deemed to be a major factor in the difficulty Chas Ferris was experiencing in getting North Harbour back to its winning form of the previous year.

The team stumbled from setback to setback despite being laden with international stars and when only one victory (a worthy one, admittedly, against Auckland at Takapuna) was registered in five NPC games, the team's plight was desperate.

There was talk of rebellion and Ferris was fortunate to retain his post.

Bunce had been supplanted by Buck Shelford as the team's assistant coach, but he, Ant Strachan and Little still had a major input into the backline strategy.

The major problem, it seemed, was that Ferris tried to stamp his authority on the team too emphatically, and many of the players reacted against this.

"Chas was a great talker," says Bunce, "and he staged far too many meetings. Talking strategy is all very well, but you're often better getting out and making things happen. Also, I believe Chas over-reacted when the team started losing. There was a major inquiry into every game, when I personally believe a little fine tuning would have solved the problem.

"Don't try and correct things that aren't broken is one of my mottos. Well, Chas tried to change Slade McFarland's throwing-in style and made Ian Jones stand in a different place for kick-offs. That pair didn't appreciate those instructions, I can tell you. Chas went about it all the wrong way."

North Harbour qualified for the play-offs out of pure desperation, putting a startling 60 points on a surprisingly unmotivated Otago side at Carisbrook. But a week later Ferris' boys had 60 hoisted against them!

The victory against Otago was achieved at the cost of a torn lower abdominal muscle for Bunce. He was assured it was a freak injury which didn't stop it hurting like hell.

Initially, he was considered to have no chance of playing in the semi-final on Eden Park but concentrated treatment on the groin area throughout the week produced a remarkable improvement and, to the Eden Park spectators' surprise – because Bunce hadn't even been named in the reserves – he took his place in the No 13 jersey for Harbour.

The decision to play wasn't the smartest one Bunce has ever made. He laboured through the game and was later berated by Laurie Mains who included him among the "new boys" when the All Blacks assembled for the tour of Italy and France.

"The way you acted after suffering a serious injury playing against Otago obviously indicates you are a new boy," he told Bunce.

Bunce recalls the semi-final against Auckland with embarrassment.

"When they hit thirty and we were behind the goalposts, I said 'Right – we're not going to let them get forty.' When they reached forty, I exhorted the troops not to concede fifty. At fifty, sixty was the no-no. But when Auckland's score clicked on to sixty, I'd given up. 'Don't let 'em hit one hundred, boys!' was my last call."

The players probably didn't need a five-week tour of Italy and France after the mental and physical demands of 1995, but it was on the agenda and, the players now being professionals, the tour was worth a cool $30,000 to each of them. That helped soften their weariness.

On the topic of weariness, the players were shattered after arriving at their first destination, Catania in Sicily. Even travelling business class didn't prevent exhaustion after a gruelling 36-hour journey that took them via Los Angeles, London and Rome.

Catania was a landmark for Bunce, being the only occasion in his entire career that he has captained a team. He can retire boasting a 100 per cent record as a leader, his All Black team outgunning Italy A 51-21, notwithstanding some eccentric decisions by the Italian referee.

Bunce managed satisfactorily but concedes he wouldn't want the responsibility on a regular basis. "There's too much to worry about. I had to tick off Justin Marshall as a new player for imitating Andrew Mehrtens and preparing too casually – Andrew helped me with that one – then I had to work on a speech for the team meeting and on the field I had to keep making decisions. Every time a penalty was awarded, the players would look at me!"

The All Blacks rumbled along in fine style, putting 70 points on Italy in the first international at Bologna, and winning easily at Toulon, Beziers and Bayonne before coming seriously unstuck against France in a roaring gale at Toulouse.

Little labels it the second strongest wind he has ever played in, topped only by the hurricane that swept down Stradey Park in Llanelli in 1989. Certainly, he's never encountered anything in New Zealand to compare with it.

"After the game, Foxy (Grant Fox) said we should have remembered Llanelli and used the same tactics," says Little, "but at Toulouse we played into the wind first and didn't control possession well enough.

"The French are gifted at seizing opportunities and we didn't pressure them consistently. The result was only our second loss in eleven tests for the year, a sad blot on our record."

The players, and particularly manager Meads and coach Mains, found life gruelling at the dinner that evening when the French president referred to the victory by their "amateurs" against the New Zealand "professionals."

"Pinetree was hopping mad about that," says Little, "because he was wanting to pressure them about their amateurism stance. It prompted him to give us a decent roasting when we got through to Nantes and starting preparing for the last two games."

Meads accused the forwards of being "soft" and the whole team of allowing the French to intimidate them.

"All Black teams traditionally do the intimidating," he reminded them.

The message got through. After a rip-roaring display by the midweekers (including Jonah Lomu) at Nantes, the All Blacks gave Mains the best possible farewell present by whipping the French 37-12 at the Parc des Princes.

Mains decided a needling attitude was necessary to stir some of his charges into producing their best rugby in the year's finale.

One he had turned on was Bunce, telling him he didn't think he was focused and ripping into him for one dropped ball and one awful pass to Lomu in training.

He offered Bunce the opportunity to pull out of the game, expressing doubt that he was ready to take on the third best team in the world. "He was," says Bunce, "totally abusive. Many of the players copped an earful, but he was particularly severe on myself, Robin Brooke and Craig Dowd. When he kept asking me at dinner on the Thursday night, 'Are you ready – do you want to pull out?' I got so annoyed I almost told him to piss off at one stage.

"I guess he knew what he was doing. I was certainly fired up when I took the field to confront these Frenchmen I was supposedly afraid of."

Volatile is an adjective traditionally associated with French rugby but the All Blacks adopted it in Paris. Heeding their manager's wishes, they intimidated the French from the opening moments. They weren't dirty but they were provocative and caused the Latin temperaments of the French players to flare.

"Once that happened, we knew we were doing all right," said Bunce.

Bunce and Little had had a few confrontations with French backs Richard Dourthe and Philippe Carbonneau at Toulouse, Dourthe, son of 1970s French centre Claude Dourthe, arrogantly pointing to the scoreboard when challenged.

"The French are unpredictable," says Bunce, "and can fly off the handle. We'd been given licence to unsettle them from the start. I think they were shocked at our attitude. Rushy was causing mayhem and there were some horrendous rucks and mauls. It was the most rugged of the dozen tests I played in 1995.

"I'm glad we had Justin Marshall at halfback. He's a feisty character, just the player to stand up to the French. Although it was his test debut, he thrived in the fiery atmosphere and came through to give an outstanding exhibition."

Mains was chaired from the field on the shoulders of Zinzan and Robin Brooke and, in buoyant mood, ranked the Paris performance on a par with the second Bledisloe Cup display and only fractionally behind the opening 50 minutes against England at the World Cup.

The rugby year complete – it had stretched from the Taupo camp at the beginning of February to the Paris test on November 18 – Bunce and Little were relieved to wing their way home to their wives and families.

Walter was surprised to find his younger son Daniel walking when he arrived at Auckland Airport. But he wasn't so thrilled when Daniel wouldn't have a bar of him at home.

Who's this man who's come into my house?

It was, says Walter, a reminder of just how often he'd been away on rugby duty in 1995.

The Class Of '95

The twenty-six players who comprised the All Black World Cup squad of 1995 were a pretty special bunch of people. They had to be to survive Laurie Mains' commando camps!

Collectively, they carried the running game to a new dimension, opening the rugby world's eyes to the stimulating possibilities available under the existing laws, if the attitude was right.

In five World Cup matches, before some witch's brew sent them reeling, they scored 41 tries, completed, for only the second time by New Zealand, a Grand Slam (at the expense of Ireland, Wales, Scotland and England) and won over the entire international rugby fraternity with their breathtaking semi-final performance against England.

They were, everyone agreed, *the* team of the tournament. There was only one drawback – they didn't get to receive the Webb Ellis Trophy. The spoilsport host nation, South Africa, denied them that.

But that's another story. What chance did the All Blacks ever have against a country whose president, having spent 26 years in prison, turned up at the final wearing Francois Pienaar's jersey!

The All Blacks took the setback stoically – they drank themselves into a stupor at their hotel the next day.

All Black players have traditionally been depicted as unsmiling giants, individuals ruthlessly dedicated to preserving their nation's status as the premier rugby nursery of the world.

While New Zealand previously went earnestly about mastering the game's basics and stultifying personalities who dared to try and introduce levity into such an important topic as rugby, other countries encouraged the personalities, the comedians, the entertainers.

Well, it should be recorded here that the All Blacks who went to South Africa in '95 in search of gold abounded in colourful personalities.

There were probably more extroverts and intriguing characters in the team than had represented the All Blacks in the past decade, although the predictably serious minded management seldom encouraged public expression of their whimsical qualities.

Frank and Walter thought it would be appropriate to present the personalities who made up the Class of '95, depicting most of them with original, and, in many cases, never-previously-revealed, stories. Irreverence has superseded team loyalty in the compilation of this chapter.

Not all the stories told here relate directly to the World Cup, but they involve World Cup veterans and are too good to leave untold. So here goes:

It's almost an injustice to incorporate **Glen Osborne**, Oz as he's popularly known, with the rest of the All Blacks, because he merits a chapter on his own.

So many Oz stories abound that one of his colleagues uses them almost exclusively to get his laughs whenever he's called out as a guest speaker.

Oz is unique. Fresh off the farm at Wanganui, he arrived in Auckland in 1992 and after his first North Harbour training session startled his fellow squad members by producing a pen and notebook and requesting all their autographs.

At one session he noticed Frank Bunce fondling a new pair of boots.

"Jeez, look at those beautiful boots," he said to Eric Rush. "I'd love to have a pair like that."

"Ask Frank," said Eric, "he's got plenty of pairs – he'll probably give them to you."

"Oh, no, I couldn't do that."

"Hey, Frank," said Eric, "Oz would like those boots. How about giving them to him."

"Okay," said Frank, and handed them across.

Oz was overwhelmed. "What do I owe you for them?"

"Nothing – don't worry about it."

"You've very kind," said Oz. "I'll give you *something* for them."

True to his word, next week he arrived with that special something, handing a sugar bag to Bunce.

Frank reluctantly took possession of the bounty. Inside were a couple of dozen lambs tails and two eels!

When the All Blacks were in Italy in late 1995, Oz stepped on the scales and was a little alarmed to find his weight had dropped below 80kg.

He pondered this for a moment, then removed from his trouser pocket his wallet which was heavy with coins.

He reached down and placed it on the scales.

"There," he said, "that's better!"

During North Harbour's visit to Brisbane in 1993 they encountered a 50-strong group of Japanese in the foyer of their hotel, preparing for a cultural festival.

Attired in kimonos and wearing attractive headbands depicting the rising sun, they were greatly impressed to discover so many All Blacks in their midst, and insisted on a group photo.

When the photograph was taken, Oz's unmistakable voice piped up from the back. "And where are you people from then?"

When his flatmate discovered the Sunlight washing-up liquid in the bathroom, he asked Oz what it was doing there.

Oz was coy and didn't give a direct answer, but his girlfriend later revealed that the previous night he'd treated himself to a bubble bath.

"No wonder," said Eric Rush when he heard the story, "that Oz is so slippery on the rugby field."

Having made a huge impact as a fullback throughout 1995, Osborne was dropped for the first test in France, a development which caused him to lose his usual chirpiness.

"Come on," said Rush, "don't go all quiet on us."

"What am I supposed to do," replied Oz, "jump for joy?"

When he was reinstated a week later, after Jeff Wilson dropped out with injury, he was so excited, he rushed off to celebrate before Laurie Mains could finish telling him of his requirements for the next few days.

Osborne's enthusiasm is infectious and has certainly livened up the All Black backline.

Eric Rush summed it up best when he declared, "We need guys like Oz."

Jeff Wilson, whose nickname is Goldie, is a far more serious minded young footballer than Oz, and he's a lot more emotional, too. He took the test losses at Twickenham in 1993 (when his goalkicking faltered) and Sydney in 1994 (when George Gregan knocked the ball from his grasp as he was diving for the winning try) very much to heart, shedding tears in the dressing room on each occasion.

A natural sportsman – he's also represented New Zealand as a one day cricketer and is nationally ranked as a basketballer – he gives everything 100 per cent. But he takes to heart events others wouldn't worry about and he allows injuries to get him down. He needs to develop mental toughness. Otherwise, he's equipped to become one of the great New Zealand sportsmen.

Jonah Lomu, known as Jonah or Joe, virtually overnight became an international sensation, yet, according to Bunce who roomed with him often during the World Cup, fame didn't alter him one little bit.

He has the world at his feet but because he's soared so high so young, if he doesn't get the right advice, he could come down just as quickly.

There was a classic example of this when Jonah in March secretly married his South African girlfriend Tanya Rutter in what became a public relations disaster.

Jonah was so disgusted at the media's intrusion into his private affairs that he lashed out at a photographer at Eden Park and threatened to give rugby away for the sake of privacy.

Fortunately, sanity prevailed and his manager, Phil Kingsley-Jones (an unpaid manager, it transpired), agreed to return to New Zealand from Wales and take charge of his affairs.

Bunce brands him the ideal room mate, finding that Jonah enjoyed nothing more than making cups of tea and coffee and would often shoot down the road for a packet of biscuits. He even ran Bunce a few bubble baths!

He never read books or magazines. While Bunce read, Lomu would listen to music on his walkman.

Jonah's small talk revolved around music, stereos and cars. He never talked about rugby, unless he found himself featured on television or in the newspapers. If it was an opponent bragging about how he would deal with him, Jonah would invariably respond by saying, "I'll waste him, man!" And, of course, he usually did.

Jonah's appetite is monumental. He eats anything and everything and is a connoisseur of McDonald's fast food. He's a sucker for pizzas also.

Bunce couldn't believe the number of phone calls that came in for Jonah while he was at the World Cup. Finally, it was agreed Frank would vet them.

"You wouldn't believe the requests, people phoning to invite him to their sister's birthday or wanting him to come for dinner. They were treating him like public property. Nobody's got that right."

Eric Rush, who answers to Rushy or Shotgun, is the guy who's as funny as Oz but through relating stories, not creating them. He can arrive at a table without knowing a person and have them all roaring with laughter in a short time.

He was the judge at the team's court sessions at the World Cup, keeping everyone amused with his throwaway lines and sharp, legal, mind.

He even entertains at training. North Harbour coach Brad Meurant had just finished lecturing his backs on the need for greater application at training. More attention to the basics, less frivolity, was his message. When the backs next swung into action, Rush, after sprinting across the tryline, twirled the ball on his finger and flipped it over his head and between his legs before forcing it.

"How's that, Brad?" he had the audacity to ask his coach.

When Rushy was first selected to become an All Black (as a replacement back in Australia in 1992) he was 'in camp' with the New Zealand XV at the Poenamo Hotel.

The team's coach Peter Thorburn came to his room before breakfast to break the news. Rush was sharing with Timo Tagaloa and the room was in darkness. Thorburn saw a pair of black feet, grabbed them, and said, "Wake up, Wake up, you're an All Black."

A startled Timo Tagaloa sat up, and said, "Am I?"

"Oh no, Timo, you're not. Sorry about that.

"Wake up, Rushy, *you're* an All Black!"

A maestro at the sevens game, Rush applied himself so completely after being told to switch from the forwards to the backs that in Italy and France in 1995 he was the most impressive winger. Considering Jonah was along, that's really saying something.

He's putting his career as a lawyer on hold after finding that the advent of professionalism – directly involving the company of which he is a partner – has endangered many rugby friendships which he treasures.

Marc Ellis, alias Macka, and now of the Auckland Warriors, related strongly to Andrew Mehrtens. They were two of a kind, strong on practical jokes.

There was a touch of the Stu Wilson about Ellis, someone capable of positively zany humour.

On the eve of the Scottish game in Pretoria during the World Cup, Sean Fitzpatrick, his mind focused on the important quarter-final ahead, was returning to his room from breakfast, when a door burst open and a person in army camouflage gear threw himself out into the hallway, rat-tat-tat-tat-ing at an imaginary enemy. It was Macka.

"Oh, hi, Marc," said Fitzpatrick, shaking his head as he wandered off.

Ellis was notorious for telling corny jokes, an example of which was the sausage and the egg in a frying pan.

"Hell, it's getting hot in here," said the egg.

"Well, what do you know," replied the sausage, "...a talking egg!"

Coach Mains always encouraged his players to relax on the morning of test matches. Ellis and Mehrtens' way of relaxing was to play pool, ribbing each other mercilessly and usually making enough noise for half a team.

On the field, however, they both gave 120 per cent. They got on famously together at the World Cup.

Alama Ieremia always answered readily to Al but not quite so enthusiastically to April. Possessed of a high pitched voice, he tended to become over-excited in onfield defensive situations, intriguing his team mates with his rapid fire gabble.

A hard case, he often used to remind his team mates that his father was a priest, a priest who never hit him. He would only have to touch his belt and Alama would burst into tears.

Ellis wasn't great as a joke teller, but Al was worse. Much worse. His so-called jokes made everyone groan and usually he was the only person laughing at the punchline!

Simon Culhane, nicknamed Nibs, gave Ellis cause for satisfaction when he was selected. No one called him Chicken Legs any more. Culhane, a builder from Invercargill, rolled his rrrrrrs in true southern fashion and slotted neatly into the team.

When he first arrived in the World Cup squad, Mains encouraged more senior players like Bunce and Little to get to know him. They did and during the summer camps came to find him a great fellow.

Having scored a world record 45 points (against Japan) in his test debut at the World Cup, he was lucky to get away to Italy and France after breaking a bone in his foot in an NPC match.

When he was undergoing a fitness test after assembly in Auckland, the doctor, by chance, put his hand straight on to the broken bone, causing Culhane to gasp in pain.

"What's the matter?" asked the doctor.

"Your hands are cold," replied Nibs, thinking quickly.

"Oh, sorry about that, I'll run them under a warm tap."

Culhane grimaced as the inspection continued, was passed fit, and went on to play five of the eight matches.

Andrew Mehrtens, Mehrts to all, the thoroughbred flyhalf born of a New Zealand Junior father and a South African mother, was another of the hundred-mile-an-hour brigade. Multi-talented, he's gregarious and one of those rare individuals who seems to befriend everyone. His departure from the touring party after seriously injuring his knee in the opening game in Italy in 1995 robbed the team of one of its most popular members.

Back in 1993 at the New Zealand Colts trial, he played 20 minutes at first-five, 20 minutes at halfback and 20 minutes at fullback, which demonstrated his exceptional skills. When he missed a couple of tackles in the international against Australia, coach Peter Thorburn asked him if he could account for these lapses. He confessed that when he wasn't handling the goalkicking duties (which were with Adrian Cashmore on this occasion) he tended to lose concentration. Which only confirms what his fellow team mates now recognise – he's a full on person *all the time.*

Mehrtens' impish sense of humour showed itsef when a female television interviewer asked him what the chances were of him going to league. "No, no, I'm much too important to the All Blacks," he replied.

"Isn't that a rather arrogant attitude?" asked the interviewer. "Why do you consider you are so important?"

"Because I'm in charge of the laundry and no one else understands the system!"

Ant Strachan was an extrovert, one of the team's strong personalities. For anyone else, Ant would be an ideal nickname, but as that *was* his name, he was called variously Strawney or Strackan. Or, in deference to his receding hairline, sometimes M Head.

Hyperactive, he wanted to be doing things all the time. And if there was nothing else offering, he'd take off his shirt and flex his muscles.

He was peculiarly susceptible to any illnesses going round. Anything that affected the team, he got it. Needless to say, he was one of the worst victims of the Johannesburg food poisoning.

At one of Mains' early meetings on tactical planning, back in 1992, the coach concluded his session by asking if there were any questions.

"Yes," said Strachan, "can we have more blankets in our room, and iced water?"

A serious student of horse flesh, he was the person to approach for advice before risking money at the TAB.

Graeme Bachop, known as Bash or Grim, was one of the quieter members of the touring party, until the evil alcohol took its effect, as it did following the massive World Cup final disappointment.

Grim was nicely under the weather when he arrived at the compulsory court session at 10am. In fact, he was in an uncontrollably giggly mood.

Now the rule is that silence prevails when the judge (Rushy, on this occasion) is presiding at such meetings.

But Grim's behaviour deteriorated. He kept interrupting and, when challenged, reacted like a stupid schoolboy. Bunce, sitting next to him, was ordered to bring him under control, but it was an impossible task.

Every time Bachop spoke out of turn, not only was he ordered to down a drink, but so was Bunce, with the inevitable result that they were both paralytic by mid afternoon.

Grim was custom made for the free-flowing game the All Blacks promoted throughout 1995 and his decision to delay his return to Japan to be available for the Bledisloe Cup series was a bonus for Mains.

Zinzan Brooke, Zinny to everyone, has to be the most competitive rugby player in the world. And if he wins anything, he's automatically the world champion at it. While the rest of the world was astonished when he slammed over a 40 metre dropped goal in the World Cup semi-final, his team mates had watched him practising droppies so earnestly, it was only a question of time before he landed one. The only surprise was that he didn't make it a greater challenge by attempting it with his left foot!

There being such widespread dissatisfaction with the method of determining the World Cup winner in the event of a draw after extra time (the loser being the side with most players ordered off during the tournament), there seemed a good argument for adapting the Touch football system.

If teams are still level after extra time in a play-off in Touch, they each drop off a player. After every minute, for as long as the scores remain tied, teams continue to diminish in size.

That system would be perfect for Zinny. He'd banish Sean

Fitzpatrick, the captain, initially and nominate the players to drop off until only he and his brother Robin remained.

After a furious argument, Robin would stalk off, knowing he could never defeat his elder brother, leaving Zinny single-handedly to defend the honour of the All Blacks against South Africa's last remaining individual.

Because Zinny can do everything, from dropkicking and goalkicking, to sidestepping and jumping in the lineouts, he would inevitably win and would go forward to accept the Webb Ellis Trophy from Nelson Mandela.

He would then, finally, be *the* world champion he's always professed to be.

Mike Brewer, Bruiser to everyone, was a serious person who put an awful lot of thought into everything with the result that he always came to team meetings with a seemingly endless set of questions.

He would often drive Laurie Mains to distraction. After twenty minutes of explaining from Laurie, which would be crystal clear to everyone else, Bruiser would invariably come in with his questions.

"Laurie, what if…?" he would start. Bruiser wanted to cover every conceivable alternative.

In the early days, when Fitzpatrick was fresh to the captaincy ranks, Bruiser called a lot of the shots, too many some felt. But as Fitzy grew in confidence in the position he didn't let Bruiser get away with so much.

Bruiser always trained himself to a standstill, becoming more and more intense as a big game drew near. In that respect he was almost identical to coach Mains.

He never did come to terms with the fact that the younger guys played up at times.

The other loosies, **Josh Kronfeld, Paul Henderson, Jamie Joseph and Kevin Schuler**, were a complex, fascinating lot.

Kronfeld, Josh to everyone, was another extremely earnest young man, who takes life terribly seriously. Criticism makes him bristle and Frank was startled to find that he reacts to it on the field.

"Josh would turn upon anyone who dared to challenge him on the field, which is unusual," says Frank. "He's not one to take things on the chin. There's always a reason for him doing something."

He would question coach Mains, too. On one occasion during the World Cup preparations, Mains had called in a referee who was explaining the complexities of the ruck. His instructions were clear to most of the All Blacks, but Josh kept challenging him.

Finally, Mains, losing his cool, turned on him.

"Oh, for God's sake, Josh – you're another bloody Herb!"

A strong personality, Josh was prepared to make a stand for issues he believed in, hence his controversial appearance for Otago wearing headgear sporting the anti-nuclear emblem.

'Ginge' **Henderson** was well known for storing money and for inventing schemes to make it. In South Africa in 1995, during a visit to an Air Force base, he and Graeme Bachop, sitting in different cockpits, made radio contact with each other. "I'm reading you," said Ginge. "Keep an eye out for fighter planes. Hey…this call isn't collect, is it?"

Schuler, who, like Bachop, came back from Japan to qualify for the World Cup – and who bears the same nickname, Herb, as his brother – got on extremely well with coach Mains and also related to Marc Ellis, obviously because he too enjoyed practical jokes.

Herb could never sit still and was always talking and/or laughing.

"Herb's a hyperactive guy, like Ant Strachan," says Bunce, "the difference being that Strawney knew when to shut up. If someone was talking when you wanted a bit of quiet, you could say, 'Is that you again, Herb?' knowing almost certainly that it would be."

Herb was similar to Bruiser (Brewer) in presenting theories and asking questions when often none was required.

Joseph, JR or Jake, was a good, hard man who seemed to spend an inordinate amount of time on the physio's table and hated it when Pinetree Meads saw him there. Meads would never say anything, just shake his head.

JR copped a lot of flak from critics for aggressive play, a good bit of which was avoidable because, says Bunce, he often went "over the top."

Joseph was one of the few players who would stand up to, and often challenge, coach Mains, for which Mains seemed to respect him.

"Laurie would often say, 'Jamie's the only one standing up to me.' He was right, but the rest of us had earlier concluded it was a no-win situation.

"JR had plenty of spunk. In South Africa in 1992 he got into a fight at training with Richard Loe over how he should pack on the side of the scrum. Laurie stood back and let them go. They continued to argue the issue in the changing room, the debate becoming decidedly heated.

"When Laurie came in, he told JR he should respect the view of Richard, who had been around a lot longer. It didn't quieten him down. Instead, he then directed his attack at Laurie!"

Joseph accepted the nickname of Jake until it was explained to him that Jake was the villainous main character in *Once Were Warriors*.

After that, he was particularly sensitive.

"Don't call me Jake," he would insist. "And don't call me black either!"

Ian Jones, called Kamo after the Northland town from which he hails, challenged Oz at times for the Stupid Comment crown.

When the All Blacks visited the Ferrari factory during their 1995 visit to Italy, they were gathered around watching Jonah Lomu pose for promotional photographs on and in a shiny red number.

"Does Ferrari only make red cars?" asked Kamo of the company representative who was showing them around.

When he asked the question, he was leaning on a yellow Ferrari and was not ten paces from a silver one!

At Toulon, the day following the All Blacks' match against the French Barbarians, Richard Fromont, one of Kamo's locking partners, did not train, remaining on the sideline throughout with his neck in a brace.

Back at the hotel, Kamo came face to face with Fromont as he entered the team room.

Kamo's penetrating question? "Have you got a sore neck, mate?"

At one stage he was being referred to as The Tight One after he took exception to criticism from management of The Tight Five. "I'm the one getting all the write-ups," he said. So they dubbed him The Tight One!

Richard Loe and Mike Brewer played a trick on him when he first joined the All Blacks, introducing him to a game in which two players sit facing each other with a spoon between their teeth and see how hard they can hit the other person on the head.

Truth is, you can't make much impact at all.

But when Jones put his head down for Loe's turn, Brewer sneaked up behind him and gave him a monstrous crack over the head.

Jones was given another turn, but again it was feeble.

Loe's second effort was another stunner.

A baffled Jones walked away, holding his damaged scalp and acknowledging the incredible power that Loe could achieve with his teeth!

Blair Larsen, the policeman from Takapuna known as Lammy, made it to the World Cup as a lock, but the truth is that he much prefers operating from the side of the scrum because he likes to run with the ball.

At one stage, after he had flirted with a career in league, he was being referred to as Bradley Clyde.

He probably prefers that to having the origins of his nickname disclosed. He was on tour with the Harbour team in a rural setting, when he spotted a ewe giving birth. "Look at that," he shouted to his colleagues, "a cow lambing!" He's been Lammy ever since.

Be prepared to confront all of Blair Larsen if you ever knock on his door, because he enjoys nothing more than lounging about in the nude.

Robin Brooke, alias Moose, is renowned for his blinking and his deep, hearty laugh. Like his brother Zinny, he can do everything well. Well . . . he likes to think he can.

He can certainly exaggerate. During a visit to Singapore with the infamous Mongrels sevens team, he told a television interviewer he could complete the hundred metre dash in better than eleven seconds.

"At least," one of his colleagues observed, "he had the grace not to say he was wearing football boots and carrying a ball at the time."

Several times during commentaries on the New Zealanders' games throughout the tournament, reference was made to his exceptional prowess as a sprinter, causing team mates to fall about laughing.

On another visit to Singapore he was rooming with Bunce and Rush when he fell ill, becoming quite feverish.

According to his unsympathetic room mates he moaned and groaned a lot before falling asleep. In his delirious state he started calling for his mother, telling her that Marty and Zinny were picking on him.

He took some time living that down!

Olo Brown, Craig Dowd and Richard Loe tended, like most front rowers, to stick together, although the favourite pastime for **Brown**, nicknamed Max, was playing chess or backgammon with Sean Fitzpatrick. They'd find a suitable cafe, sip coffee and play to their hearts' content. Max made an art form out of avoiding the media, preferring to let his strongman onfield performances do his talking for him.

Dowd, known as Jethro after the Beverly Hills character, is someone to avoid when he's under the influence but at all other times is a popular individual who is a great team man. He is amazingly supple, being able to do the splits, like his sister who is an accomplished ballet dancer.

Loe, the veteran of the team, known simply as Loey, is the exact opposite off the field from what he is on it. A dedicated family man, he loves to spend time with his wife and daughter. He's got a fund of stories and, if there's an audience, he'll play the raconteur for hours.

He can speak French and a little Italian and he knows his wines. In fact, he's rather cultured. The Richard Loe fan club would be disappointed, because off the field he doesn't live up to his notorious reputation at all.

He doesn't let things get him down. When he was booed as he ran on to the Sydney Football Stadium as a replacement in 1995, he commented that Jim Bolger "would love to be that well known over here."

Sean Fitzpatrick, Fitzy to nearly everyone but Caveman to a few, has proved a great survivor. Laurie Mains cleaned out the cliques when he arrived in 1992 and Fitzy was in the middle of that but turned around for the good of the team.

He knows how to relax. He's an excellent team man who will have a laugh and a few beers with the troops.

Norm Hewitt, Normie to his mates, is another to give a wide berth to if he's been drinking. But he acknowledges that problem and doesn't drink now. He's the team's wheeler/dealer, forever on the phone - to lawyers during the day and to his girlfriend at night. His phone bill from the tour of Italy and France stretched to $3500. He's one who has been enormously grateful for the advent of professional rugby!

Managers, Coaches
And Captains

R ugby, as we all appreciate, is a game for fifteen players, be they
towering lineout specialists, squat front rowers, tearaway loosies,
inside backs with golden boots, outside backs with blistering pace or
fullbacks who love to demonstrate their limitless courage by standing
defiantly under soaring up-and-unders.

Individually, rugby players possess all these diverse skills. And as
individuals they are invariably a fascinating mix of personalities, ethnic
backgrounds and talents. Some are self starters, others require to be
goaded into action. For every two conscientious players there's one
bound to be late, while others may not arrive at all.

In only the rarest of instances will an assortment of individuals
succeed, consistently, on the rugby field. A team's fortunes hinge largely
on how, collectively, they are welded together and how the individuals
respond to commands and leadership.

Which is where the manager, the coach and the captain come in.
They can be as weird an assortment as the players.

Managers, generally speaking, should be organised and efficient,
preferably with some business acumen. They are, effectively, their team's
managing director.

The coach ideally should be proficient with both the laws and modern
coaching methods, not stubbornly determined to instruct teams in 1996
by the same methods that moulded him two or three decades previously.
He should be personable and relate to his players and involve them in
decision making.

It's more difficult to define the captain's role, for successful captains
come in many different forms. Some lead from the front, others are

better at directing operations while still others automatically assume the captaincy mantle because they are articulate and confidently handle the speeches that would cause other players to shrivel away. Whatever the captain's style, it's essential he has the respect of his team mates.

Bunce and Little between them claim 22 years of representative and international experience and in that time they have encountered managers, coaches and captains of wildly varying type and quality.

Some have been stunningly successful, others modestly so and some not very successful at all. Frank and Walter thought it would be fitting to share their views on the men who have helped, in some cases significantly, to shape their careers.

THE MANAGERS

Focusing on the men who have been in charge of the All Blacks since 1989, when Little first represented his country, there have been three – John Sturgeon, Neil Gray and Colin Meads. To this list can be added the name Brian Lochore, who fulfilled the role of campaign manager through to and including the 1995 World Cup.

John Sturgeon, the teetotal mining official from the West Coast, was the All Blacks' boss in 1989, 1990 and 1991, through to the conclusion of the second World Cup in the UK. They were Walter's first three years at international level.

Walter came to admire Sturge, as he was known, branding him the ideal players' manager.

"He had everything planned," says Walter. "He always thought of it before you.

"I especially appreciated him on the 1989 tour of Wales and Ireland when as a teenager I was finding my way at that level. He was more like a father figure to me, always there to help and get you through any difficult phases.

"For Sturge, the players came first and his personal requirements came second.

"He didn't drink, but he accepted that others did. He set down ground rules, emphasizing that it was important to know how much you could handle.

"I remember him saying, 'If you go over the limit, I'm the one whose got to come in and sort things out.' He did, too, whenever players over imbibed and found themselves in awkward situations.

"Grizz Wyllie was the coach throughout Sturge's term as manager and although they had a couple of furious arguments, generally they worked well together."

Neil Gray, the Morrinsville farmer, succeeded Sturgeon and was in charge of the All Blacks during 1992 and 1993.

Walter had been involved with him at New Zealand Colts level when John Hart was the coach. Now he teamed up with Laurie Mains and although they forged an excellent partnership initially, they were at odds over the controversial issues, notably the involvement of Mike Brewer, that dogged the closing weeks of the 1993 tour of England and Scotland.

He remained more in the background than Sturgeon and consequently had less impact on Little.

"He was a pleasant enough person," says Little, "but without Sturge's personality. Sturge was very much his own man."

Colin Meads, who achieved legendary status as a player and who had for several years been Mr Big in King Country rugby, replaced Gray as manager and guided the All Blacks' fortunes throughout 1994 and 1995.

He was, say Bunce and Little, different again from Sturgeon and Gray, a been-there-done-that person with amazing status in rugby.

A coach who always put the players' interests ahead of his own, he made things happen.

"Presumably because of his status," says Little, "he got things done more easily than the other managers.

"His mana meant he could give the team a roasting whenever we went off the rails. No other manager I can think of, with the possible exception of Sturge, could have given us the bollocking Pinetree handed out after the Toulouse test defeat in 1995. You accepted his criticism because you recognised his own achievements. If a lesser manager had climbed into us, we'd have probably told him to go take a hike."

Brian Lochore, the Wairarapa farmer who was a hugely successful All Black captain from 1966 to 1970, joined the management for the '95 World Cup campaign. It was an inspired appointment, Lochore taking a vast amount of pressure off manager Meads and coach Laurie Mains.

He was the link between the players and management and the media, fulfilling his role brilliantly.

"Because of his status, we treated him with the same respect as Pinetree," says Little. "He made us relax. In fact, you felt he made the whole thing happen.

"There were rumours back home that the All Blacks were winning because of B.J. That was unfair on Laurie who was the tactical genius behind the team.

"Where Brian Lochore did have a huge influence was in relaxing everyone and in releasing the manager and coach to concentrate purely on their jobs."

THE COACHES

Peter Thorburn was Little's coach with North Harbour for four years, introducing him to representative play in 1988 and also being involved as a selector at All Black level. Bunce's involvement was limited to a handful of games after he transferred across from Auckland in 1991.

"Thorbs was," says Little, "a thinking coach who was always looking for players with potential and plotting means of overcoming the opposition.

"He always went to school games, which not many coaches do, looking for players he could mould."

He became more than a coach to Little, their relationship developing into a close bonding. With Walter's family in Tokoroa, Thorburn became almost a father to him in Auckland.

"I would often call into Thorbs' office for a chat. He was a great motivator and thinker, and on the giant pad on his desk he would sketch out moves or variations from tap penalties or make suggestions about the lines I should be running.

"He was my first high profile coach, and I guess I was lucky to have someone so talented and personally involved in my career."

Little says that Thorburn was always striving for original planning.

"He would often sit the Harbour team down and get us to write down what we regarded as the opposition weaknesses and ways we could get through them. He was a great competitor, always trying to outwit the other team. He was definitely a players' coach.

"He expected all team members to be aware of what was going on. The backs had to know the lineout calls and the forwards were expected to understand any moves the backs called."

Thorburn was, if not a perfectionist, certainly someone who was nervous about making mistakes.

Brad Meurant, who took over the coaching of North Harbour in 1992, becoming New Zealand's Coach of the Year in his third term, took a different approach from Thorburn.

He was more laconic, more one of the boys, seeking to create a happy family atmosphere. In his three years North Harbour twice reached the NPC semi-finals and once the final.

Little and Bunce, enormous fans of Meurant now, admit that initially they weren't sure how to take him.

"But any coach takes a while to win the players' confidence," says Bunce. "So it was with Brad. We soon appreciated that he wasn't a dictator, that having selected players for their skills, he encouraged them to use those skills.

"He possessed a keen sense of humour and was great for one-liners. This allowed him to abuse players and get away with it, such as when he referred to us as 'brown buggers' at Port Elizabeth.

"The North Harbour backline came to possess the greatest collection of characters around, who related brilliantly to Brad.

"Although he used Mike Mills to coach the backs, essentially he gave us licence to do what we wanted, with the end result that in 1994 we played the most spectacular and effective rugby of any team in New Zealand."

Little says that although Meurant never developed battle plans to the same extent as Thorburn, he worked hard to pinpoint opposition weaknesses.

When Bunce became his assistant in 1994, they formed a remarkably effective combination, claiming victories over France and Auckland at Eden Park while sweeping all NPC opponents aside until the grizzly final against Auckland.

"Brad worked with the forwards and I handled the backs," says Bunce. "I used to say, you give us quality ball and we'll score the tries.

"He allowed us free reign, only ever intervening if we began to lose the plot seriously, and that didn't happen very often."

Chas Ferris, who had guided the fortunes of New Zealand Maori, was given North Harbour in 1995 when Meurant spent a year in South Africa (coaching Border).

Little, who was with Ferris at Glenfield, is a family friend and therefore feels it would be inappropriate to pass judgment. So he handed this one over to Bunce.

"Chas," says Bunce, "goes about his coaching in a thoroughly professional manner, using time management systems. Coming after Brad, this method rather startled the guys, because it was so completely different.

"Chas would allow so many minutes for lineouts, say, then order the next routine. Trouble is, the guys might not have resolved their lineout problems. Inevitably, it led to friction.

"I knew how to take Chas, but a lot of others didn't and his dictatorial manner antagonised many of the players, which doesn't help achieve the spirit needed to create a winning combination."

Bunce says that, under Ferris, the team did far too much talking.

"There were too many bitch sessions, and not enough action at training. Chas over-reacted to losses when I personally believe only a little fine tuning was necessary to get Harbour back on track.

"Our backline had operated so free-spiritedly for so long, it was a shock to have someone suddenly making demands. He intruded where he shouldn't have, and the players resented it."

While Bunce and Little, and half a dozen other Harbour representatives, were at the World Cup, Ferris requested that team numbering be in Maori.

That wasn't appreciated by the returning All Blacks, some of whom refused point blank to go along with it.

Ferris only just survived a mid-season crisis meeting, when the team was on a serious losing streak, and was eventually replaced by Meurant upon his return from South Africa.

Laurie Mains had four full years as coach of the All Blacks, from the beginning of 1992 (in the wake of the disastrous World Cup campaign in the UK) through till the end of 1995. Throughout that time Bunce was the only player to wear the test No 13 jersey, with the exception of the 145-point romp against Japan in Bloemfontein, while Little, after being tried at centre and first-five, became from midway through 1994 Bunce's regular partner in midfield.

In that time, according to Frank and Walter, he went through several personality changes. In 1992, he was the Otago coach suddenly taking the All Blacks. It was a sharp learning curve.

"In the first couple of years," says Little, "you got the impression Laurie was fighting against the world. Perhaps he didn't use the management around him enough. He seemed to do everything himself.

"There were times when you couldn't talk to him because you didn't know what he was thinking. But he improved and was probably at his best leading into and during the World Cup campaign of '95 when the introduction of Brian Lochore as campaign manager allowed him to concentrate totally upon his role as coach."

Mains' focus was always the World Cup and, when changes in personnel were being made, he kept the players informed, stressing that he was always searching for the right combination and the right style.

"He knew New Zealanders didn't accept defeats," says Bunce, "But he was prepared to gamble on that along the way to achieve his ultimate goal of winning the World Cup.

"In 1994, when the results weren't good, he assured us we'd be playing differently the next year. There was a lot of repetition that year. He wasn't prepared to disclose his tactics before the World Cup.

"I personally thought he had it all worked out, a strategic four year plan which he adhered to. He was so methodical in his research and preparation, and analytical where opponents were concerned."

Both Frank and Walter appreciated his training methods, agonising though they were at times.

"It was back to the basics with Laurie," says Walter, "which was appreciated after Jim Blair's pussyfooting in 1991. He liked you to be aggressive at training. Usually he'd try and run the arse off you. Working with Martin Toomey, he ensured the players were as fit as they could possibly be by the World Cup."

Bunce says that Mains loved rugby and loved its traditions. "The All Blacks meant everything to him – he was big on the silver fern. And he was equally suspicious of anyone who wasn't pro rugby.

"He was accused of being anti Auckland which was an unfair call. What he did do, back in '92, was break up the cliques existing in the All Blacks and they were largely an Auckland thing.

"As an example, I can recall, in 1990 I think it was, entering the Auckland team's dining room one evening in company with Michael Jones. We took in the scene. About sixteen players were crammed on to one table designed for a dozen.

"At the other table were Gary and Alan Whetton, Sean Fitzpatrick, Grant Fox and the management.

"Michael and I looked at each other and I said, 'McDonalds?' He nodded and away we went.

"That was typical of Auckland and the All Blacks then. They were almighty and the behaviour of the senior players was accepted. People changed for the better under Laurie. Cliques are the worst thing you can have in a team, and Laurie ended them by threatening to dismiss any players who formed them."

The training camps, through the summer of 1994-95, planned by Mains and his fellow managers, were the catalysts for the dynamic rugby produced by the All Blacks throughout '95.

"The great thing was that Laurie and the players were entirely on the same wavelength about the style of game needed to win the World Cup. He ensured we were properly conditioned and together we swept all before us, stumbling, if you could call it that, at the final hurdle. No one has accurately identified what it was that made us stumble."

Alex Wyllie was coach of the All Blacks from Little's arrival in 1989 through until after the ill-fated World Cup campaign (when he was associated with John Hart) two years later.

Little found him generally to be a good coach, motivating in his team talks and methodical in his preparation – not at all the fire and brimstone individual that his reputation painted him to be.

"I'm aware that Grizz has had his detractors," says Walter, " but frankly, I found him top value, particularly on my first tour in 1989 when I was feeling my way. He came to me and explained why he was playing John Schuster ahead of me, which was because of his greater experience. Hell, I was stoked just to be on board, but it was reassuring to know Grizz was even considering me for the bigger matches.

"He was fanatical about us getting our warm-ups and training right, reasoning that we couldn't expect to perform worthily in a match unless our preparation was spot on. I remember him watching one warm-up session and blowing a fuse because we were, in his words, 'bloody pathetic.' We didn't engage in any team training that day – Grizz took charge and gave us an extended, and extremely energetic, warm-up session!"

Little says he found Wyllie always down to earth, straight and proud of his players. "He was always prepared to come and have a beer and a chat with you."

John Hart had a brief association with Bunce as Auckland's coach in 1986, he prepared the outstanding 1989 New Zealand Colts team of which Little was a key member and he became co-coach along with Wyllie of the All Blacks at the World Cup in 1991.

Little rated him highly after his experiences with the Colts. "He was an excellent motivator," says Little, "who brought life and innovation to training sessions which he organised with high enthusiasm.

"He wanted success and he achieved it. Being a halfback, he knew what made the backs fire, so those of us in midfield and beyond flourished."

Bunce, only ever on the fringe of Hart's Auckland teams, found his training sessions to be demanding mentally as well as physically.

"He liked playing mind games to develop players' concentration. For instance, instead of saying 'Frank, hit tackle bag four,' he'd say, 'Frank, tackle bag ten minus eight plus two.'

"I didn't mind that. I was super fit in 1986 but Harty, and Maurice Trapp after him, couldn't see past Smokin' Joe (Stanley)."

Little records with disappointment that Hart was "an entirely different person" when he became involved with the All Blacks in '91.

"Because I wasn't in the top line-up until the play-off in Cardiff – when Grizz prepared the team, anyway – I didn't have that much to do with him.

"Cliques held an ominous presence in the team at that stage and John became part of one with the Auckland guys."

Earle Kirton didn't ever get to be the All Black coach, but he was Mains' right hand man almost throughout his four year stint, concentrating on the backs.

He scores highly with Bunce and Little but not necessarily for the right reasons. A good natured person, they both enjoyed sharing a meal or a drink with him, partly because he was a connoisseur of wines but mainly because he didn't batter them to death with rugby theory.

Often at team selection meetings on tour, Kirton would lie on the floor reading the sports and racing pages, occasionally tossing in his two cents' worth.

The former All Black first-five was, in Bunce's opinion, strong on good ideas but often had difficulty putting them across.

"He had trouble focusing on the job," says Bunce. "He knew what he wanted, but he'd wander off into story telling. Before we received our instructions we'd hear about what some guy got up to in 1965. Then he'd say, 'Oops, here comes the boss (Laurie) – we'd better move down the other end of the field.'

"Earle had good drills and knew what he wanted. He always emphasized quick hands...bang, bang, bang out to the wing...which suited us fine, because we had great power among the threequarters and at fullback.

"In the early days when Laurie was so deadly serious, it was good to have Earle along, someone with whom you could share a joke and not be afraid to talk to."

Kirton introduced Bunce, a dedicated beer drinker, to wine. It wasn't an easy transition when Bunce tended to swill rather than taste the nectar that Kirton had just described so lovingly.

"He didn't appreciate it either when I picked up a bottle of wine and put it to my lips! He did succeed in getting me to understand wines, however, and I often drink them, red or white, in preference to beer these days."

Maurice Trapp, with Bryan Williams as his assistant, succeeded Hart and enjoyed rich success as coach of Auckland from 1987 through till 1991.

Bunce got on well with both Trapp and Beegee, but it didn't help him break into New Zealand's premier representative team, which is a shame, concludes Bunce, because Trapp's style – fifteen man rugby – was his style.

"Maurice was a methodical coach, taking copious notes and diligently working on what he deemed to be team weaknesses, although personally I don't think the Auckland team of the late 1980s had too many.

"I accepted Joe Stanley's selection ahead of me but I found it upsetting when Craig Innes jumped the queue in 1990. Probably that's when I should have gone to North Harbour instead of the next year."

Peter Schuster, brother of All Black second-five John Schuster, coached the Western Samoan team of which Bunce became a member in 1991.

Bunce thoroughly enjoyed his time under him. He was, in Bunce's view, under-rated as a coach, probably because he had difficulty expressing himself in English.

"He can be a real comedian and get quite animated. I've seen him role on the ground trying to stress a point in his broken English! He has a top understanding of the game and Western Samoa's dramatic rise from nowhere to reach the quarter-finals of the 1991 World Cup is a tribute to his talent."

THE CAPTAINS

Buck Shelford was the captain in 1989 when Little first entered the All Blacks, guiding the team through an unbeaten tour of Wales and Ireland, only to be replaced, unexpectedly, by Gary Whetton the next season, a sacking which shocked Little. Shelford was also Walter's first captain at North Harbour.

"Buck was an inspiring leader with an unbeaten record at international level," says Little. "He was at his best in the face of adversity. He could change tactics mid-game if the original battle plan wasn't working, and if all else failed, Buck would take the opposition on himself."

Little recalls an early game with North Harbour when, having taken the ball forward, he was pinned awkwardly at the bottom of a ruck, at the mercy of the opposition forwards.

"Buck threw himself on top of me, protecting my body, prepared to take the raking himself. That was when I first appreciated that this man was someone special.

"It was a tragedy he was sacked in 1990, for I'm sure he still had a lot to offer New Zealand rugby."

Gary Whetton assumed the leadership of the All Blacks in 1990, following Shelford's demise, and survived until Laurie Mains took over the coaching.

Little does not rate Whetton as an effective leader.

"When his team was winning, he was fine," says Little, "but, unlike Buck, he didn't know how to captain a losing side.

"He had been part of two all conquering teams, Auckland and the All Blacks, for so long, he really didn't know how to handle things when the wheels started to fall off in 1991.

"He wasn't a natural leader, like Buck or Fitzy, who could pull a team close together when things started going wrong. All Gary could do was get on and play his own game and look to Foxy for suggestions.

"Under Gary's leadership, the All Blacks slid from being the unrivalled champions of the world at the beginning of 1990 to a dispirited, disorganised team of also-rans at the World Cup 18 months later.

"Personally, I had little regard for Whetton because of his almost contemptuous attitude towards the younger players in 1990 and 1991. He was largely responsible for allowing the cliques to develop within the team."

Sean Fitzpatrick wasn't Laurie Mains' original preference for captain but when Mike Brewer came to grief in the 1992 trials it opened the way for Fitzy who has proved himself a grand survivor. His record of 75 test appearances, a world record 63 in succession, is testimony to his fitness and resilience.

Frank and Walter both regard him as an excellent captain who leads by example.

"He plays hard and takes no shit," says Little. "Players like to see that.

"Also, he's excellent off the field, with the capacity to pull the team around him when that has to be done. He sorts out the troublemakers and is prepared to mix with his players.

"Having said that, I have never related to him easily, which means that I've been reluctant to approach him during matches suggesting a possible change of direction.

"If, say, Zinzan Brooke had been the skipper, I wouldn't have hesitated to make a suggestion, but somehow I've never felt I should be telling Fitzy what to do. Maybe that's a hangover from the Whetton days when the team developed them-and-us factions."

Bunce says that criticism of Fitzpatrick as a captain incapable of changing tactics on the field is true to a certain extent.

"There have been a couple of classic examples when I believe the tactics should have been varied – against England at Twickenham in 1993 and the World Cup final in South Africa in 1995.

"Like Walter, I've often hesitated to suggest tactical variations when I felt I should have, although in 1995 I finally started to offer my two bob's worth.

"The World Cup final was a prime example. The forwards were giving us the ball and we were getting it wide to Jonah who kept getting cut down.

"Maybe the forwards should have kept the ball tight or we should have kicked for position. We didn't get together and discuss it – is that Fitzy's fault or ours? The thing about the final was that it was so desperately close throughout, and if Mehrts (Andrew Mehrtens) had slotted that dropped goal three minutes from time, we would have won."

If Fitzpatrick had stepped aside, were there others in the '95 All Blacks with leadership skills?

"Yes," says Little, "Zinny (Zinzan Brooke) and Kamo (Ian Jones). For me, they would have been easier to talk to."

Richard Turner, popularly known as Pod, succeeded Shelford as North Harbour's captain in 1992 and has proved a popular and effective leader, despite the number of injuries which have frustrated him.

Bunce first encountered Turner during a Harbour visit to Wanganui in 1991. As his room mate, he was intrigued with the number of pills and lotions that were stacked into his kit bag.

"He became known as The Chemist," says Bunce. "At the time of the Wanganui trip, Pod was into a particular supplement designed to give you the cutting edge. He talked me into trying it. Fifteen minutes before the game I downed a litre of fluid which would supposedly manifest itself in immense energy on the field. "Huh, it's the worst I've ever felt. The water sloshed around in my stomach throughout the game. I never took Pod's advice again!"

Bunce found entertainment in simply watching Turner make himself up after a game. "He possessed an incredible array of sprays, lotions, creams and gels. He even used an unscented deodorant so it wouldn't clash with his cologne. You name it, Pod had it.

"He was always one for the latest fad. Among his interests at the time was transcendal meditation and he talked a few other players into joining him. Often before Harbour matches there would be three or four of them meditating. Coach Brad used to wait until they were in a trance and then bang on the door."

Notwithstanding his obsession with potions and lotions, Turner has been, in Bunce's opinion, one of his better captains.

"He thinks, he speaks well, he relates to his players and he doesn't bore you with his pre-match talks. He reads a game well and, like Buck, leads inspiringly from the front. North Harbour missed him when he was injured in 1995."

Behind
Every Man...

T he wives and girlfriends of the 1995 All Blacks were assembling
at Auckland International Airport. They were being shouted a free
trip by the NZRFU to the Bledisloe Cup test in Sydney.

"Are we all here?" asked one.

"Er, I think I know who's still missing," replied Tracy Little. "MJ
hasn't arrived yet. Typical. I'll phone."

With the plane's departure just one hour away, Tracy didn't expect
Maryjane Bunce to answer the telephone. She was slightly taken aback
when she did.

"What are you doing, MJ – we're all at the airport ready to go."

"I've just stepped out of the shower. I won't be long."

"Won't be long? The plane takes off in an hour."

"I'll be there."

Fortunately, the Bunce residence in Papatoetoe isn't a great distance
from the airport. In fact, when you're sitting in their dining room, you
sometimes get the impression the giant Jumbos are landing in their back
section.

Maryjane checked in with 25 minutes to spare which, says Tracy
Little, 'wasn't too bad for a Bunce.'

"They're incredible those two, Frank and Maryjane – they're late
for everything. If Walter and I invite them to a function, we now specify
a time an hour earlier than we need them."

It's not unusual for one partner to have a reputation for tardiness.
The Bunces are famous (or maybe that's infamous) for both being late
people, which they willingly acknowledge.

Maryjane was an hour late for their wedding, Frank and Maryjane turned up at a dinner party prior to the wedding three hours (got that? three hours) late. If Frank said he'd collect Maryjane at 7 o'clock when he was dating her, she knew not to expect him before 8. If Maryjane said she'd drop in around 5pm, Frank was happy if she was there by 6 o'clock.

When Boyd Gillespie, the talented North Harbour halfback, was interviewed early in 1996 (following a disappointing season for the Takapuna based team) he said the outlook was more encouraging.

"It'll be like old times again with Brad Meurant back as coach, Richard Turner back as captain and Frank Bunce arriving late for training."

Frank and Maryjane have more in common than their inimitable ability to arrive late for functions. They are both talented sports people and both extremely competitive. There would be few couples in New Zealand who have claimed more sporting successes.

Frank's Touch football team, the Dustys, lost only one tournament in five years, registering a staggering 248 victories from 253 games in that period.

Maryjane was a big winner in her own right. She played for the champion Reds Touch team, the female equivalent of the Dustys. They, too, used to take home the winners' share of the prizemoney from virtually every tournament in which they participated.

Frank and Maryjane first became friendly at the Touch nationals in Christchurch, in 1988. Both were representing Auckland. They'd met the previous summer in Wanganui and had been aware of each other on the Touch circuit.

Their relationship was sparked in a most unusual way: Frank offered Maryjane $250 to dance for him at the social that followed the Christchurch tournament.

"You're offering me $250 to dance right here in front of you?" said Maryjane.

"Yeah," said Frank.

"Then give me the $250 and I'll do it."

Maryjane says that she and Frank had been eyeballing each other for some time, so the dance routine seemed a not unreasonable way of getting to know each other.

"Frank's never said whether he felt he got his money's worth, but I danced with a lot of passion. Wouldn't you for $250!"

Frank not only won over his Salome but she was magnanimous enough to return his $250 the next day.

She recalls their first date equally vividly. "Frank took me to McDonalds where, between us, we put away thirty dollars worth of food. I think Frank was surprised that I matched his eating capacity. I'm not far behind him when it comes to drinking either!"

Maryjane represented Auckland at Touch over a period of eight years and won New Zealand selection in 1988-89 and 1993, no mean achievement as the Bunces have five children – Janece,11, Lauren, 10 (Maryjane's children), Chance, 10, Samantha, 5, and Jordan, 2. She won the Auckland women's Touch Player of the Year title for the 1988-89 season.

A natural sportsperson, she has represented North Harbour at netball and was also a nationally ranked tennis player at 15.

The only child of Eileen Saunderson, a Devonport identity who died of cancer while this book was being written, Maryjane also plays rugby.

Her position? Centre, just like Frank. As if they didn't have enough in common, they both wear the No 13 jersey on the rugby field.

"I have to confess," says Maryjane, "that initially I didn't feel that rugby was a game for women but Anna (Anna Richards) and Chuckie (Tracey Lemon) – two New Zealand women's rugby representatives who live with Frank and Maryjane – convinced me otherwise.

"It was the comradeship that got me hooked originally, but I must say that women's rugby has come a long way in the past five years, and is now officially recognised by the New Zealand Rugby Union."

Maryjane played a season with Ponsonby and won Auckland representation although her rugby involvement in recent years has been with sevens.

While Frank and Maryjane have spent a lot of time pursuing their individual sporting interests, there are moments, delightful and agonising, when they operate together.

The agonising times are when they work out as a twosome, committing themselves to everything from roadrunning to the fearsome 150-metre sprints.

"Prior to the World Cup in 1991," says Maryjane, "Frank and I trained together twice a day. We drove each other along and both finished up incredibly fit."

More recently they've operated together in a Touch team which plays under the name of the Dirty Dozen, all of whose members, remarkably, are related.

Frank and Maryjane play alongside Frank's sisters Margaret, Sifa and Jennifer and brothers Tony, Steve and Chris, Tony's wife Erica plus Jeff Tukerangi (Sifa's husband and brother of John) and Jeff's brother and his wife.

Although not as sensationally successful as the Dustys or the Reds, the Dirty Dozen have won a championship, although they missed out on top honours in 1995.

Frank and Maryjane were married in February, 1992. As weddings go, it wasn't without its talking points.

Partly because Frank's brothers Chris and Steve, the drivers, got lost finding her house but also because she was feeling bloody minded about her husband-to-be who hadn't come home the night before,

Maryjane arrived at the church a full hour late.

"It was one time when I enjoyed making Frank wait," she said.

During the service, Frank's mother's house, where many of the wedding presents had been left, was burgled and a car converted. The discovery was made by Chris, who in his haste to alert the family before the reception started at the Manukau clubrooms, rolled the Helensville Rugby Club van that he was driving.

The Bunces refused to let these setbacks dampen a special occasion and the reception went off swimmingly. Frank had two of his great rugby cobbers from Manukau, Jonathan Tukerangi and Greg Thomas, as his best man and groomsman. Maryjane's maid of honour was Marama Tuuta.

Maryjane wasn't able to celebrate as wholeheartedly as the guests because the next morning she was on deck representing Auckland at the Touch nationals.

She admits she knew almost nothing about rugby when she first became involved with Frank. But she's glad she made the effort to familiarise herself with the laws and the tactics of the national game because of the enjoyment she now derives from watching Frank player.

Maryjane says she considers Frank always had the necessary talent to rise to the top but that his attitude sometimes let him down.

"Frank played the nice guy role for too long, I believe. Fair enough, while Joe Stanley was installed at centre for Auckland but when it came time for a replacement, it was cruel on Frank to bring in Craig Innes.

"I always felt Frank was a better player than Craig and that his overall vision and ball distribution skills were better.

"Frank has never been a pushy type and never challenged any of his coaches. It might have helped if he had."

When the opportunity to represent Western Samoa came along, Maryjane encouraged Frank all the way.

"Frank was worried he didn't have enough Western Samoan blood and that he might be seen to be pushing in where he didn't have the right to be, but Peter Fatialofa had been round and had checked the family tree thoroughly.

"Peter was happy, so I told Frank to go for it. It was a marvellous opportunity to play at the World Cup, and after that, who knows. Once Frank made the decision to go with Western Samoa, he committed himself totally, training as hard as he's ever done. He was as fit as he could possibly be went he went off to the World Cup."

Has the advent of professional rugby been welcomed by the Bunces?

"It's changed things," says Maryjane. "You can't do what you want any more, which previously suited Frank's casual attitude to life.

"The up side is that it's a guaranteed income for as long as Frank remains a top-level rugby player.

"Because of his rugby commitments he's never been able to hold down a fulltime job, and with the family, it's been difficult for me to work, and so we have struggled desperately at times.

"It was the attraction of money that took Frank close to league a couple of times, but it was always his passion for rugby that kept him for all that time in the game...and kept him poor!"

A decade ago, All Blacks were campaigning vigorously to have their wives involved at after-match functions, dinners and social occasions. Have things changed?

"I'm sure they have," says Maryjane. "The NZRFU has made the effort to involve wives and partners in recent years, and the bonus of a trip to Sydney was appreciated.

"Personally, I believe in making the most of your own opportunities. I've always followed Frank's career, which included getting to South Africa for the World Cup in 1995, which was a wonderful experience made possible because Frank's family looked after the kids.

"While it's nice to be involved in test dinners I have to confess that I sometimes find them boring. To a great degree, rugby is a man's world, and I accept that."

Who better to describe the special qualities of Frank Bunce than Maryjane?

"Frank is an easygoing person with a placid nature and a good sense of humour," says his wife. "He never judges people. He's a loving father and husband (when he's here).

"He's not an individual. He's a team man. If a team mate performs poorly, no matter how badly, Frank will never accuse him of letting the side down. He always looks at the positive side.

"Laurie Mains brought out the best in Frank, because he challenged him, and Frank, who never takes anything personally, responded. Laurie disciplined him and in return Frank strove to produce his best.

"Frank can take criticism where others can't. He'd sometimes come home and say that Laurie was really needling him. Instead of letting Laurie's comments upset him, he'd become deadly determined to succeed next time out."

There was a reasonable chance of Tracy Wishnowski finding her lifelong partner in the Glenfield Rugby Club, for her father Lew – who still plays for the renowned Glenfield Grizzlies Golden Oldies team – and brother David are both dedicated members of the North Harbour club. And Tracy was present on the sideline at Kaipatiki Park, as a zambuck, for seven winters, although Walter Little was never among the players she treated.

She can thank Isi Tuivaii, a former Glenfield player who represented Hong Kong at that country's international sevens tournament in 1996, for sparking her relationship with Walter.

Isi, playing the matchmaker, told Walter that Tracy wanted to dance with him. He then told Tracy that Walter wanted to dance with her.

Walter (God bless him) followed Isi's advice and asked Tracy for a dance. And they've been together ever since.

Tracy was born in Westport and, with her father working for the railways, lived in Taihape, Waiouru and Panmure before settling on Auckland's North Shore where she schooled at Carmel College.

Their relationship was given a boost when Walter accepted an invitation to play club rugby in England following the 1991 World Cup.

"The five months we spent in the UK was a magic time," says Tracy. "It gave us quality time together with no pressure on Walter (because of the 12-week qualification period, he played mostly for the second fifteen) we were able to travel about and visit many of England's most famous landmarks."

This included a visit to Stonehenge. However, Walter and Tracy (who had Daniel Manu in tow – he was also playing for Rugby) seriously underestimated the drive time back to Rugby, arriving just after 6.30pm to prepare for a match that kicked off at 7 o'clock.

Among the highlights was having Christmas dinner with a gang of New Zealanders at the home of Buck and Joanne Shelford in Northampton.

Another (offbeat) highlight was having Walter's great mate Craig "Postie" Innes bowl into their hotel room in Northampton one night desperate for a place to sleep.

"You're welcome to join us," said Walter, "but there's only one bed - at least it's a double."

If the scenario sounds romantic, forget it. "Postie got into bed beside Walter and for the rest of the night I had two men snoring beside me instead of one!"

The next year Walter and Tracy found themselves in Rome where Walter played (outstandingly well) for the Roma club.

"Thanks to the Corvo family, and Roberto in particular, we had the most marvellous stay there. They treated us like their own.

"The club shouted us back for a two week holiday the following year and have remained in contact."

Walter and Tracy's first child, Michael, was born while they were in Rome and created quite a stir, being blond.

"We had no trouble identifying Michael at the hospital," says Tracy. "Every other baby had black hair. Our fellow couldn't have created more interest if he'd been born with a halo over his head!"

Tracy had difficulty adjusting to Italian food because of her dislike of tomato based dishes. Which meant all their rugby friends went to extreme lengths to create non tomato dishes that Tracy would like.

"What I did fall in love with were the pizzas. They were divine, so much nicer than the pizzas they make in New Zealand."

When they travelled north for a Kiwi invitation game against Casale they stayed in Zinzan Brooke's house while he was away. There were

10 of them, all New Zealanders, including Steve and Jo Hotton, and Arthur and Charlotte Stone.

"Everyone was hankering for New Zealand food, so we had a Kiwi tucker night. We all went out searching for Kiwi products. Everyone pitched in, the result being the best Kiwi/Italian style boil-up ever. The guys peeled the spuds – it was a fun night."

Tracy's next overseas excursion was to the (100th) Bledisloe Cup in Sydney in 1995, courtesy of the NZRFU. While she appreciated the gesture, she felt the union let itself down by not attending to the small matters.

"We received our invitations late, which made for some frantic organisation. I think the NZRFU sometimes forgets that their players have families. We accepted all that because it was fun to be involved.

"What we couldn't accept, which spoiled the whole occasion, was the bus arriving late. We not only missed all the pre-match entertainment, we missed New Zealand's first try. And it looked bad, the All Blacks' wives getting to their seats fifteen minutes after kick-off."

And what are the special traits of Walter Little?

"Walter's a quiet and shy person, but once you get to know him, you love him. You can't help it.

"He's an awesome father and husband. He loves spending time with the boys and really misses them when he's away on rugby duty. He loves all kids. Whenever he's signing autographs, you'll notice he always obliges the kids first.

"He'd do anything for anybody. And he would never use his position for gain. He's just a normal guy with normal feelings."

And his bad traits?

"I don't think there are many of those. Fishing is one of his favourite hobbies, although he can't do it for nuts. And drinking's another.

"And when he's overseas he makes too many phone calls, including early morning calls, usually around 3am, wanting the phone number of Postie (Craig Innes). Wherever in the world they are, they always want to phone each other after they've had a few drinks. We have horrendous toll bills following every rugby tour."

Finally, Tracy's attitude to rugby professionalism.

"Rugby is our life. It's enabled us to do a lot more than most couples our age, to travel and make great friends. However, I don't think that friends can replace the boys' Dad.

"I'd kill for Walter to be an amateur again. Nothing to do with the amount of money he may or may not earn. But because the Chiefs have been Hamilton based, he's been away from home incessantly since the beginning of January.

"You know, it wasn't such a bad thing he returned a positive drug test and got suspended for two matches. It meant me and the boys had him home for two weeks – quite a bonus."

Testing Positive

This chapter was to have been dedicated exclusively to the advent of professional rugby. But two weeks before the manuscript was completed, Little bounded into notoriety by becoming the first New Zealand rugby player to return a positive drug test, having given a sample following the Waikato Chiefs' match against Natal at Durban on March 17.

He was found guilty by an independent tribunal appointed by the NZRFU of consuming the banned substance propoxyphene (contained within digesic which is taken as a painkiller) and suspended for two Super 12 matches.

Propoxyphene is not regarded as performance enhancing, which is as well or Little would have been looking at a two year ban.

He was shaken enough by the experience which came about through a mix of innocence and ignorance.

Little had carried digesics in his toilet bag for his troublesome knee since before the World Cup in 1995. When he mentioned them to the All Blacks' doctor, Mike Bowen, he was shocked to be told they contained a banned substance.

"I got a hell of a fright because I'd used them several times before games," says Little. "Doc Bowen dispensed more of them to me on the condition that I did not use them closer than four days to a game. They were for my knee which aches all the time and which periodically flares up.

"It was my understanding all traces of the drug passed out of your system in three days, but that you should allow a fourth day to be certain."

Little was not drug tested at the World Cup.

But he was selected for random testing while in France later in the year, testing clean. Which is interesting, because he had been using digesics again, this time for toothache.

Having been troubled by an aching tooth back in Auckland, Little had the tooth capped by his dentist prior to assembly. However, while in France, after eating a lolly, the cap fell out.

At the conclusion of the French tour, Doc Bowen gave Little, who was in considerable discomfort because of the aching tooth, more digesics which he popped into his toilet bag.

Little acknowledges that he *should* have had the bad tooth extracted at the beginning of 1996 but because of his commitments to the Hamilton-based Waikato Chiefs, as they prepared for the Super 12 series, it was something he never got around to.

After one match in Hamilton and another in Brisbane in March, the Chiefs flew off to South Africa, to do battle with Natal and Transvaal.

On the Tuesday, five days before the Natal game, the tooth began playing up. It throbbed after training, the pain intensifying to a point where Little knew he would have trouble sleeping.

So he rummaged through his toilet bag, found his favourite painkillers and popped two into his mouth. The result? A pain free night's sleep.

Following the game at Durban's Kings Park, the names of two players from each team were drawn out at random. One of those was Little.

"It's a rather unnerving experience," he says. "Two guys from the drug agency introduce themselves and follow you until you produce a urine sample in a beaker.

"I was asked if I'd taken any tablets leading up to the game. I said I had used Voltaren as an anti-inflammatory for my knee. I made no mention of the digesics, reasoning they would have completely cleared my system."

It was in Hamilton, a fortnight later, while Little was preparing for the Chiefs' game against Western Province that the bombshell dropped.

Having tweaked a muscle in his groin, he had been away swimming rather than running with the rest of the team.

He was having the leg strapped by the physiotherapist on the Friday when the Chiefs' manager, Steve Gilbert, said he and the coach (Brad Meurant) wanted to have a word with him.

"I presumed they were going to tell me I wasn't playing against Western Province. I wish that's what they'd said.

"Instead, Steve told me my drug test from South Africa had returned a positive. I had to appear before an NZRFU tribunal in Hamilton the next day.

"My heart sank. It had to be the digesics, although I found it hard to believe they still showed up after five days.

"Right at that moment I felt wretched, and my humour didn't improve when it was announced on the national news that I was the first New Zealand rugby player to return a positive drugs test."

Although he was deemed fit enough to take the field against Western

Province the next afternoon, that prospect was destroyed when Little was advised that the tribunal would convene at 1pm. The session would not conclude until 5.30pm.

Little and Dr Bowen, together with legal counsel representing both parties, appeared before the independent tribunal comprising John Laurenson QC, Brett Gould (lawyer), Peter Burke (former All Black and NZRFU president) and Dr Chris Milne (medical practitioner).

The following oral decision was released after the meeting:

We are satisfied that this has been an unintentional offence. There was proper medical justification for taking the drug, namely the painful tooth. We are satisfied from Dr Milne and Dr Bowen that the drug does not enhance performance and therefore was not taken to enhance performance.

We now have to face the question of penalty. We conclude that the matter must be decided in accordance with the New Zealand Rules.

Appendix 'A' to the NZRFU policy statement refers to the penalties involved. At this point, we are concerned only with 10(c) and (d) which state:

(c) A reprimand may be given if the Drugs Tribunal is satisfied that there has been an "unintentional offence" in that the drug was not taken to enhance performance but the participant has failed to disclose the taking of medication (as listed by the International Olympic Committee) which has led to the positive result;

(d) If a suspension is imposed for an unintentional offence, it should not exceed three months for the first offence, but subsequent offences should be treated as in (a) and (b).

These rules imply that even in cases of unintentional offences a penalty may be imposed when the player has failed to disclose the taking of medication. Mr Little did not disclose he had done so.

We have given the most careful and anxious consideration to his explanation which is, as we understand it, that because he had understood the drug would not be present after about 3 days and because the drug had been dispensed by his own team doctor, he says in effect he had good reason not to disclose it.

The fact remains he had been told the drug was banned. The question is whether this places him in a position of having a residual responsibility for taking the drug, notwithstanding the matters he has referred to. In our view, it does.

The question is, then, whether that residual responsibility should attract a penalty and, if so, how much?

The question of the use of drugs, whether they be performance enhancing or not, is of huge importance in the field of sport.

The penalty for deliberately taking performance enhancing drugs is met by a mandatory penalty of 2 years suspension.

Therefore, reviewing this down to the limits set in Rules (c) and (d), it means, we believe, more than merely a reprimand is needed in this case. A clear message is needed. If a doctor had not originally prescribed the drug, we consider a month would have been appropriate, a month's suspension.

Because it was prescribed by a doctor and taking into account that this is the first time this has had to be considered in this country, we believe that the appropriate penalty is that Mr Little be suspended for the next two Super 12 matches. That is our finding.

That tribunal's statement went on to consider "the complex issue of whether there can be justification for prescribing banned drugs to athletes."

They felt it would be inappropriate for them, as a tribunal, to make further comment on that issue.

They did conclude their statement with a tribute to Little:

We would like to make the following matter very clear. We accept that in every respect, except for this incident, he has been an asset to the game. In this case, it is sad that he has failed to properly consider his responsibilities and, harsh though it may be and despite his contributions, and a notable contribution it is, he must accept that responsibility now.

Little accepts that he was foolish to take the digesics which he used initially in innocence and subsequently in the belief they could not be traced after three to four days.

"Personally, I don't believe digesics should be banned," he says. "They are not performance enhancing, quite the opposite. The reason they are on the banned list is because they are an addictive drug.

"However, I certainly won't be using them again."

In the wake of his sensational banning – which ruled him out of the Waikato Chiefs' matches against the ACT Brumbies and Northern Transvaal – Little received sympathy and understanding from relatives, friends and rugby colleagues.

Two All Blacks, in expressing their regrets, told him they had been using Digesics themselves, in the same mistaken belief they were harmless.

"I just hope the kids who know and support me don't think I'm a drug user seeking to enhance my performance," says Little.

"I was, I consider, an innocent party who should have been more careful. I hope my experience is a timely lesson for all rugby players."

Prior to the World Cup, drug-testing methods for rugby players were not sophisticated enough to detect substances such as propoxyphene after two or three days. But the systems now in use can detect the most minute traces of drugs. In Little's case, the percentage of propoxyphene in his blood stream was 0.0056 which is almost nothing at all.

Little's dentist felt himself partly responsible for the predicament his patient found himself in and, on Easter Monday, during Walter's enforced lay-off, arranged for him to visit an oral surgeon and have the offending tooth removed...along with two wisdom teeth.

It was a sorry looking, swollen faced Walter Little who sat at home watching the Chiefs' matches against ACT and Northern Transvaal, having been docked two weeks' pay.

His final observation on the propoxyphene issue: "The oral surgeon had the devil of a job prescribing a painkilling drug for me that didn't contain a banned substance."

•

By 1996, rugby was professional, something that didn't seem possible a few years back, rugby by definition having always been an amateur game.

The major rugby nations of the southern hemisphere, New Zealand, Australia and South Africa, had been pushing for a relaxation in the game's amateurism laws for some years but had been consistently frustrated by the British traditionalists.

The breakthrough was forced upon the International Rugby Board by a series of dramatic developments in the first half of 1995.

First, there was the announcement of Super League, a daring Rupert Murdoch funded breakaway from the game's establishment. Salaries of up to $1 million were being touted for the game's leading performers. They would be recruiting rugby players, and contracts worth $1 million for three years were being talked.

At the same time, Japanese clubs – businesses in reality masquerading as rugby clubs – were tempting many of New Zealand's most prominent players with offers so tempting they were extremely hard to resist.

If that wasn't threatening enough to the grand old (amateur) game of rugby, in the wake of the World Cup in South Africa came the Kerry Packer driven World Rugby Corporation, a concept which threatened to wrest the administration of the game at the highest level from the national bodies of the major nations.

It was all rather bewildering for the average rugby player who suddenly found himself, midway through 1995, spending as much time at player meetings as at rugby trainings. It was a time of huge distraction for the game's top players.

The International Rugby Board had no alternative, when it gathered in London in August, but to "go pro."

Its revolutionary decision in August to declare the game open had already been pre-empted by the NZRFU which by then had contracted all its leading players. And the contracts were offering big bucks.

Had the NZRFU sat back and waited until the International Board sanctioned player payments, it's very likely it would not have had any players of consequence to administer.

It is believed that 13 of the 26 players who represented New Zealand at the World Cup would have defected to Super League or Japan had not the NZRFU counter-attacked which it did by despatching its newest national councillor Jock Hobbs, its deputy chairman, Rob Fisher, and its Campaign Manager to the World Cup, Brian Lochore, to 'sell' its concept to every leading player and, more importantly, get them all contracted.

And *all* of them would have been lost had the WRC succeeded with its bold takeover scheme.

Frank Bunce is in a unique position to explain the dramatic professional dealings of '95 from a player's viewpoint.

"It was obvious during 1995," he says, "that rugby was advancing towards professionalism. For the players, though, it became a perplexing issue trying to understand which route it was advancing along.

"Sky Television was first into the arena with a Super 10 concept which didn't get off the ground because it didn't involve the South African provinces.

"The All Blacks were using Sean Fitzpatrick, Eric Rush and Mike Brewer as negotiators and spokesmen and before the World Cup they alerted us to the existence of WRC and what it offered, which was, at first sight, sensationally appealing.

"WRC planned to make rugby global, dividing the playing nations into three zones, Northern, Central and Southern, with the leading teams coming forward to effectively stage a World Cup competition every year.

"The amount of money on offer was mind-boggling to those of us who, as true blue amateurs, had played out our entire careers as virtual paupers.

"The negative right from the start was what would become of the All Black jersey. Fitzy and Bruiser weren't able to give us any assurances on that, which some of the younger guys like Goldie (Jeff Wilson) and Josh (Josh Kronfeld) saw as a major concern. Fitzy said that unless WRC could involve the NZRFU, the black jersey would probably have to be sacrificed.

"By the time we headed for the World Cup there were deals going in all directions. The Japs were offering outrageous money, Super League clubs were targeting players and WRC wanted all of us at figures most of us believed could only be achieved through purchasing a winning Lotto ticket.

"Glen Osborne, for one, was considering a three year league contract worth almost $2 million. However, I'm sure the preference of all the All Blacks was rugby plus cash rather than any other sport.

"The WRC negotiations were put on hold while we went about trying to win the World Cup but back in New Zealand, before and after the first Bledisloe Cup game, the issue was a hot potato again, especially when news of WRC's existence leaked out.

"Eric Rush's firm Davenports represented WRC in New Zealand

and it was there that they told us that a sum of $US100,000 million would be available to fund the global event by November 22.

"At that stage, I had the feeling WRC's concept was going to happen, although we stressed that November 22 was too late and that they should strive to arrange the financing earlier.

"I should emphasize that Rushy was never an agent of the WRC, as some people concluded. He was merely the go-between. All he did was relay the goings-on to the players.

"By the time of the second Bledisloe Cup test in Sydney, the NZRFU was exerting pressure on the players and threatening not to select anyone for the tour of Italy and France who wasn't contracted to them.

"After playing at the Sydney Football Stadium, and winning well, the All Blacks boarded their bus and were directed to the private home of an executive of a TV channel where we received an update on the WRC situation.

"We were assured everything was coming along well, that it was all go. They wanted a commitment from the players.

"We conducted something of a straw poll which revealed equal numbers in favour and opposed to WRC, with a lot in the middle.

"I was getting sick of the whole thing by then. I was at the stage of my career when obviously a juicy contract was a good thing, and we were talking something like $US800,000 for three years, which is a phenomenal amount of money to play rugby. But to get it, we were going to have to abandon the NZRFU and that was obviously a concern, whether we thought the NZRFU had looked after its players or not.

"Some of the younger guys, like Josh, Mehrts and Goldie, were trying to relate that money to the black jersey. They were obviously fighting with themselves.

"We were aware that we had to bind together as one group. There were rumours that the senior players were pressuring the younger guys, but that was never the case.

"There seemed to be a lot of half truths at this stage. It was claimed at one point that the All Blacks were the last team in the world to sign with WRC. We were assured the Springboks and the Wallabies had all signed and that the English were waiting on New Zealand.

"I gather most of the Aussies *were* signed, and most of the Springboks too.

"It was at this point that most of the All Blacks signed a letter of intent and several signed final contracts as well, having been offered $100,000 each to sign the final contract. Those contracts were signed by us but not them.

"WRC was so confident of its competition getting off the ground that its negotiators said we could keep that money regardless. Well, for some of us that money is still in trust with Davenports and is still in dispute.

"It should be stressed that the WRC concept had enormous appeal. It was totally global, involving, of course, the island nations Western Samoa, Fiji and Tonga which were obviously going to be the big losers in the Rupert Murdoch deal with the NZRFU. I saw this as a harsh side effect, especially when you consider how Samoan rugby has benefited New Zealand in the past decade. They were going to be left out in the cold, vulnerable to league raids.

"The NZRFU, starting from way behind the eight ball but suddenly desperately urgent when it realised it was in danger of having all its leading players hijacked by WRC, began presenting us with contracts which were a big improvement on what Richie Guy had outlined prior to the World Cup, although they were still pale in comparison with what WRC was offering.

"Jock Hobbs, representing the NZRFU, offered a cash payment on signing and a deal that could see an All Black who appeared in every test in 1996 earning upwards of $250,000.

"Jock's strongest negotiating argument was that the NZRFU *had* the money in the bank. The WRC didn't.

"For some players, the money was obviously a major factor. But others had different priorities.

"I believe that the WRC was falling over before Goldie and Josh signed with the NZRFU, an event which naturally received vast publicity. Their defection was a body blow but I believe the WRC was haemorrhaging before that.

"How different things might have been had the WRC had its millions available when it first commenced negotiations, because it had the superior game plan.

"It didn't surprise me that Josh and Goldie abandoned ship, although some players have accused them of reneging on the all-for-one, one-for-all arrangement we supposedly had. They were never that happy about sacrificing the black jersey. And Goldie wanted to play his cricket too.

"Fitzy finally phoned around one day and told us to make our peace with the NZRFU.

"It was then over to every individual to negotiate the best possible deal for himself, and obviously some were in stronger negotiating situations than others.

"Oz (Glen Osborne) was the victim of dirty dealings in Wellington. He had this huge offer from Canterbury Bankstown with him when he sat down with his lawyer to discuss his contract with the NZRFU.

"One of the NZRFU councillors went out and telephoned an official of the Canterbury Bankstown club to say that Osborne was using their offer to get himself a better deal in rugby. Canterbury Bankstown in turn contacted Oz's manager John McKittrick who phoned his lawyer Graeme Halse at the meeting to advise that, in the circumstances,

Canterbury Bankstown had withdrawn its offer.

"Oz was so brassed off he almost made the decision to play league, there and then. Like a lot of us, his heart was in rugby. He didn't want to abandon New Zealand to live in Australia and become involved in the cut-throat world that is league.

"The Canterbury Bankstown offer wasn't easy to reject, being worth close to $2 million with a top-up from Super League. I don't think the NZRFU councillors appreciated the sacrifice Oz was prepared to make to stay with rugby.

"Oz and I had spent a long time discussing the offer. He didn't want the money just to be rich. He was going to use it to buy his parents a new house and do a lot of noble things.

"I took my contract to David Jones of Phillips Fox before I signed it. He asked me and Olo Brown, and a few others, whether we had given back the $100,000 signing-on fees that WRC had paid us. We said no. So his advice was not to. As far as he was concerned, WRC had promised the money, regardless of whether their competition got up and running.

"WRC is demanding the money back and the whole issue is before the courts at the moment.

"WRC is claiming its scheme fell over because we signed with the NZRFU. We argue that we signed because WRC was crumbling.

"It was a terrible time while the players were considering the rival offers of WRC and the NZRFU. North Harbour, with so many players involved, suffered more than most, I'm sure.

"Every time the Harbour players came together the conversation would turn to player contracts and professionalism. By the time I signed with the NZRFU, I was heartily sick of the whole thing.

"Now that professionalism is here, what do the players think of it?

"It's not easy to supply an unequivocal answer to that.

"Obviously, it's gratifying to be paid for playing rugby, and the $50,000 we're getting for appearing in the Super 12 series is a realistic payment.

"However, because we are professionals, and not our own people any longer, we are at the mercy of the NZRFU.

"If they order you to do something, you do it. They say we're paying you a lot of money and you're not performing (which was the Waikato Chiefs' situation after a dreadful tour taking in Brisbane, Durban and Johannesburg), so they ordered us to do another series of fitness tests in Whangarei.

"Why couldn't we have done them in South Africa when we had plenty of spare time?

"The Waikato Chiefs have been disadvantaged because the players come from far-flung unions. Those of us from North Harbour have been regularly journeying down to Hamilton since the beginning of

January for training. We've had precious little time with our families this year.

"It's all right for the Auckland Blues. They are Auckland based and several of them have retained their jobs, managing a level of employment between matches.

"There's not a solitary member of the Waikato Chiefs still working. We are all full time professional rugby players because there's no alternative.

"For the All Blacks involved, there's no problem. Once the Super 12 is completed, their salary is assured and they move on to the international phase of the season.

"But for the others, the outlook isn't so great. Will any of them be able to resurrect the jobs they've sacrificed? Who's going to employ someone who is available only from June until the NPC starts in August?

"Professional rugby is an excellent and exciting concept. And if you're one of the elite players, it's answered all your prayers.

"Spare a thought, however, for the second tier players. Fifty thousand dollars sounds pretty good for five months work, but there's tax and insurance to be paid, and a huge gap to be filled when the rugby eases off.

"How many of the players are disciplined enough to budget well and ensure that that income does them adequately for a full year?

"Time will tell."

The Last Word

I t is a Monday in mid-April and Walter Little loosens his seat belt a fraction to lean forward and take in the dramatic view of the Southern Alps as the Air New Zealand 737 makes its way towards Invercargill.

Beside him is Oz (Glen Osborne) who is having trouble sitting still because he knows that his wife Kylie, back home, is due to go into labour with their first child any moment.

Walter senses that he should be feeling downcast. His gums still ache – from the surgery that recently removed three wisdom teeth – and while he was sitting out his two match suspension for putting a banned substance into his body, the player who substituted for him, Scott McLeod, made such a huge impact that Walter has been overlooked for the Waikato Chiefs' match against the Otago Highlanders.

But Walter is more concerned for Oz than for himself. "Kylie will be fine," he assures the Chiefs' fullback. "Just think, some time in the next week you'll be a father. It's a wonderful experience."

Walter closes his eyes and sinks back into his seat. "Oz about to become a father? Wow, it's amazing what can happen in twelve months."

This time a year ago, Oz was just breaking into the All Blacks, Walter and Tracy were preparing for their wedding, rugby was still amateur, Jonah Lomu was a promising footballer, no one had heard of WRC, Super 12 was still Super 10 and Walter was innocently using digesic as a painkiller because no one had told him it contained a substance that was on the banned list.

Now he's a rugby professional, like every other member of the Waikato Chiefs. Not one of them retains an outside job. They are all contracted to the New Zealand Rugby Football Union and paid monthly by that body.

Walter looks at Oz who is dozing, apparently contentedly, for he has a smile on his face. "I wonder whether he's dreaming about tomorrow night's game and scoring a try or what it will be like to hold his new baby," Walter muses.

The baby will arrive sooner than Oz expects, while he is in Invercargill. It's a girl, Arianna, and Oz expresses his utter delight during an interview following the Chiefs' match against the Highlanders.

Some things change, some things don't. Walter Little and Frank Bunce are now professional rugby players. That's new, daringly new. Their circumstances have changed. But Frank and Walter haven't. And those who know them well, know they never will.

Walter will continue to smoke. In that respect, he was unique as an All Black at the 1995 World Cup.

"There used to be about four of us who smoked," says Walter, "Foxy (Grant Fox), Postie (Craig Innes), JT (John Timu) and me. But I'm the only survivor. Win, lose or draw, we would unwind in the dressing room with a cigarette after every game.

"I've got a partner in crime when I represent North Harbour - Brad Meurant. He's a much heavier smoker than me. The number of cigarettes he gets through is directly proportional to how his team is performing at the time. When it's a nailbiter, Brad just about smokes the packet as well!"

Walter smokes three or four cigarettes on an average training day and gets through a few more in social situations. He won't smoke when he's rooming with another player and he always steps out of the changing room before lighting up. "I seldom smoke in front of the other guys," he says, "and never in an enclosed situation."

Also, Walter will continue to strum a guitar, an instrument he took to quite naturally from an early age. He doesn't have a voice like Eroni Clarke, so he confines himself to making the music, leaving it to his team mates to do the singing.

You won't find Frank puffing on a cigarette or playing a guitar. But chances are, in a relaxed social setting, you will find him with a beer in his hand, although his consumption of alcohol has diminished as his rugby responsibilities at the highest level have increased.

If you are wanting to engage Frank in conversation and are wondering what subject to introduce, appreciating that he's probably talked enough rugby for one day, try motor cycles and classic cars.

Frank's assortment of transport over the years would, if brought together and exhibited, command high interest from connoisseurs of classic machines.

His first car was a 1958 Plymouth, a gas guzzler with fins, not the perfect mode of transport in the days when petrol was in short supply.

Then he moved on to a two-door Zephyr Mark II, a handsome machine with a suped-up engine which he bought from a neighbour who restored Fords.

In more recent times he's owned two Jaguars, the first a Mark II 3.4

litre, the other an XJ6. Both were white with red leather interiors.

Frank nominates the Mark II Jaguar as arguably his favourite. "It was," he says, "smooth, powerful and comfortable. I just loved driving that car around."

Sandwiched among the classic cars were a selection of motor cycles. Altogether, Frank owned five Triumphs and Nortons although the motor bike he drives these days is Italian, a Motoguzzi.

"Motor bikes have always been a hobby," he says. "I've been to a few rallies over the years, in New Plymouth, Taupo and Pukekohe.

"Probably my favourite machine was an Old Bonneville 650cc. I never owned a Harley Davidson."

Had rugby not hooked him as powerfully as it did, and had he not progressed to the All Blacks, Frank suspects he would have devoted more time to motor cycle rallying.

But rugby did envelop Frank, to a degree he never considered possible. And although a late starter he was to become one of the great (and hugely admired) All Black midfield backs.

He and Walter were to form the most potent midfield combination in the world in 1992 which when permitted flourished through until the World Cup of 1995 and may well extend into 1996.

It is surely fitting to conclude Frank and Walter's book with tributes from three of the celebrated coaches who helped shape their careers.

BRAD MEURANT
North Harbour coach 1992-93-94-96

Frank came to North Harbour (in 1991) in an age bracket when most players are looking to finish their careers. The change gave him a new lease of life and was extremely good for us.

He hadn't got a fair go with Auckland though to be fair there was a little indiscipline there in a team context and it took a while to knock the rough edges off.

Players do mature at different times and Frank was certainly later than a lot of the others.

In 1992, I had both Scott Pierce and Frank challenging for the centre spot. Scott had been a part of North Harbour for a long time while Frank (at 30) was effectively in his first year.

As a coach looking at centres, Scotty was the guy to pick. He was in the Bruce Robertson mould, a player who could break the line and set his wingers up beautifully. It was unfortunate that the All Black selectors never acknowledged his talents.

Frank was a different type of player, stronger, more physical, a dynamic tackler, one of the best in the game. He was the up-and-coming All Black centre.

Scott could see the writing was on the wall and went off to play in Japan.

Frank as a centre had the nature of a second-five with regard to his tackling and his confrontational approach.

He can fire a wrist pass left or right for 15 to 20 metres. People don't appreciate how well he sets up his wingers.

Frank Bunce being on the paddock would have had in my time as coach the same impact as Buck Shelford had when he was in the pack.

As a coach, I'm much more confident when Frank is there. His mere presence and the respect he is accorded from the opposition is worth six to eight points a game.

The confidence of the other players grew if Frank was there.

Punctuality was never a word Frank could spell, so when he volunteered to become assistant coach when Mike Mills stepped down, I hesitated, but I knew he and I were compatible and I knew the unique set-up we had with North Harbour. You couldn't allow just anyone to come in and coach the backs.

Everyone looked up to Frank and so being the assistant coach was a natural progression for him. We sat down at the beginning of '94 and plotted the year. It proved to be the turning point for Harbour.

I have to say he made every training session on time that year. It just shows, if you can't beat 'em, join 'em!

We had the most marvellous season, winning virtually everything except the NPC final against Auckland.

I remember the day Tabai Matson ran past Frank playing for Canterbury. He's never been allowed to forget it. It stands out because in three years I had never previously seen Frank miss a tackle.

Walter Little, who had been a North Harbour player for several seasons before I came on the scene, is one great guy. He doesn't flaunt his status as an All Black. It's not relevant to him. He seems himself as nothing but a member of the side.

I recognised that he had a close association with Peter Thorburn, almost like father and son. I had to move gently into that area.

Walter's not a person to say a lot. You wouldn't know whether he was injured or not because he never troubles you with such information.

He's the ultimate team member. If I asked him to play on the side of the scrum, he would. Against Wellington once, Warren Burton was injured and I said to Walter, "You're going to have to play first-five today."

"No problem," he replied. That's the sort of guy he is.

Other All Blacks are loath to move away from their specialist position, but it's never a problem for Walter.

As a second-five, he's reliable and unpredictable. He can do things a lot of other players can't. He can pick up a situation and read it better than any player I know. But ask him to explain it and he can't!

That's because he's an instinctive player. Some coaches have dismissed him because of that instinctiveness and others have brought him back because of it.

Put Walter and Frank together and there's no more dangerous combination in the world.

Together they have a special understanding. You know something is going to happen. There's a glorious unpredictability about them. If I don't know what's coming up, what hope has the opposition got?

I'll never forget Harbour's NPC game against Auckland at Eden Park in 1994 when Walter's try between the posts in the last minute won it for us.

Eroni Clarke was so certain he'd passed, he turned away, and Walter ran past him. You can't coach those skills into a player. You can only encourage them to use that flair and marvel at it when they do.

PETER THORBURN
North Harbour coach 1985-91
When Walter first came into the North Harbour team we had Frano Botica, Paul Feeney and Scott Pierce there. They were all free spirits. You can't control players like that because if you do, you destroy their natural strengths.

That environment suited Walter's own free spiritedness. It's the (Fijian) island way. I encouraged him to use his skill and talent and very rarely did I sit with him one on one. That was how we played the game and Walter became an integral part of it.

Frano Botica has become one of the best goalkickers, rugby or league, in the world. That's because he's worked hard at it.

Walter could have been as good a goalkicker if he'd had the mental hardness, but he was always a little bit lazy.

He uses as an excuse that his knee's troubling him. Mind you, he has had an awful lot of problems with those knees of his. That's why I told him he was crazy to ever consider playing league. With all those side-on tackles, he wouldn't have survived three months in that code.

The All Blacks wasted Walter's talent for a couple of years. They kept throwing skip passes and missing him out. I spoke to Grizz Wyllie about using Craig Innes and Walter as inside and outside centres, having Walter as the tricky player, Craig as the hard one. They were an ideal coupling, but my idea was never taken up.

Walter is above all else a confidence player. If you've got Walter in your side, you're a thirty to forty per cent better team.

People have asked me what Walter's best position is. I still don't know. I feel he would make a brilliant fullback because his thirty metre pace is explosive, although he doesn't sustain it over seventy metres.

He probably doesn't have the kicking game to concentrate on first-five, although he has played a lot of brilliant rugby for North Harbour, and the All Blacks, in that position and he certainly gets a backline moving.

I guess in combination with Frank Bunce, second-five is his ideal position. You've got to have players of contrasting strengths in midfield and those two complement each other perfectly.

LAURIE MAINS
New Zealand coach 1992-95
I couldn't have wished for a more dedicated pair of midfielders. They were a delight to coach.

Walter has that incredible, tackle-breaking style and acceleration that opens up gaps. He has magic hands in moving the ball and placing it ideally for those outside him.

Frank in my time as All Black coach was the toughest centre in the world, a rugged, gifted footballer.

He was mentally tough. On three occasions – that's all, I think – I had to get tough on him because he'd let his attitude soften. And when I say I got tough, I really got tough. Frank responded on each occasion.

As people and players, Frank and Walter were the sort of guys who make a team.

It's no secret that Frank became one of my favourites and I eventually involved him in team selections and as a giver of opinions. I valued his opinion because he was always totally honest. In selection meetings, he never looked after his mates. He did what was best for the team. That was the measure of the man.

Frank and Walter were matched up against some of the game's greatest partnerships – Tim Horan and Jason Little, Will Carling and Jeremy Guscott, Philippe Sella and Franck Mesnel – but they were never outplayed.

There was not another combination in the world better than them.

Statistics

Current till April 25, 1996
Compiled by Geoff Miller

WALTER KENNETH LITTLE

Born: October 14, 1969
Height: 1.78m.
Weight: 90kg.
Club: Glenfield.
Union: North Harbour.
Tests: 36. **Test tries:** 7.
Married to: Tracy Wishnowski.

FIRST-CLASS CAREER

Team	Period	Games	Tries	Cons	Pens	Pots	Points
North Harbour	1988-95	94	37	15	17	-	250
New Zealand	1989-95	58	13	-	-	-	61
NZ trials	1990-95	6	6	-	-	-	27
New Zealand XV	1993-94	3	2	-	-	-	10
New Zealand Colts	1989	3	3	-	-	-	12
Barbarians	1989	1	1	2	2	-	14
North Zone	1989	2	1	-	-	-	4
Waikato Chiefs	1996	5	1	-	-	-	5
		172	**64**	**17**	**19**	**-**	**383**

FRANK ENERI BUNCE

Born: February 4, 1962.
Height: 1.83m.
Weight: 93kg.
Club: Helensville.
Union: North Harbour.
Tests: 33. **Test tries:** 16.
Married to: Maryjane Saunderson.

FIRST-CLASS CAREER

Team	Period	Games	Tries	Cons	Pens	Pots	Points
North Harbour	1991-95	63	17	-	-	-	81
New Zealand	1992-95	46	23	-	-	-	111
Auckland	1984-91	20	9	-	-	-	36
Western Samoa	1991	8	2	-	-	-	8
NZ trials	1988-95	6	2	-	-	-	9
North Island	1986-95	2	-	-	-	-	-
NZ Samoa	1992	1	2	-	-	-	10
Barbarians	1989	1	-	-	-	-	-
Harlequins	1995	1	2	-	-	-	8
Manawatu XV	1986	1	-	-	-	-	-
Waikato Chiefs	1996	9	1	-	-	-	5
		158	**58**	**-**	**-**	**-**	**270**